placer county
real food
from farmers markets

healthy soil. healthy food. healthy people.

placer county
real food
from farmers markets

recipes and menus for every week of the year

Joanne Neft with Laura Kenny

Introduction by Deborah Madison

First Edition

Copyright 2010 by Joanne Neft
Photography by Keith Sutter, Wayde Carroll, and James Cole

Published by In Season Publishing Company
P. O. Box 753
Newcastle, CA 95658

www.placercountyrealfood.com

Auburn Printers, Inc., Auburn, California
Printed in Hong Kong, China

Library of Congress Cataloging-in-Publication Data
Neft, Joanne
Placer County real food cookbook/Joanne Neft with Laura Kenny; photography by Keith Sutter, Wayde Carroll, James Cole
ISBN- 978-0-615-31872-1
1. Farmers Market—California. 2. Cookery. 3. Neft, Joanne

For the Placer County agriculture community,
with honor and gratitude

AN EATER'S MANIFESTO

Eat food. Not too much. Mostly plants.

Do all your eating at a table.

Eat slowly.

Try not to eat alone.

Have a glass of wine with dinner.

Don't eat anything your great grandmother
wouldn't recognize as food.

Avoid food products containing ingredients
that are unfamiliar, unpronounceable,
or more than five in number.

Shop the peripheries of the supermarket
and stay out of the middle.

Don't get your fuel from the
same place your car does.

Pay more, eat less.

Eat well-grown foods from healthy soils.

Eat wild foods when you can.

Cook and, if you can, plant a garden.

— *Michael Pollan*

BROADSIDE PUBLISHED BY POINT REYES BOOKS ON THE OCCASION OF SLOW FOOD NATION, HELD IN SAN FRANCISCO, AUGUST 2008.
TEXT: MICHAEL POLLAN, *IN DEFENSE OF FOOD: AN EATER'S MANIFESTO*, COPYRIGHT 2008, USED BY PERMISSION OF PENGUIN PRESS.
ART: *ONIONS* BY DAVID GOINES, COPYRIGHT 1999.
PRINTED LETTERPRESS BY POINT REYES PRINTING CO.

sponsors

first edition printing

StoneBridge Properties
Café Zorro, Loomis

Aronowitz & Skidmore, Inc.

Auburn Gold Country Rotary

East Wind Quantum Wellness

Eisley Nursery

Foothill Farmers' Market Association

Julie Reader Hanson

The Lockhart Macinnes Group at Morgan Stanley Smith Barney

Jennifer Montgomery and Pat Malberg

Brad Onorato

Placer Community Foundation

Robert Weygandt, Scott & Braeden Weygandt, William & Kathy Weygandt

Carpe Vino

Kuppinger & Phillips, CPA's

Sutter Roseville Medical Center

table of contents

Menus:

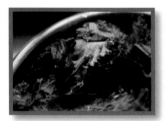

table of contents

the value of the certified farmers markets

From the farmer to the consumer: in a nutshell, that's the definition of a certified farmers market. Farmers sell what they grow directly to the consumer.

Benefits include:

• **Access to fresh, healthy food.** Health experts say diets should contain more freshly picked fruits and vegetables. Farmers markets let consumers buy just-picked, locally grown produce.

• **Safer food supply.** With the growing concern over food-borne illnesses, consumers look to farmers markets as a way to ensure a safer food supply. Consumers can meet the farmers and ask how the food was grown, what chemicals, if any, were used, all the while developing a sense of confidence in both the farmer and the foods they'll be feeding their families.

• **Local food system.** Farmers markets are vital in creating a local food system. The availability of fresh local foods at farmers markets also provides food security to communities that may otherwise have little or no access to fresh foods.

• **New products.** Farmers markets let shoppers try new produce and unusual varieties of commonly grown fruits and vegetables. It's an adventure for shoppers.

• **Variety.** The variety and freshness of food offered at the peak of flavor is incomparable.

• **Healthy eating habits.** Farmers markets encourage families to eat more fresh fruits and vegetables, and to prepare fresh foods with simple and delicious recipes.

• **Community.** Farmers markets strengthen the bond between people who live in the community and those who produce food for us.

• **Tourism.** Farmers markets attract people from outside the area, and create a snapshot of local culture.

• **Economic sustainability.** Farmers markets are important venues for small- and mid-scale family farmers to sell their products at a more sustainable retail price level. That means increased profitability, and more sustainable farms.

• **Farmland protection.** Being able to sell directly to the consumer keeps small farms economically viable and strong, and preserves farmland for this generation and potentially future generations as well.

Shopping at the farmers market, meeting farmers, running into friends, and finding vegetables and fruits you've never tried make shopping an experience.

Give yourself, and your family, the gift of that experience.

–Christine E. Turner, Placer County Agricultural Commissioner, Auburn

acknowledgements

It takes a year to write an in-season cookbook, and it takes an entire community to participate in writing a cookbook created in 52 weeks.

Thanks to the farmers who show up each week at the farmers markets with food picked the day before. No matter the weather – cold, rainy, hot or windy – our farmers are there with an amazing selection of the freshest produce available. Thanks to them, too, for their hard work behind the scenes: tilling fields, planting crops, pruning fruit trees. We feel graced with the bounty of their efforts.

Thanks to the more than 300 guests who dined with us at the big table and provided feedback and insight into the recipes, meal presentation and preparation.

Special thanks to everyone on the cookbook team for their involvement each and every Monday – and many other days, too – throughout the year.

Inspiration for recipes comes from friends, family, other cookbooks, even from the food itself. We thank the many anonymous authors who were the inspiration or creators of many fine recipes. It's important to acknowledge those cooks and authors, and to explain that we didn't just sit at the kitchen table writing all new recipes.

We did lean on a few friends for favorite recipes: Bob Roan, local farmer, for the Meyer lemon meringue pie; Carol Arnold, manager of the Foothills Farmers' Markets in Placer County, for the angel food cake with strawberries; chef Geno Duggan for the May 4 meal; chef Courtney McDonald for the August 3 meal; pastry specialist Jen Linn for the Asian pear galette with pistachio ice cream and the warm apple compote; Candee Kenny for the olallieberry cobbler; Deborah Madison for the quinoa with nectarines and pistachios; Kay McCreary for the zucchini pickles; and Peg Tomlinson-Poswall for the chicken mole.

Our bread was the best, thanks to local pediatrician Roke Whitson, who modestly offered to practice his bread-making skills for each of our Monday night dinners. His amazing and delicious bread is a grain above the rest.

Thanks, also, to Susan Loomis, Cindy Fake, Christine Turner, Dan Macon, Steve Costa, Michael Pollan, David Lance Goines, Kate Levinson, Jennifer Johnson, Bill Percy, Steve Neft, Jennifer Elliott, Robert Weygandt, Jim Holmes, Susan Dupre, Barbara Read, Cheri March, Gary Moffat, Scott Craig, Shannon Hayes, Jo Robinson, Sara Perkovic, Keith Sutter, James Cole, Wayde Carroll, Michele Tuggle, Merrill Kagan-Weston, Randy Sater, Trish Kelly, Casey Kirk, Betsy Newman, Don Albrecht, Gerry Watson, Burnelle Kenny, David Harry, Ted Gaines, Debbie Dutra, Jerry Burns, Rosemarie La Rocca, Roger Ingram, Janice Forbes, Beth Gillogly, Jim Williams, Jeff Rieger, Tony Aguilar, Chris Caballero, Dennis Kenny, Candee Kenny, Neisha Lofing, Jill Benz, Laura Read, Tom Neary, Cindy Whitson, Betony Jones, Wes Cotton and Pat Rubin. This has truly been a community effort.

Many thanks to cookbook author Deborah Madison for pointing us in the right direction, for graciously and generously sharing her experiences with us, and for inspiring us to reach further with her words of wisdom.

introduction

by Deborah Madison, Author,
Local Flavors, Cooking and Eating from America's Farmers Markets

By her own description, Joanne Neft is a Lutheran German Minnesotan, and that means she is, above all, not interested in talking about herself. Nor is she even able to. But her story is partly what makes her book especially interesting and important. So that she doesn't have to talk about herself, I will attempt to do at least a little of that for Joanne in hopes that you can see the light her life sheds on these 52 meals.

When, in 1989, Joanne moved from Southern California north to Auburn, she was struck by the rich agricultural history of her new home. Placer County had once been a source of much of the country's pears and stone fruits. In the early 20th century, 42,000 acres of orchard fruits were in production. A railroad wound through Placer County's seven little towns, from Roseville to Auburn, picking up fruit from the packing sheds. There was a packing shed in nearby Newcastle no longer in use. But it once held thousands of boxes of fruit. The green, wooden shed was enormous, and it overlooked the highway. Joanne bought it with the idea that it might once again serve as a temporary home for Placer County fruit. It hasn't yet, but she helped build a market next to the shed that features local foods, both raw and prepared, from nearby.

Perched above the floor of the Central Valley with all its heat and agricultural dust, Placer Country proved an appealing place for Californians to live. Joanne saw the farmland in this area was endangered, that development had already taken many orchards on the rolling foothills of the Sierra, and threatened those that were left. Farming and ranching were succumbing to the usual economic pressures, and the new generation looked upon farming with disinterest. "Why work so hard for so little?" young people asked themselves. Even as late as 1989, there were no farmers markets in the area that encouraged small scale farming, or a sense among residents of what foods might be local. A farmers market, though, would be a good place to start nurturing local agriculture.

The first farmers market Joanne opened was in Loomis, down the road from Auburn. I remember her putting on a big red tomato outfit and luring people off the freeway to come to the market. She cooked samples of food for shoppers to try. She promoted the market and she organized and managed it. Then she got five other markets in Placer County up and running. Clearly, Joanne believed in the future of Placer County and its food and she got other people to see its possibilities, too.

Joanne loves farmers markets, and they are part of her early history: her father was a farmer who sold produce in the St. Paul farmers market, which began before Minnesota was even a state. In her own life she has honed a vision of local and seasonal eating and how it connects to the culture of farming, the sustainability of farmland, and good health and pleasure at the table. *Placer County Real Food* grew out of "her" local markets and the kind of agriculture she helped to encourage. While Placer County might once have been known only for its pears and stone fruits, it is now known for its Satsuma mandarins, a product Joanne has worked tirelessly to promote — she started the Mandarin Festival in 1994. It now draws

40,000 people a year. Placer County is also known for a more rare and historical product, *hoshigaki*, or dried persimmon, boarded on Slow Food's Ark of Taste, which is still produced (laboriously) by Japanese farmers in the area. Joanne promoted the *hoshigaki*. Every fruit and vegetable used in this book — even the horseradish — and all the meats were found at a Placer County farmers market.

One of the drawbacks to farmers markets is the (largely false) idea that "they're only for summer!" That used to be the case with my market in Santa Fe — its season went from May to November when I first moved here. But for the past several years, it has been a year around market, and that is true of markets in many places where winter is unfriendly. Farmers generally can grow something, or they can store something. Of course, California is blessed with a most tolerant climate, far better than what the rest of the country enjoys, so many California markets easily go year around. Even so, shoppers tend to hang back when it's foggy, cold or raining. *Placer County Real Food* shows that if you don't hang back and you do go out, you can enjoy real food every week of the year, beginning in January. You may discover a certain repetition of ingredients in this collection of 52 menus (and in your own shopping experience), but this is what you would expect from a locally driven cookbook. There are lots of Meyer lemons early on, and lots of peaches and tomatoes later. But local eating is about just this— eating through the cycles of foods, enjoying them when they're plentiful, missing, perhaps, but not replacing them, when they're gone.

One of the obstacles to eating seasonally is the notion that we can have everything all the time, which is how America eats when it eats from the supermarket. Eating locally, which means seasonally as well, is about feasting and fasting on foods as they come and go, and this book is a witness to the seasons progressing bit by bit, week by week. And when there are surpluses, there is freezing, drying and canning foods, which make a raspberry and plum pie on a winter's eve and other such treasures easily possible. For most shoppers, farmers markets have been most closely associated with produce, and, not surprisingly, many cookbooks that have sprung from farmers markets have been vegetarian, or at the very least, vegetable-centric. Meat, however, has also found its place in many farmers markets, especially those in Placer County (and just within the past few years), which means that this book, as you might expect from a Lutheran German Minnesotan, is a collection of meat-driven meals with high quality meats at the center of every menu. (Vegetarians, as Joanne points out, can feast on the myriad of wonderful plant foods that can also be found at the market.) Unlike most meat and three American meals, these are all locally sourced. An option to buying feedlot meat from the supermarket, it turns out, can be accomplished when local ranching is encouraged.

I would love to see every region in our country have such a book as this one, a book that shows us what we can eat throughout the course of the year in our particular foodsheds. There were no farmers markets when Joanne moved to Placer County 20 years ago; today she has produced a book of menus based entirely on what is available from one county's farms and its farmers markets. This is no small feat, but it did happen, and hopefully, this story of local meals shared by friends and strangers every Monday night of one year, will inspire readers elsewhere to discover their "real foods" and enjoy them with others.

foreword

A dear friend, Susan Dupre, casually planted the seeds for this cookbook one chilly December day in 2008. We were having lunch: a couple of mandarins, a Fuyu persimmon, some left-over chicken pickings, winter greens and a container of homemade Cinderella squash soup. The simple soup was hot, flavorful, just right for the day and the conversation. We talked about food, real food, simple food from the farmers market.

I explained how I always arrange my week so I have time every Saturday to shop at the farmers market in my hometown, Auburn, California, and how I buy very little of my food from a commercial grocery store. After I explained I'd been shopping and eating this way for 20 years, Susan said, "I want to make the same total commitment to the farmers market, Joanne, but I don't know how to do it. Could I follow you around the Saturday market to see how you buy your food?" What a lovely idea, I said, and offered to introduce her to my favorite growers. Susan thought a while, and then said, "Yes, well, it's one thing to know what to buy, but what if you don't know what to do with the food after you get home?"

I knew by the spark in her eye she wasn't finished, so it didn't come as a complete surprise when she added, "Joanne, why don't you just write a cookbook? That will make it easier for both of us." The *Placer County Real Food* cookbook was born.

Here's the gist: Small-scale farmers are producing exceptional food all over the country. Their produce is both delicious and nutritious. And yet they make very little income for their work, so little, in fact, that small farmers find it difficult to sustain a living from the five to 100-acre plots they cultivate. Many barely scrape by. Year after year they hang on because they love farming, but those who can't support their families are forced to sell. Often a developer replaces the orchards and gardens with rows of streets and buildings.

Located in northern California, Placer County lies east to west, and links the Sierra Nevada foothills near Sacramento to the high mountains around Lake Tahoe. About 150 years ago, gold miners discovered fruits and vegetables grow really well in the soils here. Fruits, especially, mature to a fine sweetness in the cooler temperatures of these elevations, which range from slightly above sea level to elevation 3,000 feet.

Our local growers make the majority of their farmers market incomes between May and October. They have to stretch that income over the low-selling months of winter, months that were more profitable in years past when more people cooked at home using the fresh produce of the season. If the farmers could sell as much during winter, they could live more comfortable lifestyles, and perhaps their children would be more interested in taking over the farm. If farms can be sustainable, the agricultural landscape – with its animal habitat, visual beauty, and food productivity – would not be eaten up with streets and subdivisions, and more people could eat nutritious, locally grown food.

foreword

The statistics tell the story: Approximately 1,500 people shop every week at the Auburn farmers market in summer, but only 500 people shop weekly in winter. I'd love to see that number triple during both seasons. Hoping to help boost attendance, I launched this cookbook project. Susan's timing couldn't have been better.

I asked my friend, and local chef, Laura Kenny, to join the venture. We devised a plan to buy every bit of the meal, from the beef and pork to the parsnips and persimmons, at the Saturday farmers market in Auburn. We'd develop simple recipes, and serve a complete meal to test those recipes every Monday night.

On January 3, 2009, we bought lamb shanks, German butterball potatoes, carrots, onions, mandarins, kiwis, Cinderella squash and Meyer lemons at the Auburn farmers market. I had some baking apples already in my pantry. At my house, two days later, Laura and I tasted our first recipes. We had Cinderella squash soup, mandarin and kiwi salad, mashed potatoes, sautéed rutabaga, braised lamb shanks and apple pie.

"This is really a delicious dinner," we said. "It's exactly what we want to do for 51 more weeks." We were off.

Food awareness has blossomed recently. Thanks to a couple of bestseller books and excellent documentaries, there's an invigorated international discussion about where food comes from, how it's grown, how it's picked and transported, and how it nourishes our bodies. This is in sharp contrast to the previous two decades during which I worked as an agricultural marketing director for Placer County. At that time, efforts to promote local food were moving like cool molasses. Suddenly, the molasses got warmer. Now it's starting to really flow.

Farmers markets are now in towns all over America, from San Leandro, California to Jersey City, New Jersey. The timing was right this year for a cookbook that shows how easy it really is, not only in Placer County, but also across the U.S., to eat locally grown food every day of the year.

An important step was to figure out how to promote our project. I turned to the books of Malcolm Gladwell, which have provided me many ideas in the past. In *The Tipping Point*, Gladwell says you need 150 people to totally understand what you're doing in order to get a word-of-mouth buzz going about your product. It occurred to me that we could connect with our 150 people – 200 plus, actually – if we

foreword

shared our meals with four guests in my home every week. Tapping an extensive email list, I invited friends and friends of friends to Monday night dinner. The response was overwhelming, and within a few weeks, every Monday dinner for 2009 was booked.

We quickly saw results of our outreach at the Auburn farmers market. On Saturday mornings, we'd see people whom we'd served the previous Monday evening. They'd say, "That meal was so delicious. We're trying to replicate it. Tell me again how you prepared the meat." Or "Was there anything special you added to the beans?" Laura or I would answer their questions, and then walk with them to the stall where we'd bought watermelon radishes or to the farmer from whom we'd bought Romano beans or okra. This happened over and over again.

I see so many people out of touch with the sources of our food – who grows it, how it evolves from seed to stem, how it's harvested, packed, and sold. From my own experience buying local produce at farmers

markets and preparing it simply at home, I'm convinced if you understand the sources of your food, and you know the people who grow it, you'll get more enjoyment from it, and after eating fresh, nutritious food at home, you'll feel better.

For me, eating fresh, in season, locally grown food is a way of life. Shopping at the farmers market is a way of life. I want to share that with you.

Happy cooking and eating,
Joanne Neft

tips from the chef
By Laura Kenny

If I could sit down with you as you read and cook your way through this book, if I could tag along as you shop, I'd have a few tips to share. They're things that don't fit inside any recipe, just bits and pieces of knowledge that have made me a more thoughtful, better informed cook. They're snippets of information I'd like to pass along to you.

🦟 Read a recipe thoroughly before you begin.

🦟 Some cooking ingredients shouldn't be substituted for less expensive brands. It's easy to justify saving a few cents here and there buying bargain brands, but don't. There are certain items that are tried and true; they won't let you down with a greasy macaroni and cheese, or a flat cake. We don't switch to bargain brands for our favorite mayonnaise, mustards, cheese, butter and oils. Bottom line: don't skimp on what you put in your body.

🦟 A meat thermometer is your best friend. Buy a good one; it won't cost much. One of the main lessons we learned was grassfed meats cook faster than traditional grocery store brands. Refer to our Meat Temperature Chart on page 59, and eatwild.com. Remember, too, if you want to cook a roast to 135°F, pull it from the oven when the thermometer reads 130°F, and as the meat rests, the temperature will climb to your desired 135°F.

🦟 All the recipes serve eight people. This way, they can easily be halved or quartered to feed your family of four or two.

🦟 Although there is not a vegetarian meal during the 52 weeks, any menu can be adapted. Most often, we practice the 80/20 rule, meaning 80% of our dinner is grains, fruits and vegetables, and the remaining 20% is protein.

🦟 Citrus sections versus segments (also called supremes): It's your choice. In some recipes, we call for citrus sections, and in others, segments. The difference is in the pith: a section has it, and a segment does not. To make segments, cut the ends off the citrus, and carefully cut away the rind and the pith. Next, slice out each segment, being careful to avoid the pith. It's a bit time consuming, but dresses up your dish a little more.

🦟 There are a few pieces of kitchen equipment I am rarely without. These include: sharp knives (the world is a better place when they're sharp); sheet trays (cookie sheets work, but a slight edge is sometimes necessary); parchment paper; a food mill; a citrus zester; a good vegetable peeler.

🦟 Improvisation is the key. Let the farmers market inspire you. Maybe you aren't fond of fava beans, but there are beautiful snap peas and green beans at the market that week. Substitute, experiment and enjoy. If you leave this book with nothing else, know you can shop at the farmers market year around, and create a simple, wholesome, delicious meal for your family.

shanks and squash

Cinderella Squash Soup

Lettuce, Mandarin and Kiwi Salad with
Sweet & Sour Vinaigrette

Braised Lamb Shank with Meyer Lemon Gremolata

German Butterball Mashed Potatoes

Sautéed Rutabaga and Baby Carrots

Apple Pie

Serves eight

It's all about simple, easy and in season.

We want readers to learn about delicious, easy recipes that use the cornucopia of unusual, interesting and beautiful produce found at farmers markets across the country.

As I walked through the Auburn farmers market, I'd hear people asking questions about the produce. How do you cook rutabagas? What's fennel? How do parsnips taste? How long do you bake a winter squash?

Chef Laura Kenny and I decided to make it easy for people to buy unfamiliar local foods and prepare them with minimal effort and only a few ingredients so the fresh flavor of the food is what you taste.

The first recipe, Cinderella Squash Soup, is a perfect example. It's simple and basic: take one squash, simmer the seeds, fibers and rinds in water, purée the squash, add to broth and serve. Since Cinderella squashes tend to be large, there will be plenty of soup to freeze and defrost for the next dinner party. Later in the spring we'll cut fresh watercress from a neighborhood creek, make soup, and freeze it for use at a later meal. Freezing fruits or vegetables while they're in season provides us a host of opportunities to savor local flavors long past the growing season.

Simple, easy, in season.

Blessings on the seed; blessings on the root;
Blessings on the leaf and sprout;
Blessings on the fruit.

Cinderella Squash Soup

Preheat oven to 375°F.

1 Cinderella squash, 9 to 10 pounds, quartered
⅓ cup olive oil
Salt and pepper to taste
Crème fraîche

To make a stock, remove the seeds and fibers from the squash, and put them in a large stockpot. Cover with water, bring to a boil, then reduce the heat and simmer for at least an hour. Rub each piece of squash with olive oil, and place on a sheet tray. Roast until the squash is tender when pierced with a fork, about 1 to 1½ hours. Cool slightly, and then remove the tough edges and rinds with a knife, taking care to save as much squash meat as possible.

Purée the squash, put it in a bowl, and set aside. Place the skins and rinds in the pot with the seeds. If needed, add more water to cover. Bring to a boil; reduce the heat and simmer slowly for 2 hours. Set a colander over a large bowl and drain the stock. Discard the seeds and rinds. Slowly stir the squash stock into the puréed squash until the consistency is soup–like. Season with salt and pepper to taste.

Serve in small bowls and top each one with a spoonful of crème fraîche.

Any extra broth or soup can be saved in the refrigerator or the freezer.

Take a virtual tour of the cookbook by visiting our website, placercountyrealfood.com. You'll find luscious photographs, get inside information about recipes, and meet the team of cooks, photographers, guests and supporters behind it.

Lettuce, Mandarin and Kiwi Salad with Sweet & Sour Vinaigrette

2 heads red leaf lettuce, torn into pieces
6 scallions, sliced
4 mandarins, segmented
3 kiwi, peeled and sliced
½ cup pecans, chopped
½ cup blue cheese, crumbled

Sweet & Sour Vinaigrette

½ cup olive oil
¼ cup brown sugar
¼ cup apple cider vinegar
3 drops Tabasco
Salt and pepper to taste

Toss all salad ingredients together. Whisk vinaigrette ingredients together, season with salt and pepper, and add to salad just before serving.

Braised Lamb Shanks with Meyer Lemon Gremolata

Braised Lamb Shanks

½ cup olive oil

8 small lamb shanks (approximately 6 pounds)

1 cup flour plus 1 teaspoon salt
    and ½ teaspoon pepper

2 large yellow onions, thinly sliced

1 head celery, stalks cut in 4-inch lengths

4 large carrots, peeled and sliced vertically

1½ quarts vegetable broth

2 cups dry white wine

2 tablespoons Herbs de Provence

2 tablespoons parsley, chopped

Heat oil in a medium stockpot. Season shanks in flour mixture, and sear quickly on all sides. Remove shanks to plate and set aside.

Add additional olive oil to pot if necessary, and caramelize onions until limp (about 10 minutes). Place shanks on top of onions, add celery and carrots. Sprinkle Herbs de Provence and parsley over shanks.

Barely cover shanks and vegetables with vegetable broth and wine. Bring to a boil, cover, and reduce heat. Simmer gently 2 to 3 hours. When shanks are tender and beginning to fall off bone, pull them out of the liquid, remove and discard celery and carrots.

Turn up heat and simmer until braising sauce is reduced by about one-third. Season the finished sauce to taste with salt and pepper.

Warm shanks in braising sauce and place in a large serving dish. Garnish with Gremolata.

Meyer Lemon Gremolata

4 Meyer lemons, zest and juice

½ bunch parsley, finely chopped

2 cloves garlic, minced

1 cup extra virgin olive oil

Salt and pepper to taste

Combine all ingredients and season to taste with salt and pepper.

january 5

German Butterball Mashed Potatoes

4 pounds German butterball potatoes,
    peeled and quartered
Salt to taste
1 cup milk
¼ pound (1 stick) butter

Cook the potatoes in salted water until fork tender. Drain and let dry.
Heat milk in a small saucepan until scalded.
Pass the potatoes through a food mill with butter and add warm milk to desired texture.
Season to taste with salt.

Sautéed Rutabaga and Baby Carrots

2 tablespoons olive oil
2 tablespoons butter
4 pounds rutabaga, peeled and cut into
    wedges (about 4 cups)
3 pounds baby carrots, peeled and halved
    lengthwise (about 4 cups)
Salt and pepper to taste

Heat oil and butter in a large skillet. Sauté vegetables until slightly tender.
Season to taste with salt and pepper.

Apple Pie

Preheat oven to 400°F.

Two-Crust Pie Dough for 9-inch Pan

¼ cup vegetable shortening

¼ cup butter

1½ cups all purpose flour

½ teaspoon salt

¼ cup cold water

1 teaspoon half-cinnamon/half-sugar mixture

½ teaspoon Demerara sugar (optional)

Using a pie dough cutter, blend shortening, butter, flour and salt together to cornmeal stage. Place in a medium bowl and slowly add cold water, mixing with a fork, until dough comes together. Add more water if necessary. Form into a ball, cover and chill at least 2 hours before rolling out.

Cut the dough ball into two pieces, one slightly larger than the other. Roll out dough until ⅛-inch thick. Make dough 10 inches round for bottom, and 9 inches round for top.

Place filling in the shell. Apply top crust. Trim, roll and crimp edges. Sprinkle with cinnamon sugar; then sprinkle Demerara sugar on top.

Pie Filling

1 cup sugar

2 tablespoons flour

1 teaspoon cinnamon

Pinch salt

6 to 8 apples, peeled, cored and
   sliced (5 to 6 cups)

1 tablespoon butter

Blend sugar, flour, cinnamon and salt. Set aside. Layer half of the apples in pie shell and sprinkle ½ cup sugar mixture over apples. Repeat. Top with remaining sugar mixture and distribute pieces of butter evenly over fruit.

Bake pie until a toothpick inserted comes out clean, and juices are bubbling around the crust, about 50 minutes.

The key to great, flaky pie crust is chilling the crust before rolling it out. Once you've formed the dough, cover it and put it in the refrigerator for two to six hours. Take it out of the refrigerator and let it sit long enough to take the chill off before rolling it out.

we love roots

Sweet & Sour Ginger Cole Slaw

Pan Seared Pollack with Meyer Lemon Beurre Blanc

Mashed Rutabaga

Roasted Root Vegetables

Plum and Raspberry Pie

Serves eight

There weren't many shoppers at the Saturday Auburn market. Fair weather shoppers don't show up when it's cold or it looks like rain. As I walk past the stalls, I think to myself, "It's a good thing Laura and I are writing a cookbook to help people understand how important it is to support farmers throughout the year, and not just during summer months when the weather is mild." Supporting local farmers is the real reason for writing this cookbook. Between the months of November and April, when shoppers think there's nothing at the market, we'll encourage regular attendance by providing simple recipes that explain how to prepare celery root, rutabaga, turnip, parsnip roots, winter squash, cabbages, broccoli, cauliflower, chard, spinach and Brussels sprouts. We'll talk about fennel and pea shoots, the fresh tastes of kohlrabi and watermelon radishes. In addition, this is the time of year nature provides loads of mandarins, Meyer lemons, and navel oranges. Our bodies need the vitamins in citrus to remain healthy through the chilly months.

Our goal is to provide opportunities for regional growers to plant more and varied crops throughout the entire growing season. It means our hillsides will be preserved for agricultural purposes rather than for building houses. Also, it means we'll have a healthier community because nature provides us with exactly what we need to eat when we need to eat it...in season.

Sweet & Sour Ginger Cole Slaw

½ head each Savoy (or Napa), red and Irish cabbage, finely shredded (total 12 cups)
2 carrots, peeled and grated
4 kiwi, peeled and sliced
4 mandarins, segmented
¼ cup pistachios

Ginger Dressing

1 cup mayonnaise
⅓ cup rice vinegar
2 tablespoons Mirin
1 teaspoon salt
Black pepper to taste
2 tablespoons fresh ginger, peeled and finely diced

Toss cabbage and carrots together. Just before serving, add Ginger Dressing, and garnish with kiwi slices, mandarin segments and pistachios.

Note: You can make the dressing ahead of time and toss over slaw just before serving.

Pan Seared Pollack with Meyer Lemon Beurre Blanc

Meyer Lemon Beurre Blanc

1 tablespoon olive oil
2 shallots, diced
½ bunch thyme
1 tablespoon black peppercorns
1½ cups white wine
2 Meyer lemons, segmented
1 pound butter, cut into small pieces
1 tablespoon parsley, chopped
Salt to taste

Prepare lemon beurre blanc first.
To make segments, cut ends off lemon. Use a knife to cut away the rind and pith. Carefully cut out each segment, avoiding the pith in between. Put lemon segments aside for sauce. Heat olive oil in a small saucepan. Add shallots, thyme, and peppercorn. Season lightly with salt and add wine and segmented lemon bodies and pith. Reduce mixture until almost dry. Turn heat to low, and slowly whisk in butter, a little at a time until emulsified. Strain and add lemon segments and parsley. Season to taste with salt. Set aside.

Pan Seared Pollack

2 tablespoons olive oil
3 pounds Pollack, cleaned and cut into 5-ounce portions
Salt and pepper to taste

Heat oil in large sauté pan. Season fish with salt and pepper and sear for 2 to 3 minutes per side, depending on thickness.
Transfer fish to serving plate, and spoon a small amount of buerre blanc over fish. Serve remaining sauce in a small bowl. Serve immediately.

january 12

Mashed Rutabaga

4 pounds rutabaga, peeled
¼ cup butter
Salt and pepper to taste

Cook rutabaga in salted water until fork tender. Pass through a food mill with butter and season to taste with salt and pepper.

Roasted Root Vegetables

Preheat oven to 375°F.

1½ pounds fingerling potatoes
1 pound baby carrots, peeled (about 1½ cups)
1 pound beets, peeled and large diced
  (about 2 cups)
1 pound celery root, peeled and cut into wedges
  (about 1½ cups)
3 tablespoons olive oil
Salt and pepper to taste

Toss potatoes with 1 tablespoon oil and season with salt and pepper. Roast 35 minutes. Add remaining olive oil to vegetables. Salt and pepper to taste, and roast until tender, about 25 minutes. Combine with potatoes.

In the fall and winter months, local farmers bring big baskets and boxes of winter vegetables, roots and tubers to the market. You'll find a colorful display of yams, beets, carrots, celery root, parsnips, turnips, potatoes, rutabaga and more. Growers carefully cut broccoli, cabbages, and cauliflower so the heads are resting on big, protective leaves. It's a feast for the eyes as well as for the table.

This flamboyant time of year, rather than flowers for the table, I buy a head each of Irish, Savoy and red cabbage, all sitting in their oversize leaves. I put them in a basket as a centerpiece just before dinner. After the meal is over, I ask people to gather up and take home part of the centerpiece. It's a nice surprise, and gives people a chance to prepare their own fresh, local dish.

Plum and Raspberry Pie

Preheat oven to 400°F.

Two-Crust Pie Dough for 9-inch Pan

¼ cup vegetable shortening

¼ cup butter

1½ cups all purpose flour

½ teaspoon salt

¼ cup cold water

1 teaspoon half-cinnamon/half-sugar mixture

½ teaspoon Demerara sugar (optional)

Using a pie dough cutter, blend shortening, butter, flour and salt together to cornmeal stage. Place in a medium bowl and slowly add cold water, mixing with a fork, until dough comes together. Add more water if necessary. Form into a ball, cover and chill at least 2 hours before rolling out.

Cut the dough ball into two pieces, one slightly larger than the other. Roll out dough until ⅛-inch thick. Make dough 10 inches round for bottom, and 9 inches round for top.

Place the filling in the shell. Apply top crust. Trim, roll and crimp edges.

Sprinkle with cinnamon sugar; then sprinkle Demerara sugar on top.

Pie Filling

4 cups Black Amber plums, sliced

1 cup raspberries

1 cup sugar

⅓ cup quick cooking tapioca or tapioca flour

½ tablespoon lemon juice

pinch of salt

1 tablespoon butter

In a large bowl, combine plums, raspberries, sugar, tapioca, lemon and salt. Let sit at least 30 minutes. Place filling in pie pan, and top with 1 tablespoon butter cut into small pieces.

Bake 50 minutes. Cool on a wire rack.

Tapioca flour is a relatively new product for most grocery stores. Use it just as you would quick cooking tapioca. Amounts are interchangeable: if a recipe calls for ¼ cup of quick cooking tapioca, you can substitute ¼ cup of tapioca flour.

Don't be afraid to use frozen plums, peaches or berries in pies. It's a great way to extend the season, and it's such a treat for me to open the freezer and know I can still enjoy the taste of summer fruit in the middle of winter.

family style meal

Green Salad with Kiwi and Blue Cheese
and Red Wine Vinaigrette

Pork Tenderloin with Fennel and Olives

Mashed Butternut Squash

Sautéed Broccoli

Meyer Lemon Tart with Dark Chocolate

Serves eight

We serve our dinners family style.

Guests gather around the table and await big platters of fresh-from-the-farm food. We pass each dish and one person serves themselves while another holds the platter.

Dinnertime conversation focuses on the food – how it was prepared, which farmer grew it, how long it will be in season, and which oils or seasonings enhance the taste. The recipes are simple since the goal is to let the meat or vegetable or fruit reflect its true flavor. Nothing tastes better than just-picked produce, and there is no reason to alter it.

Serving the meal family style has been a unique experience for many guests. Over the years people have forgotten to appreciate the generous spirit shared when meals are served family style. For many it brings back memories of big family meals and gatherings. However, here's another reason you might want to consider serving dinners this way. Researchers discovered a common link between students who did well on SAT tests: their families ate dinner together at a table every night. Serving dinner family style – passing food from one person to another – inspires civility, encourages families to talk about their day, and reinforces a natural connection between family members. Not to mention, smarter students.

Green Salad with Kiwi and Blue Cheese and Red Wine Vinaigrette

1 large head red leaf lettuce, torn into pieces
4 kiwi, peeled and sliced
¼ pound Homestead blue cheese, crumbled

Red Wine Vinaigrette

½ cup olive oil
3 tablespoons red wine vinegar
1 Meyer lemon, juiced
Salt and pepper to taste

Toss all salad ingredients together. Combine vinaigrette ingredients, and dress salad just before serving.

Pork Tenderloin with Fennel and Olives

3 pork tenderloins (1 pound each), silver skin removed, cut into 1-inch slices, each pounded to ¾ inch thick
2 teaspoons salt
1 teaspoon ground black pepper
4 tablespoons olive oil

For Sauce

3 tablespoons olive oil
2 fennel bulbs, thinly sliced (about 3 cups)
6 garlic cloves, minced (3 tablespoons)
2 cups mandarin juice and 1 tablespoon zest from mandarins
1 cup chicken stock (recipe follows)
2/3 cup pitted green olives, sliced
5 tablespoons chopped fresh parsley leaves

Sprinkle salt and pepper over both sides of pork slices. Heat one tablespoon olive oil in heavy-bottomed pan. Brown pork slices 90 seconds on each side. Work in batches of no more than 6 slices to avoid over crowding. Transfer pork to plate.

Using medium heat, place 3 tablespoons oil in pan in which pork was cooked. Add fennel, and sauté until softened (about 2 minutes). Add garlic, sauté 1 minute more. Add juice, and bring to a boil, scraping pan bottom with wooden spatula.

Cook until liquid reduces to a glaze (about 2½ minutes). Add chicken stock.

Increase heat to high and boil until liquid reaches consistency of maple syrup (about 3 minutes). Reduce heat to medium; return pork to pan with zest, olives, and parsley, turning meat to coat. Simmer to heat and blend flavors (3 minutes). Transfer pork to serving plate and spoon sauce over meat. Serve immediately.

Chicken Stock

2 to 3 pounds chicken bones (wing tips, backs, necks, feet) or whole legs and wings
2 cups celery stalk, sliced (include leaves)
2 medium carrots, sliced
1 large onion, sliced in large pieces
1 teaspoon salt
12 peppercorns
4 whole cloves
2 bay leaves

Place bones in one gallon stockpot; add water to slightly cover. Add remaining ingredients. Cover and bring to boil; immediately reduce to simmer 1½ to 2 hours.

Strain stock and discard bones and vegetables. Return stock to pan and boil until reduced to ½ original amount of liquid. Check seasoning, and add more salt if desired.

Store covered for up to one week.

Freezes well.

Mashed Butternut Squash

Preheat oven to 375°F.

3 butternut squash, quartered
2 tablespoons olive oil
Salt and pepper to taste
¼ cup butter

Season squash quarters with olive oil, salt and pepper. Place cut side down on a cookie sheet and roast 45 to 50 minutes. Cool slightly and scoop squash into large bowl, avoiding any seeds. Mix in butter with a fork and season to taste with salt and pepper.

> Chef Laura Kenny suggests using a combination of equal parts olive oil and butter to sauté vegetables. The combination gives foods the great flavors of both.

Sautéed Broccoli

1 tablespoon butter
1 tablespoon olive oil
4 heads broccoli, cut into medium sized pieces
Salt and pepper to taste

Heat butter and oil in a large skillet over medium-high heat. Add broccoli. Sauté until tender (about 4 minutes). Season to taste with salt and pepper.

Meyer Lemon Tart with Dark Chocolate

Preheat oven to 375°F.

Tart Dough

¼ cup heavy cream
2 egg yolks
2¾ cups plus 2 tablespoons all purpose flour
¼ cup plus 3 tablespoons sugar
¼ teaspoon salt
½ pound butter

Whisk the cream and eggs together in a small bowl. Set aside.

In a mixer, combine flour, sugar, salt and butter. Mix to cornmeal stage. Slowly add cream and yolks and mix until just combined.

Divide dough in half. Form into 2 disks, wrap one and put in freezer to use later.

Roll remaining dough ¼-inch thick and fit into a 10-inch tart pan. Press in sides and use a rolling pin to cut excess from edges.

Chill for 1 hour.

Remove dough from refrigerator. Prick dough with a fork, cover with parchment paper and put beans or pie weights on top.

Bake 15 minutes, remove paper and beans, and continue to bake 10 to 15 minutes longer. Cool completely.

Filling

3 ounces bittersweet chocolate
4 eggs
3 egg yolks
1 cup plus 1 tablespoon sugar
1 cup Meyer lemon juice
10 tablespoons cold butter, cut into small pieces
Pinch salt
1 tablespoon Meyer lemon zest

Melt chocolate over double boiler and spread on cooled tart shell. Place in fridge until set. Meanwhile, make the curd by whisking eggs, yolks, sugar and lemon juice together in a heavy bottomed saucepan. Cook over medium heat, stirring constantly, alternating between a whisk and rubber spatula. When the curd has thickened to the consistency of pasty cream, remove from the heat, and whisk in butter and salt. Strain curd into a small bowl and mix in zest. Let curd cool about 8 minutes and then pour into tart shell. Chill at least 2 hours before serving.

Visiting and spending time in your home feels like floating in a cup of hot milk with honey: simply delicious.
Luthea Thomas, Truckee

Lemon zest is the aromatic, flavorful, oil-rich outer skin of a lemon. It can be peeled or grated, but be careful to only remove the brightly colored outside layer and not the white pith below the skin. Use the zest to flavor raw or cooked foods, sweet or savory dishes, or as a garnish. Zest adds a punch of lemon flavor to foods, especially pies.

rainy day dinner

Root Soup

Red Leaf Salad with Champagne Vinaigrette

German Butterball Mashed Potatoes

Beef Stew

Vanilla Ice Cream with Homemade Bittersweet
Chocolate Sauce and Mandarin Segments

Serves eight

Never throw away a bone.

Turn meat bones into stock, instead. Someone once told me the meat closest to the bone is the sweetest meat. I never miss an opportunity to make stock out of meat bones. And if I can't make it right away, I wrap the bones in plastic and put them in the freezer until I have enough bones and time.

Making your own chicken or beef stock for soup is easy, easy, easy, and stock is one of the most important ingredients in soups, stews and gravies. Talk about full flavored: homemade stock is the best.

Don't worry about a recipe because anything goes that suits your taste. Several ingredients always find their way into my stock: carrots, celery, onions, peppercorns, a bay leaf, and, in a chicken stock, a few cloves.

I guarantee once you start making your own stock, you'll never want store-bought again.

Root Soup

Preheat oven to 350°F.

1 pound each potatoes, turnips, carrots,
   rutabaga, and white sweet potatoes, peeled
2 white or yellow onions, thinly sliced
1 teaspoon dried thyme
1 teaspoon dried ground bay leaf
1 tablespoon olive oil
Crème fraîche or sour cream

Wash all roots carefully; save tops and bottoms
and peels. In a stockpot, cover peels, tops and
bottoms with water and boil 2 to 3 hours until
water takes all flavor from peelings. Strain root
tops, bottoms and peels from broth. Set broth
aside.
Cut roots in 1-inch pieces, roll in olive oil, and
sprinkle with thyme and ground bay leaf. Roast
until tender.
Meanwhile, caramelize onions in olive oil.
In a large pot, purée cooked onions and roasted
roots. Add root broth to purée. The mixture will
be the consistency of pea soup. If soup seems
too thick, add more water. Season to taste with
salt and pepper.
Serve hot and garnish with crème fraîche or sour
cream.

In recipes calling for olive oil, we use
Calolea California Extra Virgin Olive Oil.
Calolea also produces a fabulous Meyer
lemon olive oil. Taste it, and you'll swear
you've just sliced a Meyer lemon. We also
enjoy Calolea White Balsamic Vinegar.

Red Leaf Salad with Champagne Vinaigrette

1½ heads red leaf lettuce, torn into pieces
½ cup blue cheese, crumbled

Champagne Vinaigrette
½ cup olive oil
3 tablespoons Champagne vinegar
1 Meyer lemon, juiced
Salt and pepper to taste

Toss all salad ingredients together. Whisk
vinaigrette ingredients together, and add to salad
just before serving.

German Butterball Mashed Potatoes

2 pounds German butterball potatoes
3 tablespoons butter
½ cup milk

Cook the potatoes in salted water until fork
tender. Drain and let dry. Heat milk in a small
saucepan until scalded. Pass the potatoes
through a food mill with butter and add warm
milk to desired texture. Season to taste with salt.

january 26

Beef Stew

10 pounds beef shoulder roast with bones
2 cups flour with salt and pepper
½ cup olive oil
4 large carrots, sliced into 3-inch pieces
½ head celery
2 large onions, thinly sliced
2 tablespoons Herbs de Provence
2 quarts beef broth
2 cups hearty red wine
1 pound shitake mushrooms, sliced
9 cups small carrots, steamed until crisp

Remove beef from bones. Discard fat. Cut beef into 1-inch cubes.
Put flour mixture in separate bowl; set aside.
Heat olive oil in large pan, shake two large handfuls of beef in bowl with flour mixture and add to hot olive oil. Turn meat until brown on all sides. Remove to dish, add more olive oil and continue browning two handful amounts until all meat is browned and removed from pan.
Using the same pan, add 2 more tablespoons olive oil and caramelize onions on slow heat for 10 minutes. When caramelized, add enough beef broth to scrape drippings from bottom of pan. Add remaining beef broth, red wine, Herbs de Provence, meat, bones, large carrots and celery. Cover and bring to a boil; immediately put on very low heat to simmer for 2 to 3 hours.

(Note: local grassfed beef takes a much shorter time to cook.)

Taste meat for doneness and flavor. Remove carrots, celery and bones. Discard.
Five minutes before serving, add sliced raw mushrooms to pan. Immediately before serving, add cooked small carrots.
Serve with mashed German butterball potatoes.

Feasting on beef stew makes for the perfect ending to a rainy, gray January day.

Vanilla Ice Cream with Homemade Bittersweet Chocolate Sauce and Mandarin Segments

½ gallon French vanilla ice cream

Homemade Bittersweet Chocolate Sauce:

(Makes 1¼ cups)

2¼ ounces Ghirardelli bittersweet chocolate chips
(or Dagoba Chocodrops)

2 tablespoons butter

2 tablespoons light corn syrup

¾ cup heavy cream

¾ cup sugar

2 teaspoons vanilla extract

1/8 teaspoon salt

2 mandarins, segmented

In a heavy saucepan melt chocolate chips with butter and corn syrup over moderately low heat. While stirring, add cream and sugar, and cook until the sugar is dissolved.

Bring mixture to a boil at medium–high; reduce heat to medium–low and continue to boil, without stirring, for 7 minutes.

Remove the pan from heat and stir in vanilla and salt.

Serve the sauce hot over ice cream. Top with mandarins.

To store, wait until sauce is completely cooled. If you cover the sauce before it's cooled, condensation will make it grainy. Keep sauce, covered, in the refrigerator up to a month.

Fox Barrel, a micro-cidery located in the Sierra Foothills, hand crafts ciders in the tradition of Colonial America. It was our pleasure to begin every meal with a glass of Fox Barrel Black Currant Cider.

Romanesco is one of the
most beautiful vegetables.

february 2

red, white & green

Balsamic Honey Onions on Crostini

Red Leaf Salad with Sweet & Sour Vinaigrette

Lamb Chops with White Beans and Tomato
with Meyer Lemon Gremolata

Steamed Romanesco

Ice Cream Balls with Mandarin and Meyer Lemon Sauce

Serves eight

A display of Romanesco broccoli caught my eye at the Auburn farmers market one week. I stopped and stared. I went over and picked up one of them, and thought, "This is the most beautiful vegetable at the market."

Romanesco is an edible flower first documented in Italy during the sixteenth century. Rich in fiber, carotenoids, and vitamin C, the vegetable is light green in color and is considered a fractal: each bud is composed of a series of small buds and each resembles the whole flower.

During the fall season, I use a Romanesco broccoli as a centerpiece and it dependably steals the show.

We're fortunate to have Francis and Janice Thompson, owners of Twin Brooks Farm, growing rows and rows of this delicious, vitamin-rich crop. They've been involved in local farmers markets since 1989 when the Loomis farmers market opened. Ten years later, in 1999, they opened the Newcastle Produce Market. It's the big orange building visible high above Interstate 80 as it winds through Newcastle. The market specializes in fresh, locally-produced foods.

Romanesco is great slightly cooked or left raw for an appetizer. However you decide to use this gorgeous vegetable, remember, never, never overcook Romanesco.

Balsamic Honey Onions on Crostini

5 pounds yellow or red onions, thinly sliced
¼ cup butter
2 tablespoons honey
2 tablespoons balsamic vinegar
1 loaf bread, sliced and toasted to make crostini

Cook onions in butter over medium heat until onions are caramel colored and reduced to half the original volume. Add honey and balsamic vinegar, and continue cooking over medium heat until thick.
Taste; add more honey or vinegar as needed.
Serve on crostini.

"Crostini" means "little toast" in Italian, and any good artisan bread will do the trick. Slice the bread thinly, about ¼ inch, brush it with olive oil, add a pinch of salt and pepper and then bake it at 350°F 10 to 12 minutes, until crisp.

Red Leaf Lettuce with Sweet & Sour Vinaigrette

2 heads red leaf lettuce, torn into pieces
3 mandarins, segmented
2 kiwi, peeled and diced

Sweet & Sour Vinaigrette

½ cup olive oil
¼ cup brown sugar
¼ cup apple cider vinegar
Dash of Tabasco
Salt and pepper to taste

Whisk vinaigrette ingredients together. Toss lettuce with vinaigrette just before serving, and garnish with mandarin and kiwi slices.

I was thirty-two when I started cooking; up until then, I just ate.

Julia Child

Lamb Chops with White Beans and Tomato with Meyer Lemon Gremolata

Meyer Lemon Gremolata

1 Meyer lemon, zest and juice
¼ cup parsley, finely chopped
1 small clove garlic, minced
¼ cup extra virgin olive oil
Salt and pepper to taste

Combine all ingredients and season to taste with salt and pepper. Set Gremolata aside.

Lamb Chops with White Beans and Tomato

Preheat oven to 400°F.

1 pound small dry white beans
16 rib lamb chops, trimmed of fat
Salt and pepper to taste
2 tablespoons grapeseed oil
⅔ cup chopped onion
One 28-ounce can of whole tomatoes,
   finely chopped
2 tablespoons garlic, minced (about 6 cloves)
3 teaspoons finely chopped fresh rosemary leaves
1½ cups chicken broth

Soak and cook dry white beans according to directions on package. Do not add salt until after beans are cooked. Set beans aside.
Pat lamb chops dry and season with salt and pepper.
Place grapeseed oil in a large, heavy stoveproof and ovenproof casserole and heat until hot. Add lamb chops, and brown about 1½ minutes on each side. Tansfer lamb chops to plate.
Add onion to casserole and cook, stirring over moderately low heat until softened.
Add tomatoes, garlic, and rosemary and cook over moderate heat, stirring 1 minute.
Stir in chicken broth and beans and simmer 3 minutes, stirring occasionally.
Arrange lamb chops on top of bean mixture.
Roast, uncovered, on middle rack 5 minutes for medium-rare. Let lamb chops and bean mixture stand, loosely covered, 5 minutes.
Transfer lamb chops to a large serving dish.
Toss bean mixture with gremolata. Add beans to serving dish.

Steamed Romanesco

1 large head Romanesco,
  cut into medium sized pieces
Salt and pepper to taste

Steam Romanesco until tender crisp. Season to taste with salt and pepper.

Meyer lemons were imported from China in 1908 by F. N. Meyer. They're thought to be a cross between a lemon and a mandarin. The shape of a Meyer lemon is rounder, the skin smoother, the juice sweeter and less acidic, and the color more variable than commonly available lemons.

Ice cream balls are easy to make.

Ice Cream Balls with Mandarin and Meyer Lemon Sauce

Mandarin and Meyer Lemon Sauce

1 cup sugar
2 cups mandarin juice
2 tablespoons cornstarch
4 tablespoons butter
3 tablespoons Meyer lemon juice
3 tablespoons mandarin zest

Blend sugar, mandarin juice, and cornstarch. Whisk in a double boiler until thick. Remove from heat. Add butter to melt. Add lemon juice and mandarin zest. Chill.

Ice Cream Balls

½ gallon French vanilla ice cream
½ cup pecans, diced
½ cup walnuts, diced
½ cup graham cracker crumbs
8 mandarin slices

Let ice cream container sit at room temperature until ice cream is easy to scoop.
Combine diced pecans and walnuts with graham cracker crumbs. Set aside.
Once ice cream is softened, make 8 small balls or 4 large balls. Roll in diced pecan, walnut and graham cracker crumb mixture. Place balls on metal tray and immediately place in freezer. If using large balls, slice in half immediately before serving.
Top with Mandarin and Meyer Lemon sauce and a slice of mandarin.

persimmon pudding and pork

Triple Cabbage Cole Slaw with Sweet & Sour Ginger Dressing

Coffee-Rubbed Pork Shoulder Roast

Mashed Rutabaga and German Butterball Potatoes

Roasted Cauliflower, Broccoli and Fennel

Persimmon Pudding mit Schlag

Serves eight

In the months when persimmons are not in season, it's a happy day when I find another freezer bag or container packed with frozen persimmon pulp. It's a clear message the time is right for another batch of cookies or persimmon pudding.

I discovered the delights of persimmons after moving to Berkeley, California, from Colorado. I had the good fortune to be the sixth employee at Dymo Industries, where I met Dot Hummert.

Her husband was vice president of sales at the company. Dot introduced me to the wonders, flavors, textures and colors of food growing, caught, dried or pressed in California. Among the most memorable tips and recipes Dot shared was her favorite: persimmon pudding mit schlag.

For almost 50 years persimmon pudding has been a house staple, and, without fail, dinner guests are hesitant to try it. It's not a beautiful dish. So I put the pudding on the table with the schlag in a small bowl, and ask everyone to serve themselves. Just take a small amount of pudding and top it with schlag, I tell them. Try it. After just one taste they all ask for more and swear it's the best pudding they've ever tried.

Triple Cabbage Cole Slaw with Sweet & Sour Ginger Dressing

½ head each Savoy (or Napa), red, and green cabbage, finely shredded (12 cups)

½ cup scallions, finely sliced

4 kiwi, peeled and sliced

4 mandarins, segmented

⅓ cup almonds, sliced, or salted peanuts

Sweet & Sour Ginger Dressing

1 cup mayonnaise

⅓ cup rice vinegar

2 tablespoons Mirin

1 teaspoon salt

Black pepper to taste

2 tablespoons fresh ginger, finely diced

Toss cabbage and scallions together, and finish with sweet & sour ginger dressing. Garnish with kiwi, mandarins and almonds or salted peanuts.

Coffee Rubbed Pork Shoulder Roast

Preheat oven broiler to 400°F.

4 tablespoons coffee beans, ground

4 tablespoons ground black pepper

2 tablespoons kosher salt

1 teaspoon cayenne pepper

2 tablespoons ground cumin

5 pounds pork shoulder roast, without bone

Place the ground coffee on a sheet of aluminum foil. Put in oven, about 6 inches from broiler heat source. Broil about 45 seconds, shaking the foil about every 10 seconds, or whenever you see smoke. Remove from oven.

In a small bowl, stir together the coffee, black pepper, salt, cayenne pepper, and cumin. Rub onto pork and let marinate at least 2 hours.

Turn oven to 400°F, bake setting. Roast pork 20 minutes, then turn temperature down to 300°F and continue cooking 2 more hours, or until 150°F. Let meat rest 15 minutes before slicing.

Mashed Rutabaga and German Butterball Potatoes

2 pounds rutabaga, peeled and quartered
2 pounds German butterball potatoes,
   peeled and quartered
2 tablespoons butter
¼ cup milk
Salt and pepper to taste

Cook rutabagas and potatoes in water until
tender. Drain well. Add butter and milk; mash
with a mixer or potato masher. Season to taste
with salt and pepper.

*What a pleasure it was to join you for a meal
focusing on the bounties of our local farmers
market. The food was delicious, and the setting
of your beautiful home and garden made it an
extra special evening. You are definitely making
a difference in our world.*
                    Jenny and Herb Grounds, Auburn

Roasted Cauliflower, Broccoli and Fennel

Preheat oven to 350°F.

3 pounds assorted cauliflower and broccoli,
   cut into bite-size pieces
2 bunches fennel, julienne
1 large yellow onion, julienne
3 cloves garlic, chopped
2 tablespoons olive oil
Salt and pepper to taste

Toss all ingredients together in a large bowl and
season with salt and pepper. Roast on a sheet
tray until vegetables are slightly tender and
starting to
get color,
about 20 to
25 minutes.

february 9

Persimmon Pudding mit Schlag

Start this pudding when guests arrive, or about two hours before you expect to eat it, so it's ready and piping hot in time to serve at the end of the meal.

1 cup sugar

1 cup flour

2 teaspoons baking soda

1 teaspoon cinnamon

½ teaspoon salt

3 tablespoons butter, melted

1 egg, beaten

1 cup Hachiya persimmon pulp

½ teaspoon vanilla

½ cup milk

Powdered sugar

Sift together sugar, flour, baking soda, cinnamon and salt. Using a hand beater, add melted butter, egg, persimmon pulp, vanilla, milk and powdered sugar. Next, grease and sugar pudding mold. Add pudding mixture.

Heat an inch of water in a large pan. Set pudding mold on an inverted bowl to make sure mold is not standing in water. Cover pan, and let pudding steam over simmering water for at least 1½ hours. The pudding will begin to pull away from the sides of the pan when done. Remove mold from pan and let rest 5 minutes before turning onto large plate. Sprinkle pudding with powdered sugar just before serving.

Schlag

1 egg, beaten

2 cups powdered sugar

2 tablespoons melted butter

1/8 teaspoon salt

4 tablespoons brandy

1 cup heavy cream

Whisk egg, sugar, butter, salt and brandy together. Set aside. Whip cream. Fold brandy mixture into whipped cream.
Place schlag in small serving bowl. (If the sauce separates, whisk it again.)

february 16

valentine special

Endive Salad with Warm Bacon Vinaigrette

Roasted Leg of Lamb with Fennel Butter

Roasted Yellow Finn Potatoes

Sautéed Chinese Broccoli

Strawberry and Kiwi Trifle with Lemon Cream

Serves eight

Talk about feeling special. Can you imagine my surprise when one day in early February I was handed a huge box sent by my friend Rich Collins of California Vegetable Specialties, which supplies all of the endive between here and the Mississippi. In the box was a beautiful bouquet of freshly picked endive, roots and all, wrapped with a big red bow and presented in red floral paper. Lovely.

On February 9, I used the arrangement as a centerpiece and the following week we served it as a salad.

Combine fresh endive with Canadian-style bacon cured by Bob Sorenson of Coffee Pot Ranch and you have a salad fit for a king. Some people frown at using warm bacon fat in a salad, but remember, it's one or two meals a year, and we owe it to ourselves to taste something that good at least once a year.

If you don't think you can use a lot of endive very quickly, don't worry. Endive holds well in the refrigerator. However, it's important to keep it covered because it discolors in the light.

february 16

Endive Salad with Warm Bacon Vinaigrette

4 pounds endive, cleaned and sliced
Cooked diced bacon from warm bacon
    vinaigrette recipe
½ cup pecan halves, toasted
3 navel oranges, segmented

Warm Bacon Vinaigrette

½ pound bacon, diced
2 tablespoons Champagne vinegar
1 tablespoon Meyer lemon juice
¼ cup olive oil
Salt and pepper to taste

Cook bacon over low heat until crisp. Remove
bacon from pan and set aside with salad
ingredients.

In a small metal bowl, combine bacon fat,
vinegar, lemon juice and oil. Whisk to emulsify
and season lightly with salt and pepper. Place
bowl on low heat to keep warm.

Toss salad ingredients with vinaigrette. Serve
immediately.

Slurry is a thin paste of water and starch, such as flour, cornstarch or arrowroot, that is added to hot stews, soups and sauces as a thickener, says Chef Laura Kenny. Be sure the slurry is well blended into the mixture, and then bring it to a low boil to cook out the slurry's raw, flour-like taste.

A roux, pronounced "roo," is also used as a thickener. It is a mixture of flour and fat (typically butter), and is used to thicken soups, stews, gravies and more. There are three types, or colors, of roux: white, blond and brown. The color depends on how long you cook it. White and blond roux are made with butter, and you continue cooking them until they reach a golden brown color. Brown roux is made with butter or drippings, and can be cooked until it is deep brown.

Roasted Leg of Lamb with Fennel Butter

Preheat oven to 425°F.

½ pound butter

2 tablespoons fennel pollen

3 cloves garlic, chopped

3 tablespoons Dijon mustard

1 tablespoon soy sauce

1 tablespoon ground black pepper

2 teaspoons rosemary, chopped

Two 3 to 4-pound legs of lamb, boneless

Salt and pepper to taste

2 cloves garlic, chopped

4 tablespoons grapeseed oil

2 bulbs fennel, julienne

2 cups red wine

1½ cups chicken stock

In a mixer, combine butter, fennel pollen, 3 cloves garlic, mustard, soy sauce, pepper and rosemary. Mix well. Set aside.

Season the lamb with salt, pepper and 2 cloves chopped garlic. Tie with twine to form small roasts. In a large skillet, heat grapeseed oil and sear lamb on all sides. Top with half of the butter mixture and roast 20 minutes. Turn oven down to 325°F. Add fennel to pan. Cook until internal temperature of the meat registers 130°F for medium-rare, about 30 minutes. Transfer meat and fennel to platter and skim off fat from the roasting pan. Place roasting pan across two burners. Over high heat, add wine and chicken stock. Reduce by half, thicken with slurry if desired, and finish with remaining butter mixture. Slice lamb and serve with sauce and roasted fennel. Check seasoning again, and add more salt and pepper if desired.

Roasted Yellow Finn Potatoes

Preheat oven to 400°F.

3 pounds Yellow Finn potatoes, quartered
1 sprig rosemary, chopped
3 tablespoons olive oil
Salt and pepper to taste

Toss all ingredients in a large bowl and season with salt and pepper. Roast 30 to 35 minutes, or until tender.

I made the mistake of visiting the website, www.placercountyrealfood.com when I was hungry. Bad thing to do. I visited again after a meal. Also a bad thing to do. The site offers spectacular photography, talented cooking, good website design all wrapped in a wonderful idea. It's great.

Janice Forbes, Auburn

Sautéed Chinese Broccoli

2 tablespoons olive oil
3 cloves garlic, minced
3 bunches Chinese broccoli,
   trimmed and cut into small pieces
Salt and pepper to taste

In a large skillet, heat oil. Add garlic. Cook until tender crisp. Add broccoli and sauté until tender, about 2 to 3 minutes. Season to taste with salt and pepper. Serve immediately.

Chinese broccoli is also called Chinese kale. It looks a little like broccoli, and a little like kale with bright green stalks, dark green leaves and clusters of tiny white flower buds. Chef Laura Kenny describes the flavor as asparagus-like, and recommends sautéing or grilling the stalks. When shopping for Chinese broccoli, look for firm stalks and somewhat tight leaves, she says. Don't discard the leaves because they're great sautéed or grilled.

Strawberry and Kiwi Trifle with Lemon Cream

Do not preheat the oven for this cake.

3 cups cake flour
¾ teaspoon salt
1 cup butter, softened, plus additional for pan
3 cups sugar
7 eggs, at room temp
2 teaspoons vanilla
1 cup heavy cream

Generously butter and flour a 10-inch tube pan.
Sift together flour and salt. Sift three times. Set flour mixture aside.

Beat butter and sugar together in a mixer at medium–high speed until pale and fluffy, about 5 minutes. Add eggs, one at a time, beating well, and then beat in vanilla.

Reduce speed to low and add half of the flour mixture, all of the cream, then the remaining flour, mixing well each time. Scrape down bowl and then beat on medium–high speed for 5 minutes.

Spoon batter into pan and tap against work surface to eliminate any air bubbles.

Place pan in cold oven, and turn to 350°F.
Bake until golden brown, about 1 to 1¼ hours.
Cool cake in pan on rack for 20 minutes, then turn onto rack and finish cooling. Cut into 1-inch square pieces.

Lemon Cream

9 egg yolks
4 Meyer lemons, zest and juice
1½ cups sugar
2 cups whipping cream
¼ cup sugar
4 kiwi, peeled and sliced
3 pints strawberries, halved
Shaved bittersweet chocolate

Bring a pot of water to a simmer.
Combine the yolks, lemon juice and sugar in a metal bowl and whisk until smooth.
Set the bowl on top of the pot of water, without the bottom touching, and continue to whisk until curd has doubled and become thick and pale (about 10 minutes). Remove from heat, stir in zest and let cool completely. Set lemon curd aside.
Add sugar to whipping cream, and whip until stiff. Fold gently into cooled lemon curd.
To assemble the trifle, place a layer of cake pieces in a trifle dish or large glass bowl. Top with half of the lemon cream, being careful not to dirty the sides of the dish. Place half of the strawberries and kiwi on the cream layer, making sure they show from the side view. Add another layer of cake, then cream, and finish the top with remaining fruit and shaved chocolate. This dish can be made up to 4 hours ahead.

wild and fresh fish

Romaine Salad with Red Wine Vinaigrette

Wild Petrale Sole

Mashed Potato and Celery Root

Roasted Brussels Sprouts

Bread Pudding with Citrus Caramel Sauce
and Whipped Cream

Serves eight

Living on the west side of the Sierra Foothills in Northern California, we don't expect to see a lot of fresh fish in traditional grocery stores. Fortunately, at our local farmers markets there will be one or more purveyors selling fresh fish, beef, pork, lamb, goat and poultry. That makes us some of the luckiest shoppers in the country.

One of my favorites is the Little Fish Company, owned by Brand Little. He fishes out of Bodega Bay, and the fish he catches on Friday morning is packaged late Friday afternoon and available at the Auburn farmers market Saturday morning. It doesn't get any fresher than that.

I especially love the Petrale sole he brings to market. Petrale sole is actually a flounder and has excellent flavor. The meat is fine-textured and has low fat content. For this week's recipe, any thin white fish will do. Be careful never to overcook fish. We rolled the fish in this recipe so it looks attractive, is easier to handle, and is less likely to overcook.

Romaine Salad with Red Wine Vinaigrette

1 head romaine lettuce, cleaned and chopped
1 bulb fennel, thinly sliced
¼ cup walnuts, toasted

Red Wine Vinaigrette

¼ cup red wine vinegar
½ cup olive oil
¼ cup grapeseed oil
1 Meyer lemon, juiced
Salt and pepper to taste

Combine lettuce, fennel and walnuts. In a separate bowl, mix together the vinegar, oils, lemon juice, salt and pepper. Add vinaigrette just before serving and toss.

If you eat food and wear clothes, you ARE involved in agriculture –Wendell Berry

I came across this quote several years ago, and the simplicity and truth of the message struck me as profound. Our lives depend upon the farmers and ranchers who are willing to work so hard in agriculture, and who take many risks over which they have no control so the rest of us have the luxury of pursuing interests other than feeding and clothing ourselves and our families.

Farmers and ranchers are grossly underappreciated and under compensated for their work. As a community, and as individuals, we owe them our active support and heartfelt thanks.

*Christine Turner, Placer County
Agriculture Commissioner, Auburn*

Wild Petrale Sole

4 pounds Petrale sole
2 tablespoons grapeseed oil
2 Meyer lemons, sliced
2 tablespoons parsley, chopped
Salt and pepper to taste

Separate the fillets of sole by removing and discarding the backbone. You'll end up with one small fillet and one larger fillet.

To roll, place one larger fillet presentation side down, on a cutting board. Place smaller fillet on top and season lightly with salt and pepper. Starting with the tail end, roll the two up together.

Heat oil in a large skillet and sear the fish on two sides. (For larger rolls, place seared fish in 350°F oven to finish cooking, about 5 to 7 minutes.) Serve with sliced Meyer lemons and parsley.

Everything you served tasted of itself, but better. The ingredients were the stars of the show and the way they were prepared allowed the eater to taste each component of the dish, as well as the delicious combination of the ingredients. The lettuce tasted of lettuce, the chicken tasted of chicken, but Laura's delicate and deft touch in combining flavors elevated the food above the mere ingredients. There was no overwhelming of the diner's senses with lots of butter and garlic, just pure fresh foods allowed to express their true texture, color, and most of all flavor.

Jim Muck Produce, Wheatland

Roasted Brussels Sprouts

Preheat oven to 375°F.

2 to 3 pounds Brussels sprouts,
    cleaned and halved
2 tablespoons olive oil
¼ cup local honey
1 teaspoon Herbs de Provence

Toss Brussels sprouts with oil and season with salt and pepper. Place on a sheet tray and roast 10 to 15 minutes, or until tender crisp.
While Brussels sprouts are cooking, heat honey and herbs on low heat. When Brussels sprouts are slightly tender, toss with honey mixture.

Mashed Potato and Celery Root

2 pounds German butterball potatoes,
    peeled and halved
3 heads celery root, peeled and cut into wedges
½ cup whole milk
½ cup butter
Pinch of salt

Using a large pot, cover the potatoes and celery root with salted water. Cook until tender enough to mash. Drain well.
Pass through a food mill with the butter and then add the milk. Stir slightly. Season to taste with salt.

Give Brussels sprouts a chance. I guarantee you'll be surprised at the creamy texture and delicate taste of direct-from-the-farm Brussels sprouts. Remember, Brussels sprouts in grocery stores were picked 15 days ago and traveled hundreds of miles to get to your dinner table.

Bread Pudding with Citrus Caramel Sauce and Whipped Cream

Bread Pudding

Preheat oven to 325°F.

2 cups whole milk

2 cups cream

3 egg yolks

3 whole eggs

1 cup honey

½ teaspoon vanilla

2 tablespoons orange zest

8 cups bread, cut into 1-inch cubes, no crust

Combine milk, cream, egg yolks, eggs, honey and vanilla, and pour over bread. Let sit at least 2 hours.

Pour mixture in a baking dish and smash down slightly to remove any air pockets.

Cover and bake in a cake pan in a shallow water bath 45 to 50 minutes.

Check for doneness by pressing on middle; if any liquid rises, continue baking 5 to 10 minutes longer.

Let sit 15 to 30 minutes before serving.

Citrus Caramel Sauce

2 cups mandarin juice

1 cup cream

4 tablespoons butter

1 cup sugar

In small pot, cook mandarin juice over medium heat until it is reduced to the consistency of maple syrup (to about ¼ cup).

Strain reduced juice into a small bowl and add cream; set aside.

In a small saucepan, melt butter over medium heat. Add sugar and continue to cook until lightly caramelized, about 4 minutes. Add the juice mixture slowly, stirring constantly. Simmer 5 minutes longer, while still stirring, and then strain again.

Whipped Cream

½ cup whipping cream

2 teaspoons sugar

½ teaspoon vanilla

In a mixer, combine the ingredients and whip until desired thickness.

To serve, spoon out bread pudding and garnish with the caramel sauce and whipped cream.

Claudia Smith of Blossom Hill Farm sells fresh, organic eggs at the Auburn farmers market. You can depend on her being there every week.

pork loin and spring greens

Spinach and Apple Salad with Mustard Vinaigrette

Mustard Crusted Pork Loin

Roasted Fingerling Potatoes and Rutabaga

Sautéed Broccoli Rabe with Garlic and Chile Flakes

Cheesecake with Pecan Crust and Mandarin Honey Sauce

Serves eight

After a rainy, foggy, chilly winter, March means spring is either here or just around the corner, and that means you'll find colorful displays of Bloomsburg spinach, broccoli rabe, rutabaga and spring greens at growers' tables. Delicious winter squashes and root vegetables aside, it's refreshing to sample the bounty of spring.

Wheatland farmer Jim Muck grows the Bloomsburg variety and it's our first choice for spinach. This spinach has slightly curly leaves, is a rich dark green color and provides a healthy dose of vitamins A, B and C. Highly nutritious, spinach is higher in iron, calcium and vitamins than most cultivated greens.

Although it has broccoli's name, broccoli rabe is not related to broccoli. It's closely related to turnips and is probably why the leaves look like turnip greens. Stems are uniform in size and are not peeled. This vegetable is a source of vitamins A and C, as well as potassium. Wash, remove tough stems, and sauté briefly. Simple.

Many people shy away from rutabaga, but it's good peeled and roasted, and adds another flavor when served with potatoes. Roasting rutabaga is easy. My taste buds like rutabaga mashed with a big piece of real butter and a dash of salt and pepper. Delicious.

march 2

Spinach and Apple Salad with Mustard Vinaigrette

Preheat oven to 350°F.

2 bunches spinach, cleaned and torn into pieces
1 bulb fennel, thinly sliced
2 apples, thinly sliced
¼ cup pecans or almonds

Mustard Vinaigrette

¼ cup whole grain mustard
¼ cup Dijon mustard
3 tablespoons apple cider vinegar
½ cup olive oil
1 Meyer lemon, juiced
1 tablespoon shallots, minced
Salt and pepper to taste

Toast nuts until slightly browned. Toss salad ingredients together. Add vinaigrette to salad just before serving and toss together.

Mustard Crusted Pork Loin

Preheat oven to 375°F.

¼ cup whole grain mustard
2 tablespoons Dijon mustard
2 teaspoons fennel pollen
1 tablespoon minced garlic
2 teaspoons rosemary, chopped
1 teaspoon thyme, chopped
¼ cup olive oil
2 teaspoons salt
1 teaspoon pepper
4 pounds pork prime rib (pork loin with ribs attached)
½ cup white wine (Sauvignon Blanc)

Combine mustards, fennel pollen, garlic, herbs, oil, salt and pepper. Set aside.
Butterfly the loin, keeping the ribs attached. Spread half of the mustard mixture on inside of pork and roll back up. Tie with twine to secure pork loin, spread the rest of the mustard on the top and sides.
Roast 1 to 1½ hours. Let rest 10 minutes before slicing. Remove roast from pan and deglaze pan with wine. Pour over sliced pork and serve.

Don't overdo it!

Ideal internal temperatures (Fahrenheit)
for cooking reliably-sourced grassfed and pastured meats

Meat	Suggested Temperatures for Grassfed Meat	USDA Recommended Temperatures
Beef & Bison	120–140°	145–170°
Ground Meat	160°	160°
Veal	125–155°	145–170°
Lamb & Goat	120–145°	145–170°
Pork	145–160°	160–170°
Chicken (unstuffed)	165°	165°
Turkey (unstuffed)	165°	165°

www.grassfedcooking.com

Grassfed meat takes less time to cook than traditionally raised meat. Author and grass-based farmer Shannon Hayes (www.grassfedcooking.com) explains it this way:

"Since [grassfed] animals are typically smaller framed than the factory farmed animals (smaller framed animals finish better on grass), their smaller size will result in lower cooking time. Grassfed/ pastured animals will have highly variable fat content as well, which impacts cooking time. Lower intramuscular fat reduces the cooking time. That is why reducing the overall cooking temperature is so important."

About one percent of the US population regularly eats grassfed meat.

march 2

Roasted Fingerling Potatoes and Rutabaga

Preheat oven to 375°F.

2 pounds fingerling potatoes, halved
1 pound rutabaga, peeled and quartered
2 tablespoons olive oil
1 tablespoon parsley, chopped
Salt and pepper to taste

Separately toss potatoes and rutabaga with oil. Season with salt and pepper. Bake separately on sheet trays 15 to 25 minutes. Combine and garnish with parsley.

Sautéed Broccoli Rabe with Garlic and Chile Flakes

2 tablespoons olive oil
1 tablespoon garlic, chopped
3 bunches broccoli rabe
Salt and pepper to taste
½ teaspoon chile flakes

In a large sauté pan, heat oil. Add garlic and cook until fragrant, being careful not to burn. Add broccoli rabe and season with salt, pepper and chile flakes. Continue to cook until tender crisp.

For a slide show of luscious, mouth-watering photos, visit our website at www.placercountyrealfood.com. You'll leave wanting to shop at the very next farmers market.

Cheesecake with Pecan Crust and Mandarin Honey Sauce

Preheat oven to 350°F.

Crust

½ cup pecans

½ cup brown sugar, packed

2 cups all purpose flour

1 cup unsalted butter, cold and cut into
   small pieces

1 teaspoon cinnamon

1 teaspoon ground ginger

¾ teaspoon salt

In a food processor, pulse pecans with sugar
until finely ground.
Add flour, butter, cinnamon, ginger and salt.
Pulse until mixture begins to form large lumps.
Press mixture onto bottom and sides of a 9-inch
springform pan.
Bake 20 to 25 minutes. Remove from oven.
Turn oven up to 475°F.

Cheesecake

5 eight-ounce packages cream cheese

1¾ cups sugar

¼ teaspoon vanilla

1 teaspoon lemon zest

3 tablespoons all purpose flour

¼ teaspoon salt

5 eggs

2 egg yolks

¼ cup heavy cream

Beat cream cheese until smooth. In a separate
bowl, combine sugar, vanilla, lemon peel, flour
and salt and slowly add to cream cheese. Add
eggs, one at a time and then stir in cream.
Pour into pie crust.
Bake 8 to 10 minutes, then turn oven down to
200°F and continue baking 1 hour.

Mandarin Sauce

2 cups mandarin juice

¼ cup honey

2 oranges, cut into segments

To cut orange segments, cut ends off oranges,
and, using a knife, cut away the rind and pith.
Carefully cut out each segment avoiding the pith
in between. Set aside.
On medium heat, reduce mandarin juice to about
¼ cup (the consistency of syrup or a glaze).
Reduce heat to low, and add honey to reduced
juice. Remove from heat and let cool at room
temperature.
Drizzle sauce over sliced cheesecake, and top
each slice with a couple of orange segments.

the best stew ever

Red Leaf Lettuce Salad with Champagne Vinaigrette

Lamb Neck Slices Stew with Rosemary Dumplings

German Butterball Mashed Potatoes

Steamed Broccoli

Meyer Lemon Meringue Pie

Serves eight

Dan and Samia Macon named their farm Flying Mule, an appropriate name because Dan plows the land using mule power. Located on the outskirts of Auburn, the farm's mission is to produce the highest quality meats and vegetables in the most sustainable manner. We place advance orders for Dan's lamb and chickens because we like the secure feeling of knowing we always have fine lamb and poultry in the freezer.

Lamb neck slices stew is my favorite lamb dish. Meat next to the bone is always the sweetest and this stew is full of bones, lots of bones. Always simmer lamb stew slowly, the slower the simmer, the better the stew. And don't be bashful about the bones. Everyone wants to nibble on them to experience all the flavors.

Top this meal with Bob Roan's famous lemon meringue pie. At farmers market dinners, people line up for Bob's lemon pie, and feel totally left out if someone isn't willing to share a taste. By the way, Bob is a regular at the market. During late spring and summer Bob and Teri Ueki sell heirloom tomatoes, Romano beans, and creative flower arrangements.

This is a meal that should be served with your best friends, the friends who want to enjoy every last forkful on the plate.

march 9

Red Leaf Lettuce Salad with Champagne Vinaigrette

3 heads red leaf lettuce, torn into pieces

1 bunch radishes, thinly sliced

2 bunches beets, roasted, peeled and sliced

4 scallions, sliced

¼ cup blue cheese, crumbled

Champagne Vinaigrette

2 tablespoons orange juice

1 tablespoon balsamic vinegar

2 tablespoons Champagne vinegar

¼ cup olive oil

Salt and pepper to taste

Toss salad ingredients together. Whisk vinaigrette ingredients together in separate bowl, and add to salad just before serving.

Lamb Neck Slices Stew with Rosemary Dumplings

Preheat oven to 200°F.

Lamb Neck Slices Stew

5 pounds lamb neck slices with bones,
  cut into 2 to 4-inch cubes

½ cup flour seasoned with salt and
  pepper to taste

3 tablespoons grapeseed oil

2 tablespoons butter

4 carrots, medium-size, peeled and
  halved vertically

2 medium onions, thinly sliced

4 cups chicken broth

1 cup white wine (Chardonnay)

1 cup vegetable broth

1 cup navel orange juice

1 teaspoon orange zest

2 tablespoons bay leaf seasoning

4 tablespoons parsley, finely chopped

Dredge lamb in seasoned flour. Set aside. Heat the grapeseed oil and butter in a deep stainless steel pan; add the lamb and fry 2 to 3 minutes on each side, or until golden brown all over. Transfer lamb onto a plate.

Lower heat, add more oil if necessary, add onions and cook until caramelized (5 to 7 minutes).

Place fried lamb on top of onions. Add carrots, chicken and vegetable broths, wine, and orange juice. Add orange zest, bay leaf seasoning, 3 tablespoons parsley and blend with large spoon. Bring to a boil, then immediately reduce to a very slow simmer. Cook 2½ to 3 hours, or until lamb is soft and tender.

Remove lamb from broth, cover with foil, and place in oven; discard carrots.

Take out 1 cup broth and set aside for dumplings. Simmer remaining broth until it thickens to gravy consistency. Return lamb to thickened gravy. Keep warm until ready to serve.

Rosemary Dumplings

1 cup broth (set aside from recipe above)

1 quart chicken stock

2 eggs

4 tablespoons water or milk

2/3 cup flour

½ teaspoon fresh rosemary, chopped

Pinch of salt

Fifteen minutes before serving stew, heat broth and chicken stock in a large sauce pan until liquid comes to a boil.

To make dumplings, whisk eggs with water or milk; then add flour, rosemary and a dash of salt. Whisk together.

Moisten a soup spoon, and scoop ½ spoonful of dumpling batter. Place it gently in slowly boiling broth mixture.

Once all dumplings are in broth mixture, reduce heat, cover pan and simmer 10 minutes. Do not remove lid from pan until dumplings are done.

To serve: Place lamb stew in a large serving bowl. Carefully remove dumplings from broth and place on top of stew; sprinkle stew with one tablespoon chopped parsley.

www.placercountyrealfood.com

German Butterball Mashed Potatoes

3 pounds German butterball potatoes
Pinch of salt
3 tablespoons butter
¾ cup milk
Salt and pepper to taste

Cook potatoes in salted water until fork tender. Drain and let dry.
Heat milk in a small saucepan until scalded. Pass the potatoes through a food mill with butter and add warm milk to desired consistency. Season to taste with salt and pepper.

When you see German butterball potatoes at the farmers market, buy them. Hands down, they make the very best mashed potatoes. Nothing tastes like German butterballs.

Steamed Broccoli

2 teaspoons olive oil
2 heads broccoli, stems removed and
  cut into small florets
⅓ cup water
Salt and pepper to taste

Heat a large skillet, add olive oil and then broccoli. Season lightly with salt and pepper and add water. Cover and cook about 2 minutes, or until tender crisp. Check seasoning and serve.

Meyer Lemon Meringue Pie

Thanks to Bob Roan for this recipe.

Pie Shell (for a 9-inch crust)
Preheat oven to 450°F.

1½ cups all purpose flour
½ teaspoon salt
½ cup shortening
3 to 4 tablespoons cold water

Sift together flour and salt; cut in shortening until pieces are the size of small peas. Sprinkle water over mixture, gently mix with fork. Form into ball and chill in refrigerator for 20 minutes.
Flatten ball sightly and on lightly floured surface roll out dough and place in pie pan (flute the edge with your fingers).
Prick bottom and sides with a fork to reduce puffing.
Bake 10 to 12 minutes. Remove to cool.

Bob Roan is a Placer County farmer well known at the farmers market for his rhubarb and wonderful sweet onions. This lemon meringue pie recipe is one of Bob's favorites.

Filling

1 cup sugar

2 tablespoons grated lemon zest

1½ cups water

¼ cup cornstarch

¼ teaspoon salt

5 large egg yolks (farm fresh eggs work best; set whites aside for meringue)

½ cup Meyer lemon juice (use ¾ cup juice for tart flavor)

¼ cup butter

Mix sugar with zest. Whisk together sugar mixture, water, cornstarch and salt in a medium saucepan.

Bring the mixture to a boil over medium-high heat, whisking constantly. Boil until the mixture is smooth and almost transparent, about one minute. The mixture will thicken.

Remove the pan from the heat.

In a medium-sized bowl, whisk together the egg yolks and lemon juice. Add ½ cup hot cornstarch mixture to the yolk mixture and whisk to blend. (This prevents the yolks from hardening when they are added to the hot mixture).

Add yolks to the saucepan, and bring back to a boil over medium-high heat. Let boil for one minute or until thick.

Remove the pan from the heat and whisk in the butter. Fill pie shell with the filling.

Meringue

Preheat oven to 350°F.

½ cup sugar

1 tablespoon plus 1 teaspoon cornstarch

½ cup water

5 large egg whites at room temperature

Pinch salt

Whisk sugar and cornstarch together in a small saucepan. Add water and bring to a boil, whisking constantly over high heat. Boil for one minute until thick. Remove from heat.

Beat the egg whites with mixer at low speed until foamy. Increase mixer speed to high, add the salt, and beat until mixture forms soft peaks.

Pour the cornstarch mixture in a fine stream while the beaters are running and continue beating until stiff peaks form.

Put meringue over filling, making sure meringue touches the crust all around the pie. Bake 15 to 17 minutes or until golden brown.

Cool on wire rack. Cool completely before serving.

st. patrick's supper

Red Leaf Lettuce Salad with Kiwi and Oranges
and Balsamic Vinaigrette

Corned Beef with German Butterball Potatoes,
Carrots, and Cabbage

Graham Cracker Cake with
Meyer Lemon and Mandarin Cream

Serves eight

During March, the Meyer lemons on our trees are at the peak of flavor. The lemons are sweet and tangy, and the zest is pungent and deeply colored. If we're lucky, we still have Satsuma mandarins in the refrigerator from our last picking. Now is the ideal time to blend mandarin and lemon juices to make a tasty citrus cream.

As a child in Minnesota, I remember my mother baking graham cracker cake, and serving it with a hot caramel topping. I decided topping it with citrus cream would be even better. Blending Meyer lemons, mandarins, and new-crop walnuts gives the cake a distinctive California touch.

The cake calls for whole milk and the cream uses whipping cream. Generally I buy organic dairy products from grass-fed cows raised using balanced sustainable agricultural practices.

Red Leaf Lettuce Salad with Kiwi and Oranges and Balsamic Vinaigrette

Preheat oven 350°F.

3 heads red leaf Lettuce, torn into pieces
4 kiwi, peeled and sliced
3 oranges, segemented
¼ cup pistachios

Balsamic Vinaigrette

¼ cup balsamic vinegar
1 teaspoon white balsamic vinegar
¼ cup extra virgin olive oil
½ cup grapeseed or blended oil
⅓ cup Meyer lemon juice
Salt and pepper to taste

Toast pistachios until slightly browned. Toss salad ingredients together. In a separate bowl, whisk vinaigrette ingredients together, and add to salad just before serving.

Tip: Keep greens fresh longer in the refrigerator by placing them in a plastic bag or container with a paper towel. The towel absorbs the moisture, but holds it to keep the greens from drying out or getting soggy.

First, wash the greens gently in cold water, and lay them on a paper towel on the counter to dry before putting them in a plastic bag. Be careful not to break or crush the greens; they'll stay fresher when whole. The exception is basil. Place it in a vase on the counter.

We brined the corned beef ourselves for this recipe, and that's why the meat isn't the pinky-red color of store-bought corned beef. It's much healthier because it doesn't contain unpronounceable preservatives and artificial colors. Even though it's a bit time consuming, it's really easy to do, and very satisfying.

Corned Beef with German Butterball Potatoes, Carrots, and Cabbage

6 cups water

¾ cup kosher salt

⅓ cup brown sugar, packed

¼ cup pickling spices

6 pounds beef brisket

1 pound carrots, quartered

2 large onions, quartered

4 pounds potatoes, peeled and quartered

2 pounds carrots, peeled and quartered

1½ heads cabbage, each half sliced into 3 pieces

Combine water, salt, sugar and spices in a large saucepan and bring to a boil, stirring until sugar and salt dissolve. Remove from heat and let cool to room temperature.

Poke several holes in the brisket and place in a large plastic bag or bowl with a lid. Pour brine over meat, making sure it is completely submerged. Refrigerate 5 to 7 days.

To cook:

Preheat oven to 200°F.

Remove beef from the brine and place in a Dutch oven or large, heavy-bottomed pot with a lid. Add quartered onions and carrots and enough water to cover. Cover and simmer meat until tender, about 2 to 3 hours. Skim off any foam that appears.

When meat is tender, remove from pot with a large slotted spoon and place on a pan in oven to keep warm.

Remove and discard carrots and onions.

Place potatoes into cooking liquid and bring to a boil. Turn down and continue cooking until tender. Remove potatoes and add carrots. Simmer 5 minutes and add cabbage. Continue cooking until both are done and remove.

To serve, place the potatoes in a serving bowl; the carrots and cabbage together on another; slice the beef and arrange on a plate and spoon some of the cooking liquid over it.

Serve with dill, Dijon mustard or German brown mustard.

Graham Cracker Cake with Meyer Lemon and Mandarin Cream

Preheat oven to 350°F.

½ cup butter, room temperature

1 cup sugar

1 teaspoon vanilla

3 egg yolks

¼ cup cake flour, sifted

1½ teaspoons baking powder

⅓ teaspoon salt

2½ cups graham cracker crumbs

¾ cup whole milk

½ cup walnuts chopped

3 egg whites, stiffly beaten

Beat butter to soften. Gradually add sugar and cream together until light and fluffy. Add vanilla and egg yolks; beat until well mixed.

In a separate bowl, sift flour, baking powder, and salt together; add to creamed mixture alternately with graham cracker crumbs and milk, a small amount at a time. Beat after each addition until smooth. Add nuts. Fold in whites. Bake in a buttered parchment paper lined 8 x 13-inch Pyrex pan 20 to 25 minutes.

Meyer Lemon and Mandarin Cream

5 egg yolks

2/3 cup sugar

2 tablespoons Meyer lemon juice

3 tablespoons mandarin juice

2 teaspoons Meyer lemon or mandarin zest

1 cup heavy whipping cream

Beat egg yolks until lemon colored. Add sugar, 1 tablespoon lemon juice and 2 tablespoons mandarin juice.
Whisk in a double boiler until thick, stirring constantly.
Take double boiler off heat, cool slightly, add remaining juices and zests. Set aside.
Whip cream until lightly firm.
Fold egg mixture into cream.
Spoon over slices of graham cracker cake just before serving.

The bounty of good food at the table was a reminder to me that our farmers are some of the very finest found anywhere in the world. It was a privilege to be present when the farmer's produce was used with much honesty and honor.
    Michael Marks,
    Your Produce Man, Sacramento

all american pot roast

Mixed Greens with Roasted Beets and Blue Cheese
and Balsamic Vinaigrette

Pot Roast au Jus

Roasted Sweet Potatoes, Asparagus, Carrots and Leeks

Plum and Blackberry Pie

Serves eight

All the beef, lamb, pork, goat, chicken and turkey prepared in our recipes are grassfed and available at the farmers market.

One of the blessings of living in the Sacramento region is the year-round availability of local, wholesome grassfed meats. Eating grassfed meat supports sustainable agriculture, which provides environmental health, economic profitability, and social and economic equity.

Check out www.highsierrabeef.com for beef availability. High Sierra Beef produces meat in a way that is good for the animals, good for the land, and good for consumers. Best of all, grassfed beef not only tastes good, but, it has substantially less fat than grain-fed meat. In addition, the omega-3 and omega-6 fats in grassfed beef are more beneficial and there is more beta-carotene, vitamin E, and CLA (conjugated linoleic acid) "good" fat.

I challenge you to find grassfed meat wherever you live. If your farmers market doesn't have anyone selling grassfed meat, ask some of the growers whether they know someone who does. Ask them where they buy their meat.

Mixed Greens with Roasted Beets and Blue Cheese and Balsamic Vinaigrette

Preheat oven to 350°F.

1 pound mixed baby lettuces, torn into pieces
1 bunch baby beets, roasted
¼ cup green onions, sliced
¼ cup blue cheese, crumbled

Balsamic Vinaigrette

3 tablespoons cherry balsamic vinegar
½ cup olive oil
Salt and pepper to taste

To roast, trim the greens from the beets, and place beets in shallow pan with ½ cup water.
Cover pan with foil.
Roast 25 to 35 minutes, or until tender. Peel when cool and slice in wedges.
Toss with salad ingredients, and vinaigrette before serving.

I've always been fascinated with cookware. And I insist my cookware be versatile and durable, and that it works well for whatever purpose I need. This fascination began nearly 50 years ago when I invested what at that time was an exorbitant amount of money in a complete set of seven-ply construction cookware. Basically a blend of stainless steel and aluminum alloy, the cookware seals with only a minimum amount of water, thus retaining full flavor and food color.

After using the cookware for 30 years, some of the handles and knobs broke. Realizing this could happen again, I ordered a huge supply of replacement parts. Today I happily cook using the same cookware I bought 50 years ago.

My love of cookware also includes cast iron pans. Eight cast iron pans of varying sizes are in the cupboard, and are used every day. Cast iron skillets heat evenly and hold heat once a flame is removed. I like that.

For baking pies and pastry, I use Pyrex glass pans, and I have many shapes and sizes. I also prefer glass cookware for baking casseroles, gratin and stuffing.

Of course, for making large amounts of stew, soup or stock, I use giant stainless steel stockpots or a one gallon aluminum pot I remember my mother using for cooking spaghetti noodles.

Pot Roast au Jus

Preheat oven to 325°F.

Pot Roast

2 beef chuck roasts, bone-in
   (about 4 pounds each)
Salt and pepper to taste
3 tablespoons grapeseed oil
4 baby carrots
4 leek tops (reserve the bottoms)
4 tablespoons olive oil
1 cup full-flavored red wine
1 cup beef broth
1 tablespoon butter

Season the beef with salt and pepper.
In a large heavy-bottomed roasting pan, heat oil
on high, and sear roasts on both sides, about 3
minutes each side. Add carrots and leek tops.
Roast 40 to 45 minutes.

Turn the oven up to 450°F and continue cooking
10 minutes more, or until internal temperature
reaches 135°F. Let rest at least 20 minutes.
Discard carrots and leek tops.
Place beef in 200°F oven to keep warm.

au Jus

Skim some of the fat from the pan and place pan
on the stovetop. Add red wine and simmer for
a couple minutes, scraping anything that might
be stuck on the bottom. Add beef stock, bring to
a boil, and turn down to simmer. (For a thicker
sauce, add 2 teaspoons cornstarch dissolved in 1
tablespoon water.) Add butter and remove from
heat.

Cut roast into hearty slices, adding meat juices to
pan juices. Adjust seasoning and strain.
Serve immediately.

march 23

Roasted Sweet Potatoes, Asparagus, Carrots and Leeks

Preheat oven to 375°F.

4 pounds white sweet potatoes, peeled and
    cut into pieces

3 pounds asparagus, cut into 2-inch long pieces

4 leeks, halved, then sliced into
    ½-inch pieces (reserve bottoms)

2 pounds baby carrots, peeled and halved

6 tablespoons olive oil, divided

1 tablespoon garlic, minced

2 tablespoons parsley chopped

Toss sweet potatoes with 2 tablespoons oil, salt and pepper, and roast 20 to 25 minutes. Remove from heat.

Toss asparagus with 2 tablespoons oil, salt and pepper to taste, and roast 10 to 15 minutes.

Toss leeks with 2 tablespoons oil, salt and pepper, and roast 10 to 15 minutes. Remove from heat. Add carrots and garlic to leeks and roast an additional 20 to 25 minutes.

Toss all vegetables together and garnish with parsley.

Note: Vegetables can be roasted an hour ahead of time and reheated just before serving.

Plum and Blackberry Pie

Preheat oven to 400°F.

Two-Crust Pie Dough for 9-inch Pan

¼ cup vegetable shortening

¼ cup butter

1½ cups all purpose flour

½ teaspoon salt

¼ cup cold water

1 teaspoon half-cinnamon/half-sugar mixture

½ teaspoon Demerara sugar (optional)

Using a pie dough cutter, blend shortening, butter, flour and salt together to cornmeal stage. Place in a medium bowl and slowly add cold water, mixing with a fork, until dough comes together. Add more water if necessary. Form into a ball, cover and chill at least 2 hours before rolling out.

Cut the dough ball into two pieces, one slightly larger than the other. Roll out dough until ⅛-inch thick. Make dough 10 inches round for bottom, and 9 inches round for top. Place the filling in the shell. Apply top crust. Trim, roll and crimp edges. Sprinkle with cinnamon sugar; then sprinkle Demerara sugar on top.

Pie Filling

4 cups Black Amber plums, sliced (do not peel)

1 cup blackberries

1 cup sugar

⅓ cup tapioca flour or quick cooking tapioca

Juice of ½ lemon

Pinch salt

1 tablespoon butter

In a large bowl, combine plums, blackberries, sugar, tapioca, lemon and salt. Let sit at least 30 minutes.

Place filling in pie pan and top with 1 tablespoon butter cut into small pieces.

Bake 50 minutes. Cool on a wire rack.

spring is here

Watercress Salad with Bacon Vinaigrette

Pan Seared Swordfish with Citrus Relish

Calrose Rice with Leeks

Snow Peas with Spring Garlic and Almonds

Ice Cream with Strawberries and
Balsamic Reduction and Shortbread Cookies

Serves eight

As a child, I was embarrassed when my father would stop alongside moving streams, pull out his pocket knife and cut watercress. I thought people would think we couldn't afford to buy food. It wasn't until I was an adult with children of my own that I understood the value of fresh watercress, and I always carry a pair of scissors and a freezer-type bag in the car just in case I come across a patch of cress.

A member of the mustard family, watercress grows along the banks of quickly moving streams. The small, dark green leaves have a sharp, peppery flavor, almost like arugula. Keep it fresh in the refrigerator, or put it in a small vase to use as a table decoration.

There is a small window of opportunity for picking watercress. Once the weather turns hot, the watercress gets bitter. In most recipes, watercress soup excepted, you can substitute arugula when watercress isn't available. Watercress soup freezes well; freezing extends the season through hot summer months.

Watercress Salad with Bacon Vinaigrette

Preheat oven to 350°F.

8 pieces bacon
1 pound watercress, stems removed
1 head leaf lettuce, torn into bite-size pieces
¼ cup blue cheese, crumbled
¼ cup almonds, toasted

Bacon Vinaigrette

¼ cup reserved bacon fat
¼ cup olive oil
¼ cup apple cider vinegar
1 tablespoon brown sugar
½ lemon, juiced
Salt and pepper to taste

Cook the bacon on a sheet tray in oven 15 to 25 minutes, until just crispy. Set fat aside. Crumble bacon into small pieces and set aside.
Toss watercress and lettuce together. Garnish with blue cheese, almonds and bacon. Add vinaigrette just before serving.

Pan Seared Swordfish with Citrus Relish

Preheat oven to 350°F.

Pan Seared Swordfish

3 to 4 pounds swordfish, cut into 5-ounce pieces
3 tablespoons grapeseed oil
Salt and pepper to taste

Season the fish with salt and pepper. In a large cast-iron pan, heat oil and sear fish on both sides, about 2 minutes each.
Remove from pan and bake until just cooked through, about 7 to 10 minutes.

Citrus Relish

5 navel oranges, segmented
¼ cup red onion, minced
¼ cup red cabbage, finely sliced
2 tablespoons olive oil
2 tablespoons scallion, sliced
Salt and pepper to taste

Combine all ingredients and season to taste with salt and pepper. The relish can be made up to 3 hours ahead.
To serve, arrange fish on a serving platter and top with relish.

The majority of people eat over a thousand meals a year and if a man lives a normal span he has some fifty sentient years in which to enjoy more than 10,000 meals. This surely is a matter of some importance and worthy of considerable time and thought.

Frank Oliver

Calrose Rice with Leeks

3 cups Calrose rice

6 cups water

Salt and pepper to taste

1 tablespoon butter

3 leeks, chopped

2 tablespoons parsley, chopped

Rinse rice and drain well.

In a large pot, combine rice, water and salt. Bring to a boil, turn down to a low simmer, cover and cook 25 to 45 minutes, depending on the type of rice. You can also use a rice cooker.

While still hot, transfer into a large bowl and season lightly with salt and pepper.

Meanwhile, in a small sauté pan, heat the butter and add the leeks. Cook until fragrant and add to the rice with the parsley.

Calrose Rice, grown at Greco Farms in Lincoln, is one of our staples in the kitchen.

march 30

Snow Peas with Spring Garlic and Almonds

2 tablespoons olive oil
2 tablespoons spring garlic, finely chopped
2 pounds snow peas, both ends finely
   trimmed and strings removed
½ cup unsalted almonds, finely chopped

Heat olive oil in large heavy-bottomed saucepan.
Add garlic and stir briefly. Add snow peas and
sauté until tender crisp (1 to 1½ minutes). Place
snow peas on a dish and top with almonds.

Ice Cream with Strawberries and Balsamic Reduction and Shortbread Cookies

1 cup balsamic vinegar, reduced to ¼ cup
1 tablespoon butter
3 cups strawberries, halved
1 tablespoon sugar
2 tablespoons Grand Marnier
½ gallon double vanilla ice cream
8 shortbread cookies

Melt butter over medium heat in large sauté pan. Add strawberries. Sprinkle with sugar and cook about 45 seconds. Carefully add Grand Marnier and continue to cook about 2 minutes more. Portion ice cream into bowls, top with strawberry mixture and then drizzle with reduced balsamic. Add crumbled shortbread cookies to garnish.

Shortbread Cookies

Preheat oven to 350°F.

¾ pound butter, at room temperature
1 cup sugar
1 teaspoon pure vanilla extract
3½ cups all purpose flour
¼ teaspoon salt
Powdered sugar (for dusting)

In a mixer, mix butter and sugar until they are just combined. Add vanilla.
In a separate bowl, sift together the flour and salt and slowly add to the butter and sugar; mix to combine.
Dump onto a surface dusted with flour and shape into a flat disk. Wrap in plastic and chill 30 minutes.
Roll the dough ½-inch thick and cut into desired shapes (we made triangles). Bake on an ungreased sheet tray 20 to 25 minutes, until the edges begin to brown. Allow to cool to room temperature.
When cool, dust with powdered sugar.

simple lamb riblets

Watercress Soup

Watercress Salad with Bacon Vinaigrette

Beer–Braised Lamb Riblets

Lemon Pasta and Broccoli

Sautéed Chard and Beet Tops

Strawberry Pie

Serves eight

Paying attention to the food we consume gives us reason to pay close attention to the weather. Here in Placer County, April weather is often unpredictable. We know an April frost means fruits and vegetables will ripen a week or two later in the season; nectarines and peaches won't be at the market as early as we hope, and early vegetables, like Romano beans, are delayed. Mother Nature is reminding us she's in charge.

This year we had a deep chilling frost early in the month. It was great for the lilacs I planted in my back yard, but certainly nipped a few of the dogwood and early fruit tree blossoms.

In the kitchen, the cold spell gave us the perfect reason to enjoy a piping hot and uncomplicated lamb riblet dinner. Four basic ingredients, plus seasonings, and you have a delicious meal. What could be easier than that? It does take a bit of time to prepare. But it's a perfect meal to fix for good friends. I guarantee everyone will want to pick up the bones and chew through the sweet and savory meat.

The meal isn't too heavy, so there's plenty of room for a piece of freshly made strawberry pie – the first of the season.

april 6

Watercress Soup

3 cups Yukon Gold potatoes,
  peeled and quartered
3 cups yellow onions, peeled and quartered
4 cups watercress, washed, tough stems
  removed
Salt and pepper to taste
Crème fraîche

Place potatoes and onions in a large saucepan;
cover with water. Bring to a boil and reduce to a
simmer. Potatoes and onions are done when they
can be easily pierced with a fork.
Smash potatoes and onions with a potato masher.
Add watercress to potato mixture, cover pan and
bring to a boil. Reduce to a simmer.
When watercress is totally limp, use a hand
blender to purée. Season with salt and pepper to
taste.
If you prefer, place soup through a sieve to
remove any watercress stems.
To serve, heat soup and top with a small dollop
of crème fraîche.

Watercress Salad with Bacon Vinaigrette

Preheat oven to 350°F.

1 pound watercress, tough stems removed,
  leaves torn into small pieces
1 head leaf lettuce, torn into small pieces
¼ cup pistachios
8 pieces bacon

Bacon Vinaigrette
¼ cup reserved bacon fat
¼ cup olive oil
¼ cup apple cider vinegar
1 tablespoon brown sugar
½ lemon, juiced
Salt and pepper to taste

Cook the bacon on a sheet tray 15 to 25 minutes,
until just crispy. Set the fat aside. Crumble bacon
into pieces. Toss salad ingredients together.
Whisk vinaigrette ingredients together and add to
salad just before serving.

Beer-Braised Lamb Riblets

Preheat oven to 300°F.

6 to 8 pounds lamb riblets
Salt and pepper to taste
Dash of paprika
½ cup brewed coffee
2 bottles dark beer
Snow's Citrus Court Grilling Sauce

Place riblets in large baking dish (don't cut them apart). Season with salt, pepper, and paprika.
Pour coffee and beer into pan.
Bake 1½ to 2 hours, basting frequently.
Remove 2 to 3 cups liquid and pour into small sauce pan.
Baste ribs with grilling sauce and increase temperature to 425°F. Bake 20 minutes.
Meanwhile, bring liquid in saucepan to a boil, and boil at high heat until reduced to 1½ cups.
Remove ribs from oven, and cut into individual ribs. Serve reduced liquid in sauce bowl.

Lemon Pasta with Broccoli

2 cups all purpose flour

1 tablespoon salt

6 egg yolks

1 tablespoon cream

1 tablespoon extra virgin olive oil

1 tablespoon water

1 lemon, zested

½ cup semolina (for dusting)

3 cups broccoli florets

2 tablespoons butter

2 teaspoons chile flakes

Salt and pepper to taste

Pasta dough

Combine flour and salt. Make a well and add egg yolks, cream, oil and water to the middle. Slowly incorporate with your hand until dough comes together.

Continue to knead dough 8 to 10 minutes more, before wrapping in plastic and chilling for at least 2 hours or up to 2 days.

Cut the dough in quarters and roll out each piece to about ½ inch. Run dough through a pasta machine, starting with the thickest setting, about 3 times. Lower the machine one setting, and pass through 3 more times.

Sprinkle ¼ of the zest on half of the sheet of pasta and fold it over onto itself, also folding in any jagged edges. Carefully pass dough through again, and then lower another setting and pass 3 more times. Each machine is different, but we rolled it down to setting 3, which is about $1/8$ inch.

Cut pasta to desired width with a pizza cutter. (We made pappadelle about 1-inch wide and 7 to 8 inches long.)

Place cut pasta on a half sheet tray, sprinkled with semolina. Repeat process for each piece of dough, laying parchment paper in between each batch. Set pasta aside.

In a large pot of boiling, salted water, blanch the broccoli for 1 minute, and then place in a bowl of ice water to shock. (Do not discard water). Dry broccoli and place in a large metal bowl with butter and chile flakes. Season lightly with salt and pepper.

Bring the water back to a boil and cook the pasta in 3 to 4 batches, 1½ to 2 minutes each; stir gently while cooking to prevent sticking. When al dente, remove pasta from pot with a large slotted spoon and place in bowl with broccoli. Toss gently and place a lid on top to keep hot. Repeat until all pasta is cooked and tossed together.

Good cooking is an art which is easily acquired. There are only a few basic processes, and once they are mastered, even elaborate dishes seem simple to produce. No cookbook can provide the spark of genius, but it can serve as a source of inspiration and information.

Fanny Farmer

Sautéed Chard and Beet Tops

2 tablespoons olive oil

2 tablespoons garlic, minced

3 bunches chard, stems removed and cut
into 2 to 3-inch pieces

2 bunches beet tops, stems removed and cut
into 2 to 3-inch pieces

1 lemon, juiced

Salt and pepper to taste

Heat oil in a large sauté pan. Add garlic and sauté briefly. Add chard and beet tops and sauté until wilted. Season to taste with salt, pepper and lemon juice.

It's important to spend energy finding healthy food rather than spending energy to make mediocre food taste better.

There's a lot of energy (human and other natural resources) in our food system that goes into modifying products to make them taste better or more interesting to the palate.

When we discussed the simple ingredients of the food we were enjoying, it seemed clear that it is worth the effort to provide ourselves with good, nourishing food to begin with. When we care for what we eat, we spend our energy in a positive, proactive fashion that I believe produces positive ripples in other parts of our lives.

Additionally, I think the job of discovering and preparing the loveliest strawberries, bread, or fish, is another type of nourishment that we don't get if we rely on someone else to "manufacture" food for us.

Cindy Whitson, Auburn

april 6

Strawberry Pie

Pie dough (makes one 9-inch crust)

Pie dough (makes one 9-inch crust)

Preheat oven to 400°F.

¾ cup all purpose flour

¼ teaspoon salt

¼ teaspoon baking powder

1 egg well beaten

2 teaspoons water

2 teaspoons apple cider vinegar

In small bowl blend flour, salt and baking powder. In a separate bowl, blend 2 tablespoons of beaten egg mixture with water and vinegar. Add to flour and mix with a fork until dough clings together. Roll into a ball and place in refrigerator at least 30 minutes.

Roll dough and place in 9-inch pie pan. Bake 5 minutes. Pierce crust with fork to release any bubbles that form. Carefully watch crust 10 to 15 more minutes.

Remove from oven when lightly browned. Cool.

Strawberry Filling

3 baskets organic strawberries, hulled

3 tablespoons corn starch

1 cup water

1 cup sugar

Generous piece of butter

Red food coloring

1½ cup whipping cream, whipped, with 1 teaspoon vanilla flavoring and 2 tablespoons sugar

Crush 1 basket of strawberries (makes about 1¼ cups crushed strawberries). Set aside.

Dissolve cornstarch in ¼ cup water.

Mix crushed strawberries, sugar, ¾ cup water and cornstarch. Cook over medium heat until thick. Remove from heat and add butter and a few drops of red food coloring. Cool.

Line the baked pie shell with remaining 2 baskets of hulled berries; pour cooled crushed strawberry mixture over berries and chill until firm. Serve with vanilla flavored whipped cream. For a dash of color, drizzle with reduced plum or blackberry juice.

People constantly ask whether they should buy organic produce. We use both organically grown and locally grown produce and meat in our recipes. Both work well and are delicious. Both are locally grown and fresh from the farm. Experience tells me locally grown food is usually grown without the chemical regimen of traditionally grown foods. Most small, local farmers pride themselves on being good stewards of the land, and on living as lightly as possible upon this earth. Bluntly put, small farmers simply cannot afford expensive chemicals, so tend to use less, if any at all. Many practice organic methods, but haven't taken that last step to be certified organic since it can be costly.

The great thing about buying food from farmers markets is the farmer/grower is usually the person selling the food and you can simply ask how the produce was grown.

Produce that holds a lot of water, like strawberries or raspberries, also tends to hold a lot of chemicals, so I buy strawberries and raspberries organically grown whenever possible.

Correction!!!! P. 90
April 6, Strawberry Pie Dough
Pie dough (makes one 9-inch crust)

Preheat oven to 400 degrees F

¾ cup all purpose flour
¼ teaspoon salt
1/3 teaspoon baking powder
¼ cup shortening
1 egg well beaten
2 teaspoons water
2 teaspoons apple cider vinegar

In small bowl blend flour, salt, baking
powder and shortening. In a separate
bowl, blend 2 tablespoons of beaten egg
mixture with water and vinegar. Add to
flour and mix with a fork until dough clings
together. Roll into a ball and place in
refrigerator at least 30 minutes.
Roll dough and place in a 9-inch pie pan.
Bake 5 minutes. Pierce crust with fork
to release any bubbles that form. Carefully
watch crust 10 to 15 more minutes.
Remove from oven when lightly browned.
Cool.

april 13

spring barbecue

Watercress Salad with Sweet & Sour Vinaigrette

Grilled Skirt Steak with Mushroom Red Wine Sauce

Potato Gratin

Sautéed Baby Carrots and Snap Peas

Angel Food Cake with Strawberries

Serves eight

With angel food cake on the menu for this week's dinner, I decided to experiment by making two cakes – one with organic eggs from Blossom Hill Farm, the other with ordinary eggs from a local grocery store. The difference in the two cakes was dramatic. Both had good color, and baked evenly. But the cake made with organic eggs was two inches taller and had a noticeably sweet-smelling vanilla fragrance. It had a lighter, fluffier consistency, and a fresher taste. The eggs were the only difference in the recipe. Food science is not my specialty, but it doesn't take a food scientist to convince me to buy organic eggs when possible.

I topped the cake with locally grown, fresh strawberries. Strawberries have long been a popular crop in Placer County. At its heyday more than 80 years ago, about 75 to 100 acres were planted with strawberries. Traditionally, most of those strawberries were shipped outside the area. The acreage numbers are lower today, but there are still enough roadside strawberry patches to satisfy those of us willing to stop at the various strawberry stands strategically located throughout the county.

It's one of those crops you have to buy when you see it. Usually there's a four to six-week window to purchase berries; the season is over as soon as the weather warms up. The result is we eat berries as frequently as possible, and in as many different recipes as possible, for a short period of time.

april 13

Watercress Salad with Sweet & Sour Vinaigrette

1 pound watercress, tough stems removed, leaves torn into pieces
1 head leaf lettuce, torn into pieces
¼ cup pistachios
4 kiwi, peeled and sliced
½ cup scallions, sliced

Sweet & Sour Vinaigrette

½ cup olive oil
¼ cup brown sugar
¼ cup apple cider vinegar
3 drops Tabasco
Salt and pepper to taste

Toss salad ingredients together. Whisk vinaigrette ingredients together and dress salad just before serving.

Grilled Skirt Steak with Mushroom Red Wine Sauce

4 pounds skirt steak
¼ cup red wine vinegar
3 tablespoons Worcestershire
2 tablespoons lemon juice
3 tablespoons garlic, minced
2 tablespoons rosemary, chopped
½ cup olive oil

Cut steak in 4 to 5-inch pieces. Mix remaining ingredients together and pour over steak. Let marinate 20 to 30 minutes before grilling.

Mushroom Red Wine Sauce

2 tablespoons olive oil
3 pounds mushrooms, left whole (we used baby oyster mushrooms)
1 tablespoon garlic, minced
Salt and pepper to taste
1 cup red wine
3 cups beef stock
1 tablespoon butter

In a medium-sized skillet, sauté the mushrooms and garlic in olive oil, seasoning lightly with salt and pepper.
Add the wine and stock. Bring to a boil.
Reduce heat and simmer 15 to 20 minutes, or until sauce is reduced to consistency of gravy. Remove from heat and swirl in butter. Add more seasoning as desired.

I had a bit of time to spare, and thought I'd take a quick look at the website (placercountyrealfood.com). I found the gorgeous photographs lured me in, and it wasn't until many minutes later I was able to pull myself away. What a wonderful way to while away the time.

Rachel Rubin, Los Angeles

Potato Gratin

Preheat oven to 400°F.

4 pounds Yellow Finn potatoes, peeled

1 cup cream or half & half

3 cups chicken stock

2 yellow onions, julienne

2 tablespoons butter

½ pound sheep's milk cheese
   (such as Ossau Iraty), grated

Salt and pepper to taste

With a mandolin, slice the potatoes ¼ inch thick and place in a large pot with cream and stock. Season with salt and pepper. Simmer until potatoes are just tender.

Meanwhile, sauté onions in butter until caramelized.

Use a large slotted spoon to transfer a layer of potatoes to a large, buttered casserole dish. Be careful to move as little liquid as possible. Next, place a layer of onions, then a layer of cheese. Repeat until all potatoes are used or the dish is full (leave at least 1 inch of rim showing). Pour just enough liquid over the potatoes to cover. Place on a half sheet tray, and bake 20 to 30 minutes. Let sit 20 minutes before serving.

I know from bad experience not to fudge on the inch at the top of the pan for the potato gratin. I put so much love and butter and half and half and potatoes in my recipe that it filled it right to the top of the baking dish. Soon the bottom of my oven was full of burning, smoking butter and half and half. Moral of the story: Pay attention to any recipe that tells you to leave at least one inch of rim showing. Otherwise expect a floor of flame in the oven.

Sautéed Baby Carrots and Snap Peas

2 tablespoons olive oil
1 tablespoon garlic, minced
2 pounds baby carrots, peeled and
    cut into 2-inch pieces
2 pounds snap peas, cleaned
Salt and pepper to taste
½ cup water

In a large sauté pan, heat oil and add garlic. Add carrots and sauté about 2 minutes. Add snap peas. Season lightly with salt and pepper. Add water, cover and continue to cook for 2 minutes more. Serve immediately.

Angel Food Cake with Strawberries

Thanks to Carol Arnold for this recipe.

Preheat oven to 350°F.

1 cup sifted cake flour
1½ cups sugar
½ teaspoon salt
1½ cups egg whites (about 12 large) warmed
    to room temperature
1 teaspoon cream of tartar
1 tablespoon lemon juice
1½ teaspoons vanilla extract

Sift the flour, then measure, and place in a bowl. Add ½ cup sugar and the salt to the sifted flour and sift again, twice. Set aside.
Beat the egg whites in a very large, very clean bowl. When the whites are foamy, add the cream of tartar and the lemon juice. When the bubbles are uniform, start adding the remaining cup of sugar a few tablespoons at a time. Add vanilla extract. Beat the eggs until they form stiff peaks and the sugar is dissolved (when you lift the beaters a peak will form and hold).
Fold in the flour using a clean rubber spatula, using a down-the-side-and-up-through-the-batter motion. Do not over mix. When the flour is thoroughly combined, turn it into a very clean, grease-free 10-inch tube pan. Bake 50 minutes. Test for doneness by pressing lightly in the center; if it springs back the cake is done. Remove from oven and invert the pan until the cake is cool.
The cake must be lifted an inch off the counter during the cooling process. This can be done by inverting the cake over a bottle.
When cool, remove the cake by running a serrated knife around the edges of the pan. Serve with strawberry sauce.

Strawberry Sauce

2 pints strawberries, one pint diced,
   the other sliced
⅓ cup sugar
1 tablespoon lemon juice

Cook the diced strawberries, the sugar, and the
lemon juice in a small saucepan over low heat
until the sugar dissolves. Bring to boil, then
reduce heat and cook for 3 minutes. Add the
sliced strawberries. Remove from heat, place in a
covered bowl and chill for 2 hours. Serve over
angel food cake.

Carol Arnold is the manager of the
Foothills Farmers' Markets in Placer County,
California.

halibut and quinoa

Watercress Salad with Strawberries
and Sweet & Sour Vinaigrette

Halibut Cheeks

Black Quinoa with Mushrooms and Snow Peas

Sautéed Kale

Fresh Strawberries with Pistachio Biscotti
and Sabayon Grand Marnier Sauce

Serves eight

Whenever I use quinoa in a recipe, people ask for seconds. Then they ask for the recipe.

Quinoa is a grain-like crop from the Andes. For centuries it was a staple crop for the Incas. Today the crop is appreciated for its nutritional value: It contains a balanced set of essential amino acids, and is an unusually complete protein source.

I can tell you it's easy to use, has a delicious, nutty flavor, and can be served in hot or cold dishes. We especially love it served at room temperature with nectarines, peaches and nuts (recipe June 22). Quinoa is the perfect addition to your picnic basket. Recipes can be prepared ahead of time and easily transported. Variations of quinoa salad have been served at several Placer County Slow Food meals.

Watercress Salad with Strawberries and Sweet & Sour Vinaigrette

1½ pounds watercress, tough stems removed, leaves torn into small pieces
¼ cup almonds, toasted
½ cup strawberries, sliced
¼ cup scallions, sliced

Sweet & Sour Vinaigrette

½ cup olive oil
¼ cup brown sugar
¼ cup apple cider vinegar
Tabasco to taste
Salt and pepper to taste

Combine and toss salad ingredients together.
Toss with vinaigrette just before serving.

Halibut Cheeks

Preheat oven to 250°F.

3 pounds halibut cheeks
Salt and pepper to taste
3 tablespoons grapeseed oil
2 tablespoons butter
1 Meyer lemon, juiced
1 Meyer lemon, sliced
¼ cup parsley, chopped

Season cheeks with salt and pepper.
In a cast iron skillet, heat oil. Sear halibut on both sides, about 1 minute for larger cheeks. Be careful not to overcook.
Remove cheeks from pan and place on a sheet tray in oven to keep warm. Cook in batches if necessary.
After the last of the cheeks have been seared, brown the butter in the skillet. Add lemon juice, season with salt and pepper.
Place cheeks on a platter and pour butter over. Garnish each halibut cheek with parsley and a slice of lemon.

Cheeks are to halibut what caviar is to gourmet food. They're the tenderest part of any fish. Cheeks come from the head of the fish, just about where you'd think they ought to be: in a cavity just below the eyes. Flaky, sweet flavored and delicious, they take about 30 seconds to cook on each side. When done they should be slightly less transparent and slightly firm to the touch. It's imperative not to overcook this delicacy.

Black Quinoa with Mushrooms and Snow Peas

1 cup black quinoa, rinsed

3 cups warm liquid (a combination of boiling water and low-sodium vegetable or chicken broth)

1 tablespoon butter

1 pound fresh mushrooms (your choice: cremini, shiitake, porcini, chanterelles), sliced or cut into bite-size pieces

1 onion, diced

3 cloves garlic, coarsely chopped

3 to 4 tablespoons sour cream

½ pound snow peas

Several leaves fresh basil, shredded

In a heavy nonstick frying pan over medium-low heat, lightly toast the quinoa until slightly golden, about 5 minutes. Pour in 1 cup of the liquid, stirring as you go.

Meanwhile, melt the butter in a sauté pan over medium-high heat, and add the fresh mushrooms and the onion, cooking until lightly browned and softened, about 10 minutes. Add the garlic about halfway through.

When the liquid has been absorbed by the grains, add more of the liquid a little at a time, continuing until the grains have absorbed it all and are tender crisp, about 15 to 25 minutes. Stir in the mushroom mixture and sour cream; cover and remove from heat. Let stand 10 minutes, then fluff with a fork, garnish with the snow peas and basil, and serve.

Sautéed Kale

2 tablespoons olive oil
1 tablespoon garlic, minced
3 bunches kale, roughly cut
Salt and pepper to taste
2 tablespoons Mirin
1 Meyer lemon, juiced

In a large sauté pan, heat oil and add garlic. Cook
garlic until fragrant and add kale. Season lightly
with salt, pepper and Mirin.
Cook about 2 minutes, stirring frequently. Add
lemon juice and serve immediately.

april 20

Fresh Strawberries with Pistachio Biscotti and Sabayon Grand Marnier Sauce

Strawberries

3 pints strawberries
1 tablespoon sugar
Pistachio biscotti (purchased)

Slice the strawberries and place in a medium bowl with sugar. Combine and let sit for up to 2 hours before serving.

Sabayon Grand Marnier Sauce

5 egg yolks
½ cup plus 2 tablespoons sugar
¼ cup Grand Marnier
1 cup heavy cream

Put yolks and ½ cup sugar into a 2 quart mixing bowl that rests snugly on top of a slightly larger saucepan. Beat yolks vigorously with a wire whisk or portable electric beater.

Place 2 inches of water in the saucepan and bring to a boil. Do not allow mixing bowl to touch the water.

Continue beating yolk mixture for ten minutes or until yolks are thick and pale yellow.

Remove bowl from saucepan and stir in half the Grand Marnier. Allow sauce to cool, then refrigerate until thoroughly cold.

Beat the cream with 2 tablespoons sugar until it is almost but not quite stiff. Fold cream into sauce and stir in remaining Grand Marnier.

To assemble, place about ¾ cup strawberries in each bowl. Top with sabayon and garnish with pistachio biscotti.

Long time Auburn resident Cindy Whitson came to dinner one night, and I explained how I'd stopped at four fruit stands looking for the tastiest strawberries. Just any old strawberries wouldn't do, I explained. I wanted strawberries that exploded in my mouth with sweetness and taste. I wanted strawberries that excited my taste buds, and that had a complex flavor. I would know when I found them, so I went around to various fruit stands tasting the strawberries.

"I've just figured you out," she said. "You spend time and effort finding the best ingredients instead of buying ordinary ingredients and making them taste better."

When shopping at the farmers markets, ask to taste the produce. If five people are selling blackberries or strawberries, for example, ask for a taste at each stand and let your taste buds make the decision. You'll get to know the farmers and also find the most delicious produce.

april 27

rhubarb in season

Green Salad with Oranges and Pistachios
and Sweet & Sour Vinaigrette

Mint-Mustard Crusted Leg of Lamb with Artichokes

Roasted Yellow Finn Potatoes

Sautéed Broccoli Rabe with Garlic and Chile Flakes

Strawberry Rhubarb Pie

Serves eight

Dogwood trees bless us three times each year: in the spring with clear pink or pristine white flowers dangling on leafless branches, with light summer shade, and with brilliant crimson and violet autumn foliage.

Peak dogwood bloom season is in April, exactly when depends on the weather. For several years, I've been noting peak blossom dates in Placer County. This year, for 10 days, April 16-25, the 20 dogwood trees in our garden shouted white, pink, even light red, and we were again stunned and humbled by their beauty.

While the dogwoods were glorious, I noticed, again, something in the vegetable garden. The rhubarb plants were ready for the first cutting. Each year we anxiously await rhubarb harvest time. We judiciously and carefully mulch the plants with composted chicken manure and rice hulls. The rhubarb plants thank us with long red stems just right for rhubarb sauce or rhubarb strawberry pie. Oftentimes rhubarb thrives long enough to make rhubarb and raspberry sauce or rhubarb and blackberry sauce. When mixed with freshly picked berries there is no better simple dessert…the perfect finish to a meal.

I challenge you to watch for patterns and pairings in your garden. I know when the rhubarb is ready for cutting, the dogwoods are likely glorious.

Green Salad with Oranges and Pistachios and Sweet & Sour Vinaigrette

1 head lettuce, cleaned and cut into
   bite–sized pieces
2 cups watercress, stems removed,
   leaves torn into pieces
4 oranges, segmented
½ red onion, julienne
¼ cup pistachios

Sweet & Sour Vinaigrette

½ cup olive oil
¼ cup brown sugar
¼ cup apple cider vinegar
Tabasco to taste

Toss all salad ingredients together. Whisk all vinaigrette ingredients together and dress salad just before serving.

In these break-neck paced times in which we live – where we are never more than a tweet away from life's constant pressures – our Monday night meal at Joanne's was an oasis. A wise woman once told me that that "good things happen around good food." I couldn't agree more.

Rob Haswell, Auburn

Mint-Mustard Crusted Leg of Lamb with Artichokes

Preheat oven to 375°F.

2 tablespoons garlic
⅓ cup whole grain mustard
2 tablespoons Dijon mustard
¼ cup mint, finely chopped
½ cup olive oil
Salt and pepper to taste
2 legs of lamb, 3 to 4 pounds each

Combine garlic, mustards, mint, olive oil, and salt and pepper and season lamb generously. Roast 45 minutes to 1 hour, checking internal temperature (remove at 130°F internal temperature and let rest for medium rare).

Artichokes

3 artichokes, cleaned and quartered
2 lemons, cut in half
1½ tablespoons olive oil
1 teaspoon sea salt

Place artichokes in large pot and just cover with water. Squeeze lemons and place in water with artichokes. Bring to a boil and simmer until tender, about 25 minutes. Remove from water and drain to cool.

In a large sauté pan, heat oil and sear artichokes on both cut sides. Remove from pan and sprinkle with sea salt and lemon juice. Lightly dress with garlic aioli. Put remaining garlic aioli in a bowl and pass around.

Garlic Aioli

½ to ¾ cup olive oil
8 cloves garlic

In a small saucepan, heat oil and garlic until just simmering. Turn off heat and let sit about 20 minutes, until garlic is soft. Keep 2 cloves for the aioli, use 2 to 3 cloves for the broccoli rabe, and reserve the rest for another time. The garlic will keep up to 2 weeks in the refrigerator.

2 cloves garlic, from above minced
1 egg yolk
½ lemon, juiced
½ to ¾ cup garlic seasoned olive oil from above
Salt and pepper to taste

In a small bowl, whisk together garlic, egg yolk and lemon juice. While still whisking, slowly add olive oil until thick. Season with salt and pepper. Arrange lamb on plate, and surround with artichokes.

april 27

Roasted Yellow Finn Potatoes

Preheat oven to 375°F.

4 pounds Yellow Finn potatoes, cut into eighths
3 tablespoons olive oil
Salt and pepper to taste
¼ cup parsley, chopped

Toss potatoes with oil; season with salt and pepper. Place on a sheet tray and roast 25 to 35 minutes. When tender, place in a large bowl and toss with parsley.

Sautéed Broccoli Rabe with Garlic and Chile Flakes

2 tablespoons olive oil
2 bunches broccoli rabe
2 to 3 cloves garlic from aioli above, minced
Salt to taste
½ teaspoon red chile flakes

In a large sauté pan, heat oil and add garlic. Add broccoli and sauté, 1 to 1½ minutes. Season to taste with salt and chile flakes.

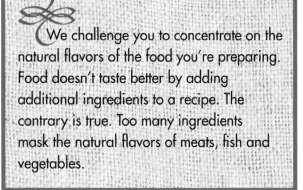

We challenge you to concentrate on the natural flavors of the food you're preparing. Food doesn't taste better by adding additional ingredients to a recipe. The contrary is true. Too many ingredients mask the natural flavors of meats, fish and vegetables.

Strawberry Rhubarb Pie

Preheat oven to 400°F.

Two-Crust Pie Dough for 9-inch Pan

¼ cup vegetable shortening
¼ cup butter
1½ cups all purpose flour
½ teaspoon salt
¼ cup cold water
1 teaspoon half-cinnamon/half-sugar mixture
½ teaspoon Demerara sugar (optional)

Using a pie dough cutter, blend shortening, butter, flour and salt together to cornmeal stage. Place in a medium bowl and slowly add cold water, mixing with a fork, until dough comes together. Add more water if necessary. Form into a ball, cover and chill at least 2 hours before rolling out.

Cut the dough ball into two pieces, one slightly larger than the other. Roll out dough until ⅛-inch thick. Make dough 10 inches round for bottom, and 9 inches round for top.

Place the filling in the shell. Apply top crust. Trim, roll and crimp edges.
Sprinkle with cinnamon sugar; then sprinkle Demerara sugar on top.

Filling

⅓ cup tapioca flour or quick cooking tapioca
¼ cup orange juice
3 cups sliced rhubarb
2 cups strawberries, halved
1¼ cups sugar
2 teaspoons orange zest
1 tablespoon butter

Mix tapioca, orange juice and zest. Let sit at least 25 minutes. Mix fruit with sugar and add to tapioca. Let sit again at least 20 minutes. Top with pieces of butter evenly over fruit.
Bake 50 minutes, or until golden brown and bubbly.

geno's feast and lilacs

Asparagus Salad with
Cranberry and Raspberry Mayonnaise

Pork Roast Rubbed with Mustard and Herbs
with Apple Garnish

Carrots and Fava Beans

Polenta with Italian Cheese

Flourless Chocolate Cake with Fresh Strawberries

Serves eight

Recipes written and prepared by guest Chef Geno Duggan

During May, the garden shouts lilacs: heavenly scented clusters of flowers in pure white, rich purple, dark violet, pale pink. We can grow lilacs this far west because our garden is high enough above the American River canyon for occasional frosts and plenty of cold nights. A good crop of winter chill means beautiful blossoms, and a garden full of lilac's sweet, heady scent. For me, the perfume is unforgettable. No other flower in my garden brings back so many fond memories.

The fragrance is synonymous with spring in Inver Grove Township, Minnesota, where I was born and raised on a farm homesteaded in 1853 by my great grandfather. I remember skipping through the Korfhage family farm gardens on the first warm spring day, and deeply inhaling what to me were the best scents of life on the farm.

Lilac shrubs like to be pruned, so I feel I'm doing the bushes a favor when I gather huge armloads and place big bouquets on each and every empty table or countertop throughout the house.

Asparagus Salad with Cranberry and Raspberry Mayonnaise

2 bunches thin asparagus, cut evenly
Boiling salted water

Cranberry and Raspberry Mayonnaise

1 cup mayonnaise
1 tablespoon Dijon mustard
¼ cup Earth & Vine Cranberry Raspberry Purée
¼ cup balsamic vinegar

Drop asparagus in boiling salted water for 1 minute, then plunge in ice water.
Whisk vinaigrette ingredients together and spoon over asparagus.

We're so honored to be part of your amazing initiative. You're all brilliant! What a superb idea you have and congratulations on being an important part of a SOLUTION for America.
Tee May and Geno Duggan, Tahoe Vista

Pork Roast Rubbed with Mustard and Herbs with Apple Garnish

Preheat oven to 375°F.

4½ pounds pork roast, bone-in, tied with netting
    brought to room temperature
1 white onion, sliced
1 quart water
½ cup salt
1 teaspoon black pepper

Mix together water, salt and pepper. Using an injector (available at BBQ supply stores), inject pork roast with brine in several places. Let sit until it comes to room temperature. Rub with mustard and herbs mixture.
Place roast in cast iron roasting pan. Surround roast with onion slices.
Roast 1 hour and 20 minutes or until internal temperature reaches 140°F.
Let rest on cutting board 10 to 15 minutes before slicing.
Places slices on warm platter for service.

Rub for Pork Roast

½ cup Dijon mustard
¼ teaspoon allspice
3 cloves finely chopped, mashed fresh garlic
1 teaspoon Two Spicy Ladies Bay Seasoning
1 tablespoon fresh chopped rosemary
½ tablespoon Herbs de Provence
½ tablespoon sea salt
1 tablespoon black pepper
¼ cup Snow's Citrus Court Grilling Sauce

Mix all ingredients together. Set aside one 1 tablespoon rub mixture for apples.

Apple Garnish

1 tablespoon olive oil
8 Gala apples, peeled and thinly sliced
1 large white onion, thinly sliced
¼ cup brandy
1¼ cups chicken stock
¼ teaspoon allspice
¼ teaspoon cayenne pepper
1 teaspoon finely chopped mashed garlic
⅓ cup maple syrup
1 tablespoon rub for pork roast

Place olive oil in cast iron pan, and lightly sauté apples over low to medium heat, covered, for 20 minutes.

When the pork roast is out of the oven and on the cutting board, use the cast iron pan that the roast was cooked in to finish the apple garnish. Add onion and apples. Add brandy, ¾ cup chicken stock, allspice, cayenne pepper, garlic, maple syrup and pork roast rub.

As the sauce is reducing, add ¼ cup chicken stock and continue to heat. Add another ¼ cup chicken stock, and continue cooking until reduced to desired consistency.

Carrots Garnished with Fava Beans

3 pounds whole fava beans, tough outer
   skins removed
3 tablespoons butter
4 bunches young carrots, trimmed of tops
   and peeled
Salt and pepper to taste
1 teaspoon marjoram
1 teaspoon thyme

Poach shelled beans in boiling water 30 to 60 seconds, then plunge in ice water.
Pop beans out of pods.
Gently reheat beans in 1 tablespoon butter and season with salt and pepper. Set beans aside.
Drop peeled carrots into rapidly boiling salted water. Cook for 2 minutes and cool in ice water.
Reheat carrots with 2 tablespoons butter, toss with marjoram and thyme, and season with salt and pepper. Place carrots in bowl and garnish with fava beans.

Polenta with Italian Cheese

2 cups chicken stock
2 cups milk or half and half
1 cup polenta
1½ cups Italian cheese, grated (Asiago or
   Parmesan)
Dash nutmeg
Salt and pepper to taste

Bring chicken stock and milk to gentle boil.
Add polenta and stir constantly with whisk.
When thickened, add Italian cheese, nutmeg, salt and pepper.
Keep warm over simmering water until ready to serve.

Flourless Chocolate Cake with Fresh Strawberries

Preheat oven to 300°F.

12 ounces bittersweet chocolate

6 ounces butter

5 eggs

1 cup sugar

1½ teaspoons vanilla extract

¼ teaspoon salt

2 tablespoons water

¼ cup cocoa powder

Lightly butter the bottom of a 9-inch springform pan and line with a round of parchment. Lightly butter the parchment and sides and dust with cocoa powder.

Melt the chocolate and butter together over a double boiler and let cool slightly. Set aside.
In a mixer fitted with the whisk attachment, combine the eggs, sugar, vanilla, salt and water. Beat on medium speed until foamy and doubled in volume, about 2 minutes. Reduce the speed and pour in chocolate. Mix to combine. Add the cocoa and mix to combine, about 30 seconds. Pour the batter into the prepared pan and bake 40 to 45 minutes, until a toothpick inserted in the middle comes out looking wet with small gooey clumps. Don't over bake. Let cool in the pan on a wire rack for 30 minutes.
Run a knife along the sides to release and remove the ring. Invert the cake onto the bottom of a sheet tray to remove parchment and place on plate.
Refrigerate at least 6 hours before serving.

Glaze

1½ ounces butter

¼ pound semi-sweet Mexican chocolate

2 pints strawberries, sliced

Melt butter and chocolate over a double boiler, stirring until smooth. Pour the warm glaze over the chilled cake and spread with a spatula to coat evenly. Refrigerate 20 to 30 minutes.
Let cake return to room temperature before serving. Cut with a warm knife and top with fresh sliced strawberries.

Ceramics by Dick Ketelle

a little asian

Green Salad with Sesame Vinaigrette

Teriyaki Glazed Salmon with Oyster Mushrooms

Ginger Rice with Fava Beans

Roasted Asparagus

Apple and Cherry Crisp

Serves eight

Almost without fail, when farmers market shoppers see fava beans on a grower's table, they ask, "How do you fix these beans? I don't have a clue how to use them."

Fava beans, also called broad beans, are beloved for their buttery, slightly tangy, yet nutty flavor. They're a bit more work than other types of beans, but worth the effort.

First, remove the bean from the pod. Blanch the beans in boiling salted water a scant 30 seconds, one minute tops. Plunge the beans in ice water until cool. Next, peel the outer skin from the bean.

There are several ways to cook fava beans. They're good boiled, steamed, mashed, added to rice or vegetables, even sautéed and spread on crackers. They have zero cholesterol, lots of protein and fiber, but little sodium or fat. Here's a secret: use fava beans as a garnish with another vegetable. By using them as a garnish you don't have to peel so many beans thus reducing preparation time.

Buy them when you see them, because favas are available only a few weeks each spring.

Green Salad with Sesame Vinaigrette

2 heads lettuce, torn into pieces
1 pound snap peas, cleaned and julienne
1 carrot, peeled and thinly sliced
1 tablespoon sesame seeds

Sesame Vinaigrette

3 tablespoons rice wine vinegar
2 tablespoons sesame oil
2 teaspoons Mirin
¼ cup olive oil
Salt and pepper to taste

Mix all salad ingredients together. Whisk vinaigrette ingredients together and dress salad just before serving.

Teriyaki Glazed Salmon with Oyster Mushrooms

3 pounds salmon
1 tablespoon butter
1 spring onion, julienne
2 pounds oyster mushrooms
¼ cup Mirin
2 tablespoons oil
Salt and pepper to taste
3 tablespoons teriyaki sauce
Parsley, chopped

Cut salmon into 4 to 5-ounce portions, and set aside.

Melt butter in a large pan. Add onion and sauté lightly. Add mushrooms and continue cooking, browning the mushrooms slightly. Deglaze with the Mirin and season to taste with salt and pepper. Remove mushrooms from pan and keep warm.

In the same pan, heat oil. Season salmon with salt and pepper, and sear on both sides (1 to 2 minutes depending on the thickness of the fish). Brush the fish with teriyaki sauce. Place in broiler to continue cooking if desired.

Place on a large platter. Top with mushrooms, then garnish with parsley.

Ginger Rice with Fava Beans

3 cups rice
6 cups water
Salt and pepper to taste
1 teaspoon ground ginger
4 to 5 pounds fava beans

Rinse rice and drain well.

In a large pot, combine rice, water and salt. Bring to a boil, turn down to a low simmer, cover and cook 25 to 45 minutes, depending on the type of rice. You can also use a rice cooker.

While still hot, transfer into a large bowl and season lightly with salt, pepper and ginger.

Meanwhile, shuck the fava beans from their outer pod, blanch in boiling, salted water for 30 seconds and then transfer immediately to a bowl of ice water.

When cool, peel favas from their remaining shell. Add the beans to the rice and stir to combine.

Cooking is at once one of the simplest and most gratifying of the arts, but to cook well one must love and respect food.
Craig Claiborne

may 11

Roasted Asparagus

Preheat oven to 375°F.

2 bunches asparagus, trimmed
2 tablespoons olive oil
Salt and pepper to taste
1 tablespoon parsley, chopped

Toss asparagus with olive oil. Season lightly with salt and pepper.
Roast on a sheet tray 8 to 15 minutes, depending on thickness. Garnish with parsley.

Crisps, crumbles, cobblers, and buckles, oh my! Actually, they're all dessert variations.

A crisp is made by mixing fruit with sugar and spices, and then topping it with butter, sugar and either flour or oatmeal, then the mixture is baked.

A crumble is similar to a crisp, with a British twist. Crumbles call for the fruit mixed with sugar and spices on the bottom of the baking pan, then you make a topping of butter, flour and sugar. The topping for a crumble is often called a streusel.

A cobbler is fruit topped with biscuit-like dough, then baked until the crust is golden brown and the fruit steaming. In Great Britain, however, a cobbler might be made with meat.

A buckle is an old American term for single layer cake made with fruit, mainly berries. Often the fruit is sprinkled on top of the batter before the cake is baked. It makes a very beautiful and unusual dessert.

Apple and Cherry Crisp

Preheat oven to 375°F.

5 apples, peeled and sliced
2 cups red cherries, pitted
¼ cup sugar
2 teaspoons cinnamon
1 teaspoon vanilla
1 cup oats
½ cup brown sugar
¼ cup flour
¼ teaspoon salt
4 tablespoons butter
Vanilla ice cream

Combine apples, cherries, sugar, cinnamon and vanilla. Place in a greased baking dish. Set aside. Combine oats, brown sugar, flour and salt in a small mixing bowl. Cut in butter until well mixed. Top fruit and bake until golden brown, about 30 to 35 minutes.
Serve with vanilla ice cream.

It is more important to make classic dishes properly (which means deliciously with the best available ingredients, following fundamental principles), than to keep trying to come up with new concoctions just for the sake of originality.
Julia Child

steak and cherries

Red Leaf Lettuce Salad with Cherries
and Cherry Balsamic Vinaigrette

Grilled Flank Steak with
Sauteéd Mushrooms and Chimichuri

Roasted Fingerling Potatoes

Sautéed Cauliflower with Onions

Strawberry Shortcake with Whipped Cream

Serves eight

I love driving the back roads of Placer and nearby counties, and watching the fruit trees blossom. Cherry trees, along with nectarine, plum, peach and pear, provide visual candy for those of us lucky enough to trek through the hills. Cherry season at the farmers market is reason to celebrate. Early cherries make an appearance at the farmers markets during May, and are available through the second or third week of June. The more complex flavored cherries are available near the end of the season. One of the reasons we have such a long season is our growers come from several different climates and elevations, all within a short distance.

We put cherries in salads, compotes, glazes and deserts. Over the years I've canned cherry sauce, preserved cherry jam, made cherry cordials, and frozen bags of cherries. My family is especially fond of hot flaming cherries served over homemade vanilla ice cream; it's a frequent request for birthday celebrations.

Red Leaf Lettuce Salad with Cherries and Cherry Balsamic Vinaigrette

2 heads red leaf lettuce, torn into pieces
1 pint cherries, pitted
½ cup toasted almonds

Cherry Balsamic Vinaigrette

¼ cup cherry balsamic vinegar
½ cup olive oil
Salt and pepper to taste

Combine lettuce and cherries. Whisk vinaigrette ingredients together. Dress with vinaigrette just before serving and garnish with almonds.

Grilled Flank Steak with Sautéed Mushrooms and Chimichuri

Preheat grill.

Grilled Flank Steak

2 flank steaks, about 2 pounds each
1 tablespoon olive oil
2 cloves garlic minced
Salt and pepper to taste

Rub the flank steak with olive oil, garlic, salt and pepper. Grill on high, about 7 minutes per side, depending on thickness.
Slice the steaks thinly, against the grain, making diagonal slices. Place slices on serving platter, top with mushrooms, and gently pour Chimichuri sauce over meat.
Pass remaining sauce in a small bowl.

Sautéed Mushrooms

2 pounds crimini mushrooms, quartered
2 tablespoons olive oil
Salt and pepper to taste
1 teaspoon rice vinegar
2 tablespoons sake

Combine mushrooms, oil, salt and pepper. Sauté on high heat, about 4 minutes then add vinegar and sake. Add more salt and pepper if desired.

Chimichuri

1 bunch flat leaf parsley

8 cloves garlic, minced

¾ cup extra virgin olive oil

¼ cup red wine vinegar

¼ lemon, juiced

1 tablespoon diced red onion

1 teaspoon dried oregano

Salt and pepper to taste

In a food processor combine all ingredients
and pulse until mixture is at sauce consistency.
Season to taste with salt and pepper.

Sautéed Cauliflower with Onions

2 tablespoons olive oil

1 tablespoon butter

2 tablespoons garlic, minced

1 sweet onion, sliced

2 to 3 heads cauliflower, cut into ¾-inch pieces

Salt and pepper to taste

In a large skillet, heat oil and butter. Add garlic
and onion, cook until fragrant.

Add cauliflower, searing on one side before
stirring. Season to taste with salt and pepper.

Cauliflower isn't just white anymore. Pale green, luscious purple, even stunning orange varieties are gaining in popularity. The colored varieties tend to be sweeter than the typical white cauliflower. Adding a few tablespoons of vinegar to the blanching water helps colorful varieties retain their color. Interestingly, when roasted or sautéed, they don't lose as much of their color.

Roasted Fingerling Potatoes

Preheat oven to 350°F.

3 pounds fingerling potatoes, halved
¼ cup olive oil
Salt and pepper to taste

Toss potatoes in oil, then season with salt and pepper.
Put on sheet tray, evenly spread out, and roast 30 minutes.

As for butter versus margarine, I trust cows more than chemists.
Joan Gussow

Strawberry Shortcake with Whipped Cream

Strawberries

5 to 6 cups strawberries, halved

¼ cup sugar

Toss together in a medium bowl and set aside.

Shortcake

Preheat oven to 350°F.

4 cups all purpose flour

1 teaspoon salt

¼ cup sugar

2 tablespoons (heaping) baking powder

5 ounces cold butter, cubed

2½ cups cream plus 1 tablespoon for
   brushing tops

½ teaspoon Demerara sugar (optional)

Sift together flour, salt, sugar and baking powder in a large bowl. Cut in butter until almost cornmeal stage. Add 2½ cups cream a little at a time, stirring to incorporate, but be careful not to over mix. Roll dough out on a floured surface, about ½ to ¾-inch thick. Cut in 3¼-inch rounds; brush the tops lightly with remaining cream and sprinkle with Demerara sugar.
Bake 14 minutes.

Whipped Cream

2 cups heavy whipping cream

¼ cup sugar

1 teaspoon vanilla

In a medium bowl, whisk cream until slightly thickened. Add sugar and vanilla and continue to whip until thick.
To serve, cut biscuits in half, placing bottom on a small plate. Spoon strawberries over biscuit, add cream and top with other half of the biscuit.

shoots r us

Pea Shoot Salad with Citrus Vinaigrette

Pan Seared Butterfish with Cherry Compote

Cauliflower Gratin

Sautéed Kale with Mirin

Peach and Blueberry Cobbler

Serves eight

You'll notice Chef Laura likes to sprinkle leafy greens or miniature vegetables over or around bowls of salad or plates of meat. It adds pizzazz, a dash of color, something unexpected to the finished product. It turns an ordinary meal into something extraordinary and beautiful. It tells you the cook cares what the meal looks like, as well as how delicious it tastes.

It's only natural we get very excited when we see pea shoots, sunflower sprouts, even wheatgrass at the markets. As well, we have our eyes open looking for baby carrots, unusual eggplant, colorful varieties of okra, tiny cabbages or little peppers to use as a garnish.

It's so easy. Watch for growers who have been especially careful in picking fruit and vegetables not only for the taste but for their beauty. We're exceedingly grateful to growers who pick or cut produce leaving a few choice leaves or tendrils attached. It makes shopping at the farmers market much more fun.

Pea Shoot Salad with Citrus Vinaigrette

½ head cabbage, finely sliced
One 8-ounce bag sunflower sprouts
One 8-ounce bag pea shoots
2 carrots, peeled and grated
½ cup almonds, chopped

Citrus Vinaigrette

¼ cup orange Muscat vinegar
1 tablespoon red wine vinegar
½ cup olive oil
Salt and pepper to taste

Toss cabbage, sunflower sprouts, pea shoots, and carrots. Whisk vinaigrette ingredients together. Dress salad with vinaigrette just before serving and garnish with almonds.

Pea shoots are the top end of the pea vine, and include the long, thin tendrils and uppermost leaves of either snow peas or snap peas (not to be confused with ornamental flowering sweet peas, *Lathyrus odoratus*, which are poisonous). Pea shoots definitely taste like peas, albeit more subtle. They're crispy, yet tender at the same time.

The Natural Trading Company in nearby Newcastle, California, is our source for pea shoots. The pea shoots come bagged in two sizes. The farm grows them in greenhouses so they're available fresh year-round. We love them raw in salads, in a stir-fry, in soups, even pasta. In fact, you can use them wherever you use spinach. I've read they contain more Vitamin C than blueberries and more Vitamin A than tomatoes.

We store our pea shoots in the refrigerator wrapped in a slightly damp paper towel inside a plastic bag. You'll love them so much and find so many uses for them you won't have to worry about storing them for very long.

The Natural Trading Company also grows sunflower sprouts and wheatgrass, two additional nutrition-packed greens making their way into more farmers markets, natural food stores and even traditional grocery stores.

We are indeed much more than what we eat, but what we eat can nevertheless help us to be much more than what we are.
Adele Davis

Pan Seared Butterfish with Cherry Compote

Pan Seared Butterfish

3 to 4 pounds butterfish, cut into 5-ounce pieces
2 tablespoons grapeseed oil
Salt and pepper to taste

Season fish with salt and pepper.
In a large cast iron skillet, heat oil and sear fish, about 1½ minutes per side.
Transfer fish to serving plate.
To serve, spoon some of the cherry compote over fish. Serve remaining compote in a small bowl.

Cherry Compote

2 cups cherries, pitted
5 cloves garlic
1 tablespoon olive oil
2 tablespoons butter
2 tablespoons flour
1 quart chicken stock
1 tablespoon raspberry vinegar
½ teaspoon honey

In a large sauté pan, slowly caramelize the cherries and garlic in the olive oil and 1 tablespoon of butter (about 30 minutes).
Add the flour and brown slightly.
Add stock and reduce by 2/3 over medium heat.
Add vinegar and honey to taste and finish by swirling in remaining tablespoon of butter.

Cauliflower Gratin

Preheat oven to 450°F.

1 head cauliflower, cut into 1-inch florets,
    reserving the core
1 teaspoon white vinegar
1 tablespoon salt
2 tablespoons shallots, minced
1 bay leaf
1 sprig thyme
2/3 cup water
1 cup heavy cream
Salt and pepper to taste
1/3 cup sheep's milk cheese, grated
1/4 cup bread crumbs

Cut the core into small pieces and pulse in a food
processor until puréed (makes one cup of purée).
Set aside.

Bring a large saucepan of water to a boil and
season with the vinegar and 1 tablespoon salt.
Blanch the florets about 2 minutes and remove
with a slotted spoon into a large bowl. Pour out
the water and, in the same saucepan, add the
butter and shallots. Cook gently over medium
heat 1 to 2 minutes. Add the bay leaf and thyme.
Add the cauliflower purée and water. Continue to
cook gently 5 to 6 minutes, until most of the
water has evaporated. Add the cream, bring to a
simmer and continue to cook 2 minutes.
Remove from heat and discard the herbs.

Pour mixture into a blender. Let cool 5 minutes
and then begin to purée, slowly at first to let the
heat escape.

Toss with the florets and season to taste with salt
and pepper.

Transfer the cauliflower to a casserole dish and
refrigerate at least 30 minutes to allow flavors to
blend.

Sprinkle with grated cheese and bread crumbs
before baking 15 to 20 minutes, until bubbly.
Brown under broiler if not yet golden brown.

Sautéed Kale with Mirin

2 tablespoons olive oil
1 tablespoon garlic, minced
4 bunches kale, roughly cut
Salt and pepper to taste
2 tablespoons Mirin
1 Meyer lemon, juiced

In a large sauté pan, heat oil and add garlic.
Cook until fragrant, and add kale. Season lightly
with salt, pepper and Mirin. Cook about 2
minutes, stirring frequently. Add lemon juice and
serve immediately.

Peach and Blueberry Cobbler

Preheat oven to 375°F.

4 ounces butter, melted
1 teaspoon lemon juice
2 cups fresh blueberries, rinsed and drained
4 cups peaches, sliced
2 cups sugar
1 cup self-rising flour
1 teaspoon vanilla
½ cup milk

Butter an 8-inch square baking dish. Set aside.
In a mixing bowl, combine lemon juice, blueberries and peaches. Add 1 cup sugar and mix well. Add butter.
Place fruit mixture in the baking dish. Do not stir. Combine flour, remaining sugar, vanilla and milk in a small bowl. Pour over the fruit and bake until golden brown, about 45 minutes.

summer squash and chops

Arugula Salad with Blue Cheese Vinaigrette

Grilled Pork Chops with Apricot and Lavender Chutney

Sautéed Summer Squash with Garlic and Basil

Grilled Chinese Broccoli

Olallieberry Cobbler

Serves eight

Summer is a glorious kaleidoscope of colors and shapes at the farmers markets. Growers' tables groan with the early summer abundance.

One welcome crop on everyone's table is summer squash. Suddenly summer squash is everywhere in every imaginable shape: crookneck, zucchini, and patty pan, all in various colors. Look for yellow, white, or dark green zucchini, bright yellow or bicolor crooknecks, white scallop squash or pale green patty pan. Imaginative growers pay attention to shapes and sizes. It's always fun to find quirky looking crookneck squash or miniature zucchinis. Our dinner guests are fascinated with a big basket centerpiece full of hand-picked unique looking squash – something never seen in a grocery store.

For something different, we stuff summer squash with sautéed ground lamb or pork, top with a sprinkling of cheese, and then pop it in the oven until it's piping hot.

june 1

Arugula Salad with Blue Cheese Vinaigrette

2 bunches arugula, stems removed,
   leaves torn in pieces
1 pint cherry tomatoes
½ red onion, julienne
¼ cup blue cheese, crumbled
¼ cup almonds, toasted and chopped

Blue Cheese Vinaigrette

2 tablespoons cream
¼ cup sour cream
¼ cup blue cheese, crumbled
1 teaspoon red wine vinegar
Salt and pepper to taste

Toss arugula, tomatoes, onion and blue cheese together.
Whisk vinaigrette ingredients together. Dress salad just before serving and garnish with almonds.

Many people have an expiration date mentality when it comes to buying fresh produce. We've gotten used to buying only enough vegetables and fruit to last a few days because they seem to go bad so quickly. They really don't. Consider this: grocery store produce has to be picked, then stored for shipment, shipped again and stored again before arriving at the grocery store where it sits once more in cold storage before being put on the shelf. By the time you put it in your grocery cart, it's likely traveled hundreds of miles and been sitting for weeks.

Farmers market produce is picked within days of selling, and has a life expectancy of two to three weeks, often more in the refrigerator. Sadly, only two to three percent of the US population eats locally grown food.

Bottom line: buy enough produce to last the whole week, or even a couple of weeks.

Grilled Pork Chops with Apricot and Lavender Chutney

Apricot and Lavender Chutney

2 tablespoons butter
½ leek, diced
1 teaspoon lavender flowers, chopped
4 cups apricots, pitted and sliced
1 teaspoon honey
Salt and pepper to taste

In a sauce pan, heat butter and lightly sauté leeks, about 5 minutes.
Add lavender and cook until fragrant. Add apricots and continue to cook until just heated through.
Season to taste with honey. Add salt and pepper. Remove from heat and set aside.

Grilled Pork Chops

Preheat grill.

8 pork chops
1 tablespoon olive oil
Salt and pepper to taste

Season the pork chops with olive oil, salt and pepper. Grill on high, about 2 minutes per side, depending on thickness.
Serve on a large platter with reheated apricot and lavender chutney.

Art, music, wine, farmers markets, slow food, community, conversation all go together. They all tap into higher needs and our better selves.
Burt Harlan, Rancho Santa Margarita

june 1

Sautéed Summer Squash with Garlic and Basil

2 tablespoons olive oil
1 tablespoon butter
1 tablespoon garlic, minced
2 to 3 pounds summer squash,
    cut into ¾-inch pieces
Salt and pepper to taste
2 tablespoons basil, finely sliced

In a large skillet, heat oil and butter. Add garlic and cook until fragrant.
Add squash, searing on one side before stirring. Season to taste with salt and pepper, and then add basil.

Grilled Chinese Broccoli

Preheat grill.

3 bunches Chinese broccoli
2 tablespoons olive oil
Salt and pepper to taste

Season the broccoli with oil, salt and pepper. Grill on high heat, about 2 minutes. (Can be grilled ahead of time and reheated in a 350°F oven.)

Olallieberry Cobbler

Thanks to Candee Kenny for this recipe.

Preheat oven to 375°F.

Filling

8 cups olallieberries
1 cup sugar
¼ cup tapioca flour or quick cooking tapioca
½ lime, juiced
Pinch of salt

Combine all ingredients and let sit at least 20 minute before transferring to a 3-quart baking dish.

Topping

1 cup all purpose flour
1 cup sweetened, shredded coconut
¾ cup sugar
¾ cup pecans, chopped
½ teaspoon baking powder
¼ teaspoon salt
½ cup cold butter, cubed
1 egg
1 cup whipping cream, whipped

Mix together flour, coconut, sugar, pecans, baking powder and salt.
Cut in butter. Knead with your fingertips until mixture resembles course sand.
Blend in the egg, and then arrange topping over berries in clumps, covering evenly.
Bake until golden brown and bubbly, about 40 to 45 minutes. Serve with whipped cream.

I'm still licking my chops over dinner the other night. Between the fabulous food and the great company, I had a wonderful time.
    Jan Christofferson, Meadow Vista

onions and chickens

Arugula Salad with Strawberries and
Balsamic Honey Vinaigrette

Herb Roasted Chicken with
Grilled Walla Walla Onions

Smashed German Butterball Potatoes

Roasted Broccoli and Cauliflower

Cherries over Vanilla Ice Cream

Serves eight

People ask why I love onions. Maybe it's genetic. I'm convinced my father lived into his 80s because he ate onions with everything, in every way, shape and form.

Lucky for us, our local growers search catalogs for the best onions available, and they come up with some interesting types. We can buy Placer Sweets (our version of the Vidalia onion), Walla Walla, Torpedo, and, of course, Stockton Reds and Whites.

Early Placer Sweets and Walla Wallas are sweet and delicate, just right for eating raw like an apple, roughly diced on salads or simply sliced on sandwiches. If roasting, be careful not to overcook sweet onions.

If you're fortunate to spot some green early garlic, still on the stems, buy it. It's not as pungent and fragrant as dried garlic, and when it goes to flower, the flowers are tasty too. If not for cooking, grab the flowering garlic and use the flowers for garnish.

june 8

Arugula Salad with Strawberries and Balsamic Honey Vinaigrette

3 bunches arugula, stems removed,
  leaves torn into pieces
2 pints strawberries, halved
¼ cup unsalted almonds, toasted and chopped

Balsamic Honey Vinaigrette
¼ cup balsamic vinegar
¼ cup olive oil
1 teaspoon honey
Salt and pepper to taste

Toss arugula and strawberries together. Whisk vinaigrette ingredients together, and dress salad just before serving. Garnish with almonds.

They say if you grow Walla Walla onions anyplace except Walla Walla, Washington, they aren't really Wallas Wallas. Well, that may be, but Walla Walla onions grown in Placer County are definitely tasty.

Walla Walla onions are available at farmers markets from June to September. Their skin is golden brown, the meat white. The flavor is mild and sweet. In fact, it's so mild some folks say you can eat a Walla Walla like an apple.

The story behind this wonderful onion is interesting, even romantic. A French soldier found a sweet onion seed on the island of Corsica and brought it to Walla Walla. It became so popular, so sought after, that farmers began selecting the best, tastiest and hardiest onions each year to save for seed. The onion was named Washington's state vegetable in 2007.

It's an open pollinated variety, not a hybrid, so you can save your own seeds each year and produce your own crop of Walla Walla onions. The Walla Walla is a long-day type onion, which means it needs 12 to 15 hours of daylight to grow well. Typically, long-day type onions do best in the north. Germination takes about a week, and from planting time to harvest is about 115 days.

www.placercountyrealfood.com

Herb Roasted Chicken with Grilled Walla Walla Onions

Grilled Walla Walla Onions

Preheat grill.

4 large Walla Walla onions
2 tablespoons olive oil
Salt and pepper to taste
1 beef bouillon cube, crushed

Cut off stem of onion, and peel. Cut an 'x' into the top, about halfway through the onion.
Combine oil, salt, pepper and bouillon cube and season each onion with the mixture.
Place each onion in the center of a square piece of foil, and wrap tightly, making sure the onion is covered completely.
Place on a hot grill and cook until tender, about 15 minutes.
Remove from the grill, careful not to spill any of the juices that are now in the foil packet.
Open over a medium bowl so that nothing is lost and let cool slightly.

Herb Roasted Chicken

Preheat oven to 375°F.

2 whole chickens, about 4 pounds each
2 lemons, halved
2 sprigs rosemary
¼ bunch parsley
2 tablespoons butter or olive oil

Clean and stuff chickens with lemon halves and herbs. Rub with butter and oil and season with salt and pepper. Roast 1 to 1½ hours, until internal temperature reaches 165°F.
Let rest at least 10 minutes before carving.
Remove legs and thighs from the chickens and then carve out the breasts.
Serve on a platter with onions (and their juices), and garnish with chopped herbs.

june 8

Smashed German Butterball Potatoes

3 pounds German butterball potatoes,
   skins on, cut in quarters
¼ cup butter
Salt and pepper to taste

Place the potatoes in a large pot, cover with water, and bring to a boil over high heat. Reduce heat to medium and cook until tender. Drain well and place back into the pot, off the heat.
Mash using a hand masher or a rotary mixer. Add butter and season to taste with salt and pepper.

Roasted Broccoli and Cauliflower

Preheat oven to 375°F.

1 head broccoli, cut into florets
1 head cauliflower, cut into florets
¼ cup olive oil
Salt and pepper to taste
1 leek, sliced in half moons, ½-inch thick
2 pounds oyster mushrooms, sliced
1 pint cherry tomatoes

In a medium bowl, season broccoli and cauliflower with olive oil, salt and pepper. Place on a sheet tray and roast about 20 minutes. Meanwhile, season the mushrooms with the leeks and tomatoes the same way and place on a separate tray to roast about 15 minutes. Toss all together and check seasoning.

I want less processed food. I don't like it at all. Instead, I want lots of fresh food and lots of people cooking it.

Julia Child

Cherries over Vanilla Ice Cream

4 cups Bing cherries, pitted
¼ cup sugar
2 tablespoons butter
½ cup brandy
1 quart double-bean vanilla ice cream

Melt butter in a large frying pan, add sugar and cherries. Cook on medium heat, stirring frequently, until cherries soften, but are not falling apart, about 7 to 10 minutes.
In a small saucepan, heat brandy until very warm. Carefully light flame to brandy and slowly pour over cherries until flames disperse (see sidebar). Spoon ice cream into eight small bowls and top with cherries.

Important: It's impressive to light the brandy in front of guests and pour it over the cherries. But be very careful. The brandy flames up very quickly, almost instantly, and the flame can be a bit high.

barbecue and blenheim apricots

Red Leaf Salad with Blueberries and Lemon Vinaigrette

Barbecued Leg of Lamb with
Grilled Walla Walla Onions and Fennel

Grilled Summer Squash

Sautéed Baby Bok Choy with Crispy Shallots

Sautéed Kale with Mirin

Apricot Upside-down Cake

Serves eight

Years ago, I remember stopping at a farm stand to buy apricots. The apricots were small and lightly colored. The farmer told me they were old-fashioned, heritage Blenheim apricots. He explained Blenheim apricots tend to be smaller than today's modern, hybrid types of apricots. "It's okay to have small apricots when they're the best tasting apricots you've ever put in your mouth," he said.

I bought them, and admit loudly and often the farmer was right. I made the best apricot jam ever with those Blenheim apricots. When we decided to plant a couple of apricot trees, it was only natural we looked for Blenheim, or Royal Blenheim as they are sometimes called.

No other apricot has the flavor and texture of a Blenheim. You won't find them in big-chain grocery stores because they're so delicate they can't be shipped. It's worth the trouble to find them at local farm stands or farmers markets. Treat these fragile beauties with care. Our local Newcastle Produce carries dried Blenheims.

I'll warn you now: after you eat one, you'll never buy a dried Turkish apricot again.

Red Leaf Salad with Blueberries and Lemon Vinaigrette

2 heads red leaf lettuce, torn into pieces
1 pint blueberries
¼ cup pecans, chopped

Lemon Vinaigrette

1 lemon, juiced
¼ cup olive oil
2 tablespoons Champagne vinegar
Salt and pepper to taste

Toss lettuce and blueberries together.
Whisk vinaigrette ingredients together, and dress
salad just before serving. Garnish with pecans.

Barbecued Leg of Lamb with Grilled Walla Walla Onions and Fennel

Preheat grill.

Grilled Walla Walla Onions and Fennel

4 large Walla Walla onions
6 fennel bulbs, halved
3 tablespoons olive oil
Salt and pepper to taste
1 beef bouillon cube, crushed

Cut off stem of onion, and peel. Cut an 'x' into the top, about halfway through the onion. Combine 2 tablespoons oil, salt, pepper and bouillon cube and season each onion with the mixture.

Place each onion in the center of a square piece of foil, and wrap tightly, making sure the onion is covered completely.

Place on a hot grill and cook until tender, about 15 minutes.

Remove from the grill, being careful not to spill any of the juices that are now in the foil packet. Open over a medium bowl so that nothing is lost and let cool slightly.

Season fennel with remaining oil, salt and pepper.

Grill fennel until tender crisp.

Barbecued Leg of Lamb

3 boneless legs of lamb, about 3 pounds each, butterflied
3 tablespoons olive oil
Salt and pepper to taste
6 cloves garlic, chopped
1 tablespoon fresh thyme, chopped

Season lamb generously with oil, salt, pepper, garlic and thyme. Cook on a hot grill until desired internal temperature is reached, about 15 to 18 minutes for medium rare. Remove from grill and let rest at least 10 minutes. Reheat onions and fennel. Arrange on a platter with the sliced leg of lamb. Pour the juices over and serve.

Grilled Summer Squash

Preheat grill.

2 to 3 pounds summer squash, cut into ¾-inch pieces
2 tablespoons olive oil
Salt and pepper to taste
½ bunch basil, sliced thinly

Season squash with olive oil, salt and pepper and grill on high until slightly tender, about 4 minutes.

Remove from grill and place in a serving bowl. Garnish with basil.

Sautéed Baby Bok Choy with Crispy Shallots

1 cup grapeseed oil
2 shallots, thinly sliced
3 bunches baby bok choy, about 12 heads,
    cut in quarters
Salt and pepper to taste

In a small saucepan, heat oil to about 350°F. Fry shallots until golden brown, remove from oil with a slotted spoon and place on a paper towel to drain.

Heat a large skillet and add 2 tablespoons of oil that was used to fry shallots. Place quartered bok choy in skillet and sauté until tender crisp and slightly browned on all sides. Season with salt and pepper while still hot.

Place on serving dish and top with crispy shallots.

A lot of people simply walk past the shallots at the market. They take a quick look, perhaps pick one up, then put it back and keep going. Shallots are a mystery for most cooks. Let's solve that problem right now.

They're related to onions (and can make you cry when you peel them), but are more garlic-like in their growth habits. They form clusters of "cloves" in the ground, like garlic. Each clove is covered with a smooth, shiny brown paper-like skin. Their taste is almost always described as mild, although subtle is a better word. It's a little like garlic, a little like a mild, sweet onion. Their texture is firm and crisp, and they can be lightly fragrant.

june 15

Sautéed Kale with Mirin

3 tablespoons grapeseed oil
2 teaspoons garlic, minced
3 bunches kale, ribs removed and cut
   into 2–inch pieces
⅓ cup Mirin
Salt and pepper to taste

In a large sauté pan, heat oil and add garlic. Add kale and sauté about 1 minute. Add Mirin and continue to cook 1 to 2 minutes longer, until kale begins to wilt. Season to taste with salt and pepper. Remove from pan and serve.

Apricot Upside-down Cake

Preheat oven to 375°F.

¾ cup brown sugar, packed
1 tablespoon honey
8 fresh apricots, halved and pitted
1¾ cups all purpose flour
1½ teaspoons baking powder
½ teaspoon baking soda
½ teaspoon salt
½ cup butter, softened
¾ cup sugar
1½ teaspoons vanilla extract
¼ teaspoon almond extract
2 eggs, at room temperature
¾ cup buttermilk
Whipped cream

Use cast iron or Pyrex for baking the apricot upside-down cake because both products heat evenly. Nothing else works as well.

Lightly butter a large cast iron skillet and place a round of parchment paper on the bottom. Place skillet on medium heat and melt butter until foamy.
Reduce heat to low and sprinkle brown sugar and honey evenly, and then cook for 2 to 3 minutes. Stir gently and arrange apricot halves, cut sides down, close together on top of the sugar mixture. Remove from heat.
Sift together flour, baking powder, soda and salt into a small bowl. Set aside.
Beat together butter, sugar and extracts in a large bowl with an electric mixer at medium speed until pale and fluffy. Beat in eggs one at a time, then beat until mixture is creamy and doubled in volume, about 2 to 3 minutes.
Reduce speed to low and add flour mixture in 3 batches, alternately with buttermilk, beginning and ending with flour mixture, and beat just until combined.
Gently spoon batter over apricots and spread evenly.
Bake cake in middle of oven until golden brown and a wooden pick inserted in the center comes out clean, 40 to 45 minutes.
Immediately invert the cake onto a large plate by placing it over the skillet and firmly pressing while flipping. Cool to warm or room temperature. Serve with whipped cream.

june 22

berries everywhere

Cucumber and Tomato Salad

Pan Seared Halibut with Peach Salsa

Quinoa with Nectarines and Pistachios

Sautéed Romano Beans

Apricot and Blackberry Pie

Serves eight

Beginning in late spring and through most of summer, we live in Berryville USA.

The California foothills have oodles of small streams, creeks and rivulets, the ideal growing conditions for blackberries. At slightly higher elevations locals have their favorite spots to pick a yearly supply of wild elderberries or gooseberries. Literally, our hills are alive with berries.

Each year, sometime in late May or early June, we schedule an early raspberry picking trip to Amber Oaks Farm on Shanley Road on the outskirts of Auburn. We pick 30 pounds of raspberries, enough for eating fresh, canning, adding to rhubarb sauce, and storing in the freezer. In June, Brenner Ranch begins picking blueberries, and throughout the season other growers, including Beauty Ranch, sell boysenberry, wild blackberry, olallieberry, triple crown blackberry, and Chester berry, to name a few.

Peek in our freezer and you'll be sure to see several bags of berries. We like berries in cobblers or pies, made into a sauce, added to sweet breads, or simply layered in a buttered pan with other fruits, topped with brown sugar and baked.

june 22

Cucumber and Tomato Salad

8 to 10 medium cucumbers, thinly sliced,
   about 1/8-inch thick
1 red onion, julienne
¼ cup sea salt
¼ cup rice vinegar
1 pint cherry tomatoes, cut in wedges
1 bag pea shoots

In a medium plastic container or flat-bottomed
bowl, place a single layer of the cucumbers, a
thin layer of red onion, then lightly salt. Repeat
until all ingredients are layered. Cover with
plastic wrap, and refrigerate 2 to 8 hours.
Remove from refrigerator. Drain water
from the cucumbers and onions by pressing
firmly (do not rinse). Drizzle vinegar over and
toss to combine.
Place the cucumbers on a plate and garnish with
tomato wedges and pea shoots.

Pan Seared Halibut with Peach Salsa

Peach Salsa

3 peaches, small diced
2 tomatoes, small diced
1 red onion, small diced
2 tablespoons cilantro, chopped
1 teaspoon olive oil
½ teaspoon cayenne pepper
½ lime, juiced
Salt and pepper to taste

In a small bowl, combine peaches, tomatoes,
onion, cilantro, olive oil, cayenne, and lime juice.
Season with salt and pepper and refrigerate.

Pan Seared Halibut

3 to 4 pounds halibut
Salt and pepper to taste
2 tablespoons grapeseed oil

Season halibut with salt and pepper.
Heat grapeseed oil in a large sauté pan and sear
halibut on high, about 1½ minutes, depending on
thickness. Flip just to sear the other side and
remove from pan.
Place on a platter and top with peach salsa. Serve
remaining salsa on the side.

Quinoa with Nectarines and Pistachios

Thanks to Deborah Madison for the basic recipe.

2 lemons, zested

2 tablespoons lemon juice

1 tablespoon cilantro or parsley, chopped

½ teaspoon paprika

½ teaspoon ground cumin

½ teaspoon ground coriander

½ teaspoon salt

½ cup olive oil

2 cups quinoa

4 cups water

Salt and pepper to taste

8 apricots, small diced

4 nectarines, small diced

2 tablespoons scallions, cut into small rounds

½ cup red bell pepper, small diced

½ cup pistachios, chopped

Combine the lemon zest, juice, spices, herbs and salt in a bowl.

Stir to combine; then whisk in olive oil. Taste and adjust flavors, adding more lemon juice if desired.

Thoroughly rinse quinoa in a bowl of cold water; pour into a fine meshed strainer and rinse again under running tap water.

Bring 4 cups water to a boil, add salt to taste, and stir in the quinoa.

Lower heat, cover the pan, and cook 15 minutes. Taste the grain – there should be just a little resistance, and the opaque spiraled ring of germ should show. If necessary, continue cooking until done, then pour into a strainer and drain over a bowl. (Save the liquid which can replace the oil in the dressing or be used in soups.)

While quinoa cooks, place fruit and vegetables in a large bowl. Toss with warm quinoa and lemon juice vinaigrette. Top with pistachios.

While somewhat new to American cooks, Quinoa, pronounced "keen-wah," can be traced back to the Inca civilization.

According to our seed catalog, quinoa contains more protein than any other grain. In fact, it contains all eight essential amino acids. Quinoa is also higher in unsaturated fats and lower in carbohydrates than most grains.

The ivory-colored grains – it also comes in black – cooks more quickly than rice, and can be used as a side dish, in salads and soups.

You can replace the fresh nectarines and apricots in this recipe with dried fruits, such as cranberries, currants, raisins, dried persimmons or apricots if you want to make this dish other times of the year.

june 22

Sautéed Romano Beans with Vinaigrette

2 tablespoons rice vinegar
2 tablespoons Mirin
½ cup grapeseed oil
Salt and pepper to taste
2 tablespoons olive oil
1 tablespoon butter
1½ pounds Romano beans

To make vinaigrette, combine vinegar, Mirin and grapeseed oil. Season lightly with salt and pepper. Set aside
Heat olive oil and butter in a large sauté pan and add Romano beans. Sauté until tender crisp, about two to three minutes. Toss with vinaigrette and serve immediately.

Apricot and Blackberry Pie

Preheat oven to 400°F.

Two-Crust Pie Dough for 9-inch Pan

¼ cup vegetable shortening

¼ cup butter

1½ cups all purpose flour

½ teaspoon salt

¼ cup cold water

1 teaspoon half-cinnamon/half-sugar mixture

½ teaspoon Demerara sugar (optional)

Using a pie dough cutter, blend shortening, butter, flour, and salt together to cornmeal stage. Place in a medium bowl and slowly add cold water, mixing with a fork, until dough comes together. Add more water if necessary. Form into a ball, cover and chill at least 2 hours before rolling out.

Cut the dough ball into two pieces, one slightly larger than the other. Roll out dough until ⅛-inch thick. Make dough 10 inches round for bottom, and 9 inches round for top.

Place the filling in the shell. Apply top crust. Trim, roll and crimp edges.

Sprinkle with cinnamon sugar; then sprinkle Demerara sugar on top.

Food is central to developing community. I'm remembering all the "food" events that brought our family, friends, neighbors, cultural groups together in the past, and every event focused on oodles of food. Good things always happen around good food.

Joanne Neft, Auburn

Pie Filling

2½ cups fresh apricots, sliced

2½ cups blackberries

1 cup sugar

⅓ cup tapioca flour or quick cooking tapioca

2 tablespoons lemon juice

1 teaspoon zest

1 tablespoon butter

Gently combine apricots, blackberries, sugar, tapioca, lemon juice and lemon zest. Let stand for 20 minutes at room temperature. Add filling to shell, and top with pieces of butter.

Bake 45 to 50 minutes. Remove from oven when filling is bubbly.

june 29

eating independently (happy 4th!)

Tomato Gazpacho

Cucumber and Tomato Salad

Grilled New York Steaks with Walla Walla Onions

Sautéed Dragon Tongue Beans and Green Beans

Corn and Basil Salad

Fresh Berry Galette

Serves eight

Neft family tradition says July 4th is the day to have a picnic and watch fireworks. The picnic always includes corn, tomatoes and cucumbers.

For the 20 years we lived at Lake Tahoe, the picnic was on the beach. We'd pile everyone into the back of the pick-up truck and park as close as possible to Tahoe City's Commons Beach for the fireworks. In Auburn, family and friends enjoy a picnic on the deck overlooking the American River. When it gets dark the group hikes to the top of the hill to watch the fireworks exploding over the Gold Country Fairgrounds.

This week's corn salad is an all-time favorite and a perfect addition to a July 4th meal. Everyone wants the recipe. Local sweet corn is the No. 1 ingredient, and it's easy to replace the squash with fresh uncooked cucumbers or mild radishes. Add basil dressing at the last minute if it's necessary to transport your picnic meal; it's tastier that way.

Tomato Gazpacho

2 pounds large tomatoes, halved

½ pound country-style bread, crust removed,
  cut into ½ inch pieces (about 3 cups)

¼ cup sherry vinegar

1 to 2 cucumbers, peeled and chopped
  (about 1 cup)

1 red onion, chopped

1 clove garlic, minced

½ teaspoon ground cumin

½ teaspoon paprika

½ cup water or tomato juice

½ cup extra virgin olive oil

Salt and pepper to taste

Fresh basil, chopped

Place a mesh strainer over a large bowl. Gently squeeze tomato halves to release seeds and juices. Discard seeds.

Chop tomatoes, and add to juices. Add bread to juices. Add vinegar, cucumbers, onion, and garlic.

Let sit at room temperature 30 minutes.

Blend with a hand blender. Add spices and water or juice. Continue blending while slowly adding the olive oil. Continue blending until smooth.

Season with salt and pepper.

Chill at least 2 hours before serving.

To serve, place 3 to 4 ounces in small sipping cups, and garnish with basil.

Cucumber and Tomato Salad

8 to 10 medium cucumbers, thinly sliced,
  about 1/8-inch thick
1 red onion, julienne
¼ cup sea salt
¼ cup rice vinegar
1 pint cherry tomatoes, cut in wedges
1 bag pea shoots

In a medium plastic container or flat-bottomed bowl, place a single layer of the cucumbers, a thin layer of red onion, then lightly salt. Repeat until all ingredients are layered. Cover with plastic wrap, and refrigerate 2 to 8 hours. Remove from refrigerator, and drain the water from the cucumbers and onions by pressing firmly (do not rinse). Drizzle vinegar over and toss to combine. Place the cucumbers on a plate and garnish with tomato wedges and pea shoots.

Grilled New York Steaks with Walla Walla Onions

Preheat grill.

4 New York steaks
2 teaspoons olive oil
Salt and pepper to taste
2 cloves garlic
2 teaspoons thyme, chopped
2 Walla Walla onions, julienne
2 tablespoons butter
2 tablespoons balsamic vinegar
Salt and pepper to taste

Season steaks with olive oil, salt, pepper, garlic and ½ of the thyme. Let sit 10 to 15 minutes at room temperature.
Meanwhile, heat a medium sauté pan and melt butter. Add onions and sauté until they begin to caramelize. Deglaze with vinegar and season to taste with salt and pepper. Set aside.
Grill the steaks on high, about 2 minutes per side, depending on thickness.
Let rest at least 10 minutes and slice to serve.
Garnish with onions and remaining thyme.

"The only time to eat diet food is while you're waiting for the steak to cook."
Julia Child

Corn and Basil Salad

6 ears corn

1 bunch basil, chopped

½ cup olive oil

Salt and pepper to taste

1 teaspoon butter

3 summer squash, small diced

2 cloves garlic, diced

1 bunch green onions, sliced

2 tablespoons red wine vinegar

Salt and pepper to taste

In a large bowl, shuck corn and slice kernels away from the cobs. Set aside.

In a small bowl, combine basil and oil until well blended. Season with salt and pepper. Set aside.

In a medium pan, heat butter and sauté squash with garlic until it begins to brown and is still crisp. Remove from the pan and add to a large bowl with corn. Add green onions. Drizzle basil oil over and toss to combine. Add vinegar and season with salt and pepper.

You can substitute cucumbers for the summer squash. Hint: pick a young cucumber with few seeds and don't peel it.

The main thing to remember about dragon tongue beans is they cook quickly. Don't even blink your eyes. They cook so fast – about two minutes, tops – that if you look away they'll be overdone.

Dragon tongue beans can be used like snap beans, or left on the vines to mature and used as dry beans. They're mottled with purple streaks. When cooked, the purple fades. Best of all, they're stringless.

Sautéed Dragon Tongue Beans and Green Beans

1 pound green beans

1 pound dragon tongue beans

2 tablespoons butter

1 tablespoon olive oil

2 cloves garlic, minced

Bring a large pot of salted water to a boil and blanch green beans 45 to 60 seconds. Remove and immediately place in a bowl of ice and water to stop cooking. When cool, remove.

Heat butter and olive oil in a large sauté pan and add green beans and dragon tongue beans. Season lightly with salt and pepper and continue to cook until slightly tender, about 2 to 3 minutes.

Arrange on a platter and serve.

Fresh Berry Galette

Preheat oven to 375°F.
Position oven racks on the middle and bottom rungs.

1 cup plus 3 tablespoons all purpose flour
¼ cup finely ground cornmeal
½ teaspoon salt
½ cup sugar, plus 1 tablespoon for the crust
½ cup butter, cut into small cubes and chilled
1 large egg yolk
¼ cup sour cream
2 tablespoons cornstarch
½ teaspoon ground cinnamon
6 cups fresh berries (raspberries, blueberries, blackberries)
1 tablespoon heavy cream
1 tablespoon Demarara sugar

For the dough

Combine the flour, cornmeal, salt, and 1 tablespoon of the sugar in a food processor; pulse briefly to combine. Add the butter; pulse until the mixture is the texture of coarse meal. Transfer to a medium bowl.

In a small bowl, beat together the egg yolk and sour cream. Stir this mixture into the dough, using a fork to blend. Gather the dough into a ball, wrap it in plastic, and compress into a disk. Chill for at least 1 hour but no longer than a day.

To assemble the tart

Remove the dough from the refrigerator and let it sit for about 10 minutes. (This takes the chill off and lets you roll it without cracking).

On a lightly floured surface, roll the dough into a 15-inch round. Transfer to a rimmed baking sheet lined with parchment.

In a small bowl, combine the remaining ½ cup sugar, the cornstarch, and cinnamon.

Put the berries in a medium bowl and toss gently with the sugar mixture to combine.

Pile the filling in the center of the dough circle, leaving a 2½-inch border all around. Pleat the tart, being careful not to rip the dough. Brush the cream onto the edge crust and sprinkle with the Demarara sugar. Bake on the middle rack 20 minutes. Move the tart to the bottom rack; reduce the oven temperature to 350°F, and bake an additional 25 to 30 minutes, rotating the pan if needed, until the crust is golden brown.

fig fantasy

Mixed Greens with Figs, Blue Cheese
and Honey Balsamic Vinaigrette

Grilled Figs and Peaches with Proscuitto

Roasted Chicken with Fig Glaze

Creamy Polenta with Fig Compote

Romano Beans with Almond Pesto and Figs

Vanilla Ice Cream with Fresh Figs and Blackberries

Serves eight

Ripe figs, mainly Kadota and Black Mission, are abundant and delicious this time of year, so we vowed to do an entire menu focused on figs.

To get things started, we grilled figs wrapped with prosciutto. I've been looking forward to this appetizer all year. The roasted chicken with fig glaze is particularly tasty, and the result is a platter that looks good and tastes good.

Figs were introduced to the region during the gold rush days. Every miner planted a fig tree. Kadota figs have a green skin, pale fruit inside, and are best in salads and desserts. Black Mission figs are purple-black, great for chutney, glazes, or grilling.

In the Northern California foothills, we have two crops of figs. Depending on the weather, the first crop ripens mid-June and lasts about three weeks. These figs are fat and plump, but there are fewer of them and they are less flavorful than the later crop. The second crop typically ripens in mid-August and lasts four to six weeks. While the figs may be smaller, they are delicious. Figs love warm weather, and the second crop has the benefit of a California summer which means lots of sun and temperatures flirting with the century mark.

The second crop is the best for making fig jams and compotes, and it's the crop that makes the flavorful pickled figs that go so well with lamb and pork.

july 6

Grilled Figs and Peaches with Proscuitto

Preheat grill on high.

6 thin slices prosciutto
6 figs, cut in half lengthwise
3 peaches, cut in quarters
Olive oil
Salt and pepper to taste
Lavender flowers, to garnish

Cut or tear each slice of prosciutto into 4 pieces and wrap the fruit with one piece each. Brush lightly with olive oil, salt and pepper.
Place on a hot, clean grill for about 45 seconds per side (there should be nice grill marks). Remove from grill and set aside. Sprinkle with lavender flowers when ready to serve.

Mixed Greens with Figs, Blue Cheese and Honey Balsamic Vinaigrette

1 head green leaf lettuce, torn into pieces
¼ pound Manchego cheese, shaved
8 to 10 figs, stems trimmed, cut in quarters
¼ cup pecan halves, toasted

Honey Balsamic Vinaigrette
¼ cup balsamic vinegar
2 tablespoons honey
¼ cup olive oil
Salt and pepper to taste

Combine all salad ingredients except pecans. Whisk together vinaigrette ingredients, and dress salad just before serving. Garnish with pecans.

Some items don't belong in the refrigerator. They include figs, garlic, onions, potatoes, tomatoes, and stone fruits (like peaches and nectarines, until they are completely ripe). Basil should be kept fresh in a small vase of water.

Roasted Chicken with Fig Glaze

Preheat oven to 375°F.

Fig Glaze

3 cups figs, diced
½ cup water
2 tablespoons agave nectar
¼ teaspoon cayenne
1 tablespoon Dijon mustard
2 tablespoons lemon juice

Combine all ingredients in a food processor and process until coarsely pureed. Set aside.

Roasted Chicken

2 whole chickens, about 3 to 4 pounds each
3 cloves garlic, minced
½ bunch thyme, chopped
Salt and pepper to taste
1 lemon, halved

Season the chickens with olive oil, garlic, thyme, salt and pepper. Place one lemon half in each body cavity. Roast one hour.

Using a pastry brush, coat the chickens evenly with the glaze. Reduce oven temperature to 325°F and continue baking 20 to 30 minutes longer, until drumsticks are easy to move. Remove from the oven and let rest at least 15 minutes.

Remove the legs and thighs and breasts from the chicken and arrange on a large platter. Place grilled figs and peaches around, sprinkle with lavender and serve.

placercountyrealfood.com

Creamy Polenta with Fig Compote

4 cups chicken stock
3½ cups milk
Salt and pepper to taste
1½ cups white polenta
2 tablespoons butter
¼ cup blue cheese

Heat stock and milk in a medium pot; season lightly with salt and pepper.
When almost simmering, slowly whisk in polenta. Reduce heat to medium-low, periodically stirring with a rubber spatula. When almost all the liquid is absorbed, reduce heat to low and add butter and blue cheese. Whisk to combine and season to taste with salt and pepper. Keep warm on a low burner until serving.

Fig Compote

1 tablespoon butter
½ Walla Walla onion, diced
¼ cup red wine
3 cups figs, stems removed, cut in quarters
1 tablespoon rosemary, minced
2 tablespoons honey
Salt and pepper to taste

In a small pan, sauté onions in butter until translucent. Deglaze with red wine and add figs and rosemary. Cook over medium-heat for about 5 minutes, until figs have cooked down. Stir

in honey and season to taste with salt and pepper.
To serve, spoon polenta in a large bowl and then make a small well in the center for some of the fig compote. Serve remaining compote on the side.

july 6

Romano Beans with Almond Pesto and Figs

1 clove garlic
½ cup almonds
1 orange, zest and juice
1 teaspoon thyme, chopped
¾ cup olive oil
Salt and pepper to taste
2 tablespoons butter
2 pounds Romano or dragon tongue beans,
   ends removed
6 to 8 figs, stems removed, cut in quarters

In a small food processor, combine garlic,
almonds, orange zest, juice, thyme and half
of the olive oil. Pulse until coarsely chopped.
With machine running, stream in remaining oil.
Season to taste with salt and pepper and place in
a large bowl.
In a large pan, heat butter and sauté beans until
barely tender. Remove from pan and place with
almond mixture and figs. Toss to combine. Place
on a platter and serve.

Vanilla Ice Cream with Fresh Figs and Blackberries

Vanilla ice cream
8 to 10 figs, stems removed, cut in half
2 cups blackberries

Scoop ice cream into bowls and garnish with fruit.

peaches, peaches, peaches

Chilled Peach Soup

Mixed Greens Salad with Radishes and Tomatoes
and Cilantro Dressing

Slow Roasted Pork Shoulder Tacos with
Peach Salsa and Tomatillo Salsa

Black Beans

Corn with Cumin

Peach and Blackberry Pie

Serves eight

You know summer peaches have arrived when you take a bite of a beautiful, fragrant peach and the juice runs down your chin and arm. It's vital to have a tissue to catch the drips.

Peaches are stars of the show this week. The color, flavor and texture of this versatile fruit are just a few of the reasons to include them in recipes. On market days like this, Laura and I stand at boxes of peaches. We mentally envision, and talk, about how peaches will complement salads, meats and desserts. It's fun to choose fruits and vegetables with someone who appreciates fresh food the same way you do.

Four Placer County orchards raise excellent peaches: Twin Peaks Orchard, the Brenner Ranch and Beauty Ranch are located off Highway 193 between Newcastle and Lincoln. Pine Hill Orchard is off Horseshoe Bar Road in Loomis. These orchards have been providing freshly picked peaches for many years and all have nice selections of early to late harvest peaches.

Be sure to talk with the growers about the complex flavors of the many varieties available. Remember that one variety may be best for cooking, another variety just right for canning.

july 13

Chilled Peach Soup

4 peaches, very ripe, cut in quarters
1 lime, juiced
1 tablespoon honey
1 cinnamon stick
½ cup water
2 to 3 cups Champagne

In a small saucepan, heat the peaches with lime juice, honey, cinnamon stick and water. Blend with a hand blender until smooth. Chill at least 1 hour.

To serve, slowly stir in Champagne until desired consistency and serve in chilled glasses.

A produce market should include the earthy scent of freshly dug potatoes, the sharp, nose-wrinkling aroma of onions, and the syrupy sweet fragrance of fresh peaches. A produce market should be as much a feast for the nose as the eyes.

The grocery store might have the most colorful, mouth-watering assortment of produce, but one thing will always be missing: the fragrance of freshly picked fruits and vegetables. Walk into any big chain grocery store and stroll through the produce section. Nothing fragrant jumps out at you. Oh sure, you can take a cantaloupe and push it against your nose to check for that heavenly aroma. But if it was really fresh, the scent would draw you in when you walked by.

Mixed Greens Salad with Radishes and Tomatoes and Cilantro Dressing

1 bag baby greens
2 bunches radishes, thinly sliced
1½ pounds mixed tomatoes,
   cut into 1-inch pieces
3 lemon cucumbers, thinly sliced

Cilantro Dressing

1 lime, zest and juice
½ cup crème fraîche
¼ cup cream
¼ cup cilantro, chopped
¼ teaspoon cayenne

Toss salad ingredients together. Whisk together dressing ingredients and toss with salad just before serving.

Slow Roasted Pork Shoulder Tacos with Peach Salsa and Tomatillo Salsa

Preheat oven to 425°F.

¼ cup cumin seeds
¼ cup sea salt
Olive oil
2 bone-in pork shoulder roasts, about 4 pounds each
½ cup onion, diced
¼ cup peppers, sliced
½ bunch cilantro
Tortillas

Toast cumin seeds over medium heat until fragrant. Remove from heat and grind with the salt in a spice grinder.

Brush pork lightly with olive oil, and season liberally with two-thirds of the cumin salt mixture. Save remaining cumin salt for corn recipe.

Cover with foil and bake 15 minutes. Turn oven down to 300°F and continue cooking 3 to 4 hours longer.

When meat is tender and can be shredded, remove from oven and let rest for at least 15 minutes. To serve, shred pork and place on a large platter, pouring any pan juices over top. Garnish with diced onion, peppers and cilantro. Serve with tortillas.

Peach Salsa

3 peaches, small diced
2 tomatoes, seeds removed, small diced
1 red onion, small diced (about ½ cup)
¼ cup cilantro, chopped
½ teaspoon cayenne
2 tablespoons olive oil
Salt and pepper

Combine all ingredients and season to taste with salt and pepper.

Tomatillo Salsa

Preheat oven to 375°F.

1 pound tomatillos
1 red onion, quartered
1 tablespoon olive oil
Salt and pepper to taste
¼ cup cilantro
2 limes, juiced
½ teaspoon cayenne

Clean tomatillos by removing husks and washing. Toss in a medium bowl with onions, olive oil, salt and pepper. Roast on a sheet tray 20 to 25 minutes, until soft and beginning to caramelize. Remove from oven and let cool slightly.

Place tomatillo onion mixture in a food processor or blender and process until smooth. Place in a bowl and let cool to room temperature before adding cilantro and lime juice. Season to taste with cayenne. Add more salt if desired.

july 13

Black Beans

1 onion, diced (about 1 cup)
6 cloves garlic, minced
2 tablespoons olive oil
3 cups black beans, soaked overnight
2 quarts chicken stock
1 lime, halved and juiced
Salt to taste
2 teaspoons cayenne

In a medium pot, sauté onion and garlic in olive oil until translucent.
Add beans, chicken stock and lime (juice and lime halves).
Bring to a boil and then turn down to a low simmer. Continue to cook until tender. Remove lime. Season to taste with salt and cayenne.

Corn with Cumin

6 to 7 ears corn, kernels removed from the cobs
2 tablespoons butter
Salt and cumin mixture to taste (from pork recipe)

Heat a large sauté pan and melt butter. Add corn and sauté until tender, about 1 minute. Add cumin salt and serve.

Peach and Blackberry Pie

Preheat oven to 400°F.

Two-Crust Pie Dough for 9-inch Pan

¼ cup vegetable shortening
¼ cup butter
1½ cups all purpose flour
½ teaspoon salt
¼ cup cold water
1 teaspoon half cinnamon/half sugar mixture
½ teaspoon Demerara sugar (optional)

Using a pie dough cutter, blend shortening, butter, flour and salt together to cornmeal stage. Place in a medium bowl and slowly add cold water, mixing with a fork, until dough comes together. Add more water if necessary. Form into a ball, cover and chill at least 2 hours before rolling out.
Cut the dough ball into two pieces, one slightly larger than the other. Roll out dough until ⅛-inch thick. Make dough 10 inches round for bottom, and 9 inches round for top.
Place the filling in the shell. Apply top crust. Trim, roll and crimp edges.
Sprinkle with cinnamon sugar; then sprinkle Demerara sugar on top.

Peach and Blackberry Filling

5 cups ripe peaches, sliced (skin left on)
⅔ cup sugar
⅓ cup tapioca flour or quick cooking tapioca
1 teaspoon pure almond extract
1 cup blackberries
1 tablespoon butter

Combine peaches, sugar, tapioca and almond extract in a 2-quart dish. Stir gently to moisten sugar and tapioca flour. Add blackberries. Let stand at least 20 minutes.
Add filling to pie shell. Cut butter into small pieces and sprinkle over top of pie filling.
Bake until pie bubbles, about 50 minutes.

a taste of summer

Tomato and Lemon Cucumber Salad with Tomato Vinaigrette

Pan Seared Salmon with Cucumbers
and Crème Fraîche

Creamy Corn with Mushrooms

Sautéed Baby Carrots and Zucchini

Plum and Blackberry Pie

Serves eight

During July the farmers markets are loaded with farmers trucks squeezed tightly against each other. Tables overflow with freshly picked food. The market is crowded with hundreds and hundreds of people who have come to shop for the freshest produce in town. These are people who value food raised on family farms. It seems everyone at the market is celebrating the bounty and abundance of good food. Everything on the tables tastes like summer.

Summer is a time for lighter meals, and fresh fish fits the bill. Our Auburn farmers market is lucky to have Brand Little selling his weekly catch from the waters off the California coast. Each week he emails a list of what's available so it's easy to plan meals with fish a few days in advance.

Of course, we can't find everything we need at a farmers market. We buy mushrooms at Newcastle Produce Market, Whole Foods, or at the local Raley's Market. My taste buds like a hearty mushroom: both Portobello and crimini have rich full flavors. However, if hearty mushrooms are not available, a lighter mushroom is better than no mushroom at all.

Tomato and Lemon Cucumber Salad with Tomato Vinaigrette

1½ pounds mixed tomatoes
1 red onion, julienne
4 lemon cucumbers, thinly sliced
¼ cup basil, sliced thin
1 bag baby greens

Tomato Vinaigrette

Juice from tomatoes
¼ cup red wine vinegar
⅓ cup olive oil

Cut tomatoes into 1-inch pieces and place in a colander over a bowl, reserving all the juices. After about 20 minutes of draining, combine tomato juices with vinegar and oil and season to taste with salt and pepper.

Toss half the dressing with tomatoes, onion, cucumber and basil and place in the center of a large platter.

Toss greens with remaining dressing, and use them as a garnish.

Pan Seared Salmon with Cucumbers and Crème Fraîche

Cucumber and Crème Fraîche

4 cucumbers, sliced 1/8-inch thick (about 4 cups)

1 small red onion, diced

2 tablespoons sea salt

2 tablespoons rice wine vinegar

1 tablespoon dill, chopped

¼ cup crème fraîche (you can substitute sour cream or yogurt)

In a medium plastic container or flat-bottomed bowl, place a single layer of the cucumbers, sprinkle with some red onions and then sprinkle with salt. Repeat this 4 to 5 more times, until all the ingredients are layered.
Cover and refrigerate 2 to 8 hours.
Drain the water from the cucumbers and onions by pressing firmly (do not rinse). Add vinegar and toss to combine.
Just before serving, stir in dill and crème fraîche.

Pan Seared Salmon

3 to 4 pounds of salmon

3 tablespoons grapeseed oil

Debone and cut salmon into 4-ounce pieces.
In a large sauté pan, heat grapeseed oil and sear salmon. When slightly caramelized, flip the salmon and cook just long enough to sear the other side (for medium-rare to medium). Remove from pan and place on platter with cucumber and crème fraîche relish and serve.

Creamy Corn with Mushrooms

6 ears corn
4 tablespoons butter
1 Walla Walla onion, diced (about ½ cup)
1 pint cream
¼ cup parmesan cheese
1 to 2 teaspoons truffle salt (optional)
¾ pound cremini mushrooms, sliced
2 cloves garlic, minced
Salt and pepper to taste

Shuck corn, and cut kernels away from cob; reserve the kernels and one cleaned cob, broken in half.

In a medium pot, sauté onions in 2 tablespoons butter until translucent. Add corn kernels, cob and cream. Slowly bring to a boil while stirring, then turn down to a simmer.

Continue cooking, while stirring, until thickened slightly, about 20 minutes.

Meanwhile, sauté mushrooms with garlic and remaining butter. Set aside.

When the cream mixture is done, remove from heat, discard cobs, and place about one-third of the mixture in a blender, and blend until smooth. Add the blended portion back to the pot, and stir in parmesan cheese, mushrooms and truffle salt. Season to taste with salt and pepper.

Sautéed Baby Carrots and Zucchini

3 bunches baby carrots
16 to 18 baby zucchini, stems removed, cut in half lengthwise
2 tablespoons butter
1 tablespoon olive oil
2 cloves garlic, minced
2 tablespoons parsley, chopped

Clean baby carrots by removing tops, peeling and halving, if necessary.

In a large pan, sauté half the garlic in half of the butter and oil. Add carrots and sauté until just tender.

Remove from the pan and repeat the process for the zucchini.

Toss with parsley and serve.

Plum and Blackberry Pie

Preheat oven to 400°F.

Two-Crust Pie Dough for 9-inch Pan

¼ cup vegetable shortening

¼ cup butter

1½ cups all purpose flour

½ teaspoon salt

¼ cup cold water

1 teaspoon half-cinnamon/half-sugar mixture

½ teaspoon Demerara sugar (optional)

Using a pie dough cutter, blend shortening, butter, flour and salt together to cornmeal stage. Place in a medium bowl and slowly add cold water, mixing with a fork, until dough comes together. Add more water if necessary. Form into a ball, cover and chill at least 2 hours before rolling out.

Cut the dough ball into two pieces, one slightly larger than the other. Roll out dough until ⅛-inch thick. Make dough 10 inches round for bottom, and 9 inches round for top.

Place the filling in the shell. Apply top crust. Trim, roll and crimp edges.

Sprinkle with cinnamon sugar; then sprinkle Demerara sugar on top.

Filling

5 cups Black Amber plums, sliced, pits removed (leave skins on)

1 cup blackberries

1 cup sugar

⅓ cup tapioca flour or quick cooking tapioca

1 teaspoon almond extract

½ lemon, juice

Pinch salt

1 tablespoon butter

In a large bowl, combine plums, blackberries, sugar, tapioca, almond extract, lemon juice and salt. Let sit 30 minutes.

Add filling to pie shell. Cut butter into small pieces and sprinkle over top of pie filling.

Bake 50 minutes.

summer vegetables galore

Chilled Tomato Soup

Tomato and Cucumber Salad with Goat Cheese

Grilled Sirloin Tip Roast
with Slow Roasted Tomatoes and Grilled Onions

Roasted Baby Potatoes

Sautéed Green Beans with Garlic

Chocolate Blackberry Cake

Serves eight

You can take a girl away from the farm, but you can't take the farm away from the girl. That explains my lifelong connection with farms and food.

Our family moved from the Inver Grove Township farm to St. Paul, Minnesota in the early 1940s. My father's hired hands were drafted, it was impossible to run the farm without help, so he signed up to work at Northwest Airlines building airplanes. But the Korfhage family never went without a garden.

Dad bought a couple acres on Stryker Avenue and planted a Victory Garden. Two acres holds an abundance of fresh vegetables and the most fun was at picking time. Dad always planted kohlrabi. When my sister, Ruth, and I visited the garden, he'd pull a couple kohlrabi bulbs, brush off the dirt on his trousers, tear away some of the larger stems, and braid the remaining stems into a handle. With his pocket knife he quickly peeled the small round bulb, and we'd have our own vegetable on a stick for a snack.

Often there were too many vegetables for our family to eat. Dad would fill our wagons with produce and tell us what we could charge for two cucumbers, three ears of corn, or some tomatoes. Ruth and I pulled wagons from door to door and sold the day's harvest. Sometimes we'd make 15 cents or 20 cents, big money for girls ages 5 and 7.

No wonder both Ruth and I turned into marketers.

july 20

Chilled Tomato Soup

4 large tomatoes, halved, seeds removed
2 teaspoons balsamic vinegar
1 tablespoon olive oil
2 tablespoons fresh basil, diced
Salt and pepper to taste
¼ cup crème fraîche

Grate tomato using a large box grater. Discard skins. Add balsamic vinegar, olive oil, and basil.
Season to taste with salt and pepper.
Use a hand blender if you want a smoother consistency.
Place soup in refrigerator for two hours.
Stir crème fraîche with a spoon and swirl a full teaspoon of crème over soup.
Garnish with a small basil leaf (optional).

Tomato and Cucumber Salad with Goat Cheese

3 to 4 pounds heirloom tomatoes,
   cut into 1-inch pieces
4 lemon cucumbers, sliced
1 red onion, julienne
¼ cup basil leaves, chopped
¼ cup red wine vinegar
2 tablespoons olive oil
Salt and pepper to taste
3 ounces goat cheese, crumbled

Gently toss tomatoes, cucumbers, onion and basil with the vinegar and oil. Season lightly with salt and pepper. Sprinkle goat cheese over the salad and serve.

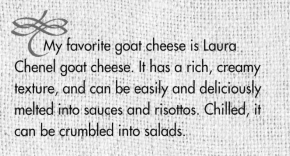

My favorite goat cheese is Laura Chenel goat cheese. It has a rich, creamy texture, and can be easily and deliciously melted into sauces and risottos. Chilled, it can be crumbled into salads.

Grilled Sirloin Tip Roast with Slow Roasted Tomatoes and Grilled Onions

Preheat oven to 250°F.

Slow Roasted Tomatoes

2 pints Juliet tomatoes (or other small
  Roma-type tomatoes)
2 tablespoons olive oil
Salt and pepper to taste
1 tablespoon dried basil

Cut tomatoes in half and season with olive oil, salt, pepper and basil. Place on a sheet tray and roast for 2 to 2½ hours. Let cool on tray. (These can be made a day ahead.)

Grilled Sirloin Tip Roast and Walla Walla Onions

Preheat grill.

4 pounds beef sirloin roast
2 tablespoons olive oil
Salt and pepper
3 cloves garlic
2 sprigs rosemary
2 pounds Walla Walla onions, halved
1 tablespoon olive oil
3 tablespoons balsamic vinegar

Season the roast with 1 tablespoon olive oil, salt, pepper, garlic and rosemary. Set aside.
In a small bowl, season the onions with salt, pepper and 1 tablespoon olive oil.
Place the roast on the grill to sear the first side for about 3 minutes. Turn to sear the other side.
Turn the grill down to medium heat and arrange the onions on the grill around the beef, turning and rotating until they begin to caramelize.
Cook the beef to 110°F internal temperature, and then remove it from the grill and let rest for at least 20 minutes for medium-rare.
When the onions are soft, roughly chop them and drizzle with balsamic vinegar.
To serve, place sliced meat on a platter and garnish with onions and slow-roasted tomatoes.

Roasted Baby Potatoes

Preheat oven to 400°F.

3 to 4 pounds assorted new potatoes
1 yellow onion, julienne
4 to 5 thyme sprigs, leaves picked
1 tablespoon chopped parsley
¼ cup olive oil
Salt and pepper

Cut the potatoes to uniform size and toss in a large bowl with onion, thyme, parsley, oil, salt and pepper. (Set a small amount of thyme and parsley aside to use as a garnish.)
Place potatoes on a half sheet tray and roast 20 to 25 minutes or until tender. Garnish with chopped thyme and parsley before serving.

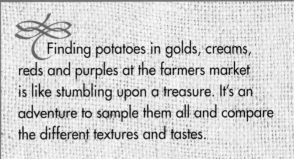

Finding potatoes in golds, creams, reds and purples at the farmers market is like stumbling upon a treasure. It's an adventure to sample them all and compare the different textures and tastes.

Sautéed Green Beans with Garlic

3 cloves garlic, minced
2 tablespoons butter
2 tablespoons olive oil
2 pounds green beans
Salt and pepper to taste

In a large sauté pan, cook garlic in butter and olive oil until fragrant. Add green beans and sauté until just tender; season to taste with salt and pepper.

Chocolate Blackberry Cake

Preheat oven to 350°F.

2 cups all purpose flour
1 teaspoon baking soda
1 teaspoon baking powder
½ teaspoon salt
1 cup plus 3 tablespoons cocoa powder
1 cup boiling water
2 cups sugar
3 large eggs
¾ cup butter
1 cup buttermilk
1 teaspoon vanilla

Butter the sides and bottom of two 8-inch cake pans. Line the bottom with parchment paper and then butter the paper. Dust with cocoa powder, tapping out any excess.

Sift flour with baking powder, soda and salt in a medium bowl. Set aside.

Sift cocoa powder into another bowl. Pour boiling water over cocoa and whisk to blend. Set aside. Using an electric mixer, beat sugar and eggs until light and fluffy, about 2 minutes. Add butter to egg mixture and beat until well blended. Beat in cocoa mixture. Add buttermilk and vanilla, beat to blend. Add dry ingredients and beat on low just to blend. Transfer to prepared pans. Smooth tops.

Bake until a toothpick inserted into the center comes out clean, about 30 to 35 minutes. Cool cakes completely in pans on rack before turning out. (This cake can be made a day ahead.)

Blackberry Filling

4 cups berries
1 cup water
¼ cup sugar
¼ teaspoon salt
½ lemon, juiced
3 tablespoons tapioca flour

In a small saucepan, heat 3 cups of the berries, water and sugar. Cook over medium heat until slightly thickened, about 25 minutes. Strain out some of the seeds if desired. Stir in lemon juice, tapioca flour and salt, and simmer 2 more minutes. Remove from heat, stir in remaining cup of berries. Let cool completely.

Chocolate Frosting

¾ cup butter, melted
1¼ cups cocoa powder, sifted
4½ cups powdered sugar, sifted
½ cup milk
1½ teaspoons vanilla
1 pint fresh berries

In a mixer, blend butter with cocoa powder. Add sugar and milk, alternating, and beat until combined. Add vanilla and beat to desired consistency.

To assemble, place one of the cakes on a cake plate. Using a pastry or plastic bag, pipe a rim of frosting around the edge of the bottom layer of cake.

Fill the center with the berry mixture and top with the other cake.

Frost with remaining frosting and garnish with fresh berries.

courtney's creations

Watermelon and Heirloom Tomato Salad Greek Style

Braised Lamb Shoulder with Olive Salsa Verde

Roasted Potatoes with Spiced Eggplant and Peppers

Roasted Peaches with Lemon Verbena
and Sheep's Milk Ice Cream

Serves eight

Recipes written and prepared by guest Chef Courtney McDonald

From the beginning, this cookbook has been a community effort. When a new crop appeared on the scene, farmers told us about it and offered ideas on preparation and pairings. Friends shared favorite family recipes, and some offered to prepare an entire meal. Courtney McDonald picked the first Monday in August to perform her magic in the kitchen.

Courtney is an Auburn girl. In 2001, she graduated from the Culinary Institute of America in Hyde Park, New York, and worked in fine dining restaurants across the country for 14 years. Most recently she served as co-executive chef of Carpe Vino in Old Town Auburn. Carpe Vino's philosophy has always been to feature local, seasonal ingredients on its menus.

This year, Courtney is pursuing a yearlong internship with Flying Mule Farm; she's learning about grassfed lamb, goat, beef and pastured poultry. This week's lamb dinner highlights the peak of summer bounty.

The Sheep's Milk Ice Cream stole the show. Never have I tasted such a rich and creamy ice cream. Fortunate is the person who finds sheep milk to make Courtney's recipe.

august 3

Watermelon and Heirloom Tomato Salad Greek Style

1 small seedless red or yellow watermelon

2 pounds mixed heirloom tomatoes,
   cut into ¼-inch slices

1 small Armenian cucumber, thinly sliced

½ cup thinly sliced red onion

4 cups baby arugula

2 tablespoons dark balsamic vinegar

⅓ cup extra-virgin olive oil

½ cup crumbled Greek feta cheese

2 tablespoons chopped fresh mint

Salt and pepper to taste

Using a large knife, remove both the ends of the watermelon so you can see the colored flesh. Stand the melon on one end and, beginning from the top of the melon, cut the rind from the melon following its natural curve. Dice the watermelon into 1-inch cubes and set aside.

Using a large platter, begin layering the tomatoes, watermelon, cucumber, red onion and arugula, seasoning with salt and pepper as you go.

Drizzle each layer with a little balsamic vinegar and olive oil.

Crumble the Greek feta over the top of the salad and garnish with the chopped mint. Serve immediately.

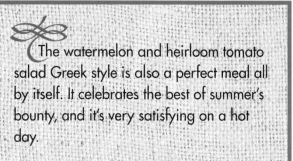

The watermelon and heirloom tomato salad Greek style is also a perfect meal all by itself. It celebrates the best of summer's bounty, and it's very satisfying on a hot day.

I like simple food, made with the best ingredients available, cooked with care and as quickly as possible to taste as fresh as possible.
Nika Hazelton

Braised Lamb Shoulder with Olive Salsa Verde

Preheat oven to 150°F.

Braised Lamb Shoulder

4 pounds boneless lamb shoulder

¼ cup chopped Italian parsley (set aside 2 tablespoons for the salsa verde)

3 tablespoons chopped fresh rosemary (set aside 1 tablespoon for the salsa verde)

2 tablespoons chopped garlic

Salt and pepper to taste

6 cups extra virgin olive oil

Trim the lamb shoulder of excess fat. Cut the lamb into 8 portions of similar size and shape. Place in a medium-sized mixing bowl. Season with parsley, rosemary, garlic, salt and pepper. Toss the lamb mixture to evenly coat.

Transfer the lamb into a narrow, deep baking dish such as a large loaf pan (or 2 smaller ones). Add the olive oil to cover, until all of the lamb is just submerged. (You may not need all 6 cups of olive oil.) Cover tightly with foil and place in the center of oven. Let the lamb braise, undisturbed, for at least 7 hours or overnight.

The lamb is finished cooking when a meat fork inserted into the thickest part comes out with no resistance. When the lamb has finished cooking, allow to cool slightly at room temperature and transfer to the refrigerator to chill until you are ready to use it.

To serve, remove the chilled lamb from the olive oil and drain off the excess oil (reserve ½ cup for the salsa verde).

Preheat a large cast iron skillet over medium high heat on the stove. Add the lamb portions and cook, turning occasionally, until brown and crispy and heated through. Serve with olive salsa verde.

Olive Oil Salsa Verde

One 8-ounce container mixed Greek olives, pitted and chopped.

½ cup reserved olive oil (from recipe above)

2 tablespoons chopped Italian parsley (from recipe above)

1 tablespoon chopped fresh rosemary

2 tablespoons chopped fresh chives

2 tablespoons chopped fresh mint

Pepper to taste

Combine all ingredients, stir and serve.

This is a great dish to prepare in advance since it can be stored submerged in the olive oil for up to two weeks in the refrigerator. But don't discard the olive oil. It can be used in a number of ways, from roasting potatoes to sautéeing onions, to a dip for some locally baked, crusty bread.

Roasted Potatoes with Spiced Eggplant and Peppers

Preheat oven to 400°F.

2 pounds very small potatoes,
   washed and trimmed
1 cup extra virgin olive oil
¼ cup water
10 cloves garlic, thinly sliced
1 large yellow onion, peeled and thinly sliced
1½ tablespoons smoked Spanish paprika
1 pound mixed sweet peppers, stems and seeds
   removed, thinly sliced
1 pound eggplant, peeled and diced
   into ½-inch cubes
2 cups baby arugula
Salt and pepper to taste

In a medium-sized bowl, toss the potatoes with ¼ cup olive oil, water, and a pinch of sliced garlic.

Season to taste with salt and pepper.

Transfer to a roasting pan, and cover tightly with foil.

Roast the potatoes until they are fork tender, about 20 to 30 minutes.

Remove from the heat and set aside.

In a medium short-sided stockpot, heat the remaining ¾ cup of olive oil over low heat.

Add remaining garlic and onion, and cook, stirring occasionally, until onions are translucent, about 15 minutes.

Increase heat to medium-high and add paprika and peppers. Cook, stirring frequently, until the peppers have softened, about 3 minutes. Add eggplant and cook until soft, about 15 to 20 minutes. If the mixture begins to get too dry, lower the heat and add a little water. Season to taste with salt.

Just before serving, add the still-hot potatoes to the pot and mix well. Layer the eggplant-potato mixture with the arugula on a large platter and serve immediately.

Roasted Peaches with Lemon Verbena and Sheep's Milk Ice Cream

Ice Cream

3 cups fresh sheep's milk

1 cup organic heavy cream

¼ vanilla bean

8 egg yolks

½ cup plus 1 tablespoon granulated sugar

½ teaspoon salt

In a small saucepot over medium heat, heat the sheep's milk and cream to just below boiling. Split the vanilla bean in half lengthwise and scrape the pulp into the milk–cream mixture. While the cream is heating, place the egg yolks into a medium–sized mixing bowl. Whisk in the sugar and salt and continue whisking until yolks are lemon yellow colored and slightly thickened. Very slowly pour the hot cream mixture into the egg yolks, one ladle at a time, while whisking constantly. Once half of the cream has been added, pour the egg yolk mixture back into the pot with the remaining cream. Place the pot back on the stove and, over low heat, whisk constantly. Gently heat the mixture until it thickens enough to coat the back of a wooden spoon.

DO NOT BOIL the mixture; boiling curdles the egg yolks and ruins the texture and flavor of the ice cream.

Once the ice cream mixture has reached the proper consistency, strain through a fine-meshed strainer and cool over an ice bath. Chill at least four hours. Freeze in ice cream freezer per manufacturer's instructions. Once the ice cream is frozen, let set in the freezer until firm enough to scoop, about 3 hours.

Roasted Peaches with Lemon Verbena

Preheat oven to 400°F.

8 ripe peaches, halved

2 tablespoons honey

2 tablespoons butter

Pinch of salt

8 sprigs fresh lemon verbena

Line a shallow baking sheet with foil or parchment paper and place the peaches, cut side up, on top.

Drizzle the peach halves with the honey and place a small piece of butter on each peach. Sprinkle very lightly with salt and evenly divide the lemon verbena over the top of the peaches.

Roast until just heated through and beginning to soften, about 5 to 10 minutes. Remove the lemon verbena sprigs and serve hot topped with sheep's milk ice cream.

Fresh sheep's milk can be difficult to find. You can substitute good quality goat's or cow's milk. If you use goat's or cow's milk, use 2 cups milk and 2 cups heavy cream instead of 3 cups sheep's milk and 1 cup heavy cream.

chickens from the farm

Baked Eggplant with Tomato Sauce
and Mozzarella Appetizers

Panzanella Salad

Braised Chicken with Mushrooms and White Wine

Sautéed Chard with Bacon

Sautéed Green Beans with Garlic and Almonds

Crème Brûlée with Almond Shortbread

Serves eight

My uncle raised chickens, and we ate chickens from the farm. As a child, I remember Sunday noon-time chicken dinner as a familiar favorite. During summer months there was always a cucumber salad, a platter of tomatoes, green beans, and mashed potatoes, and chicken gravy on the menu. The fruit that was in season ended up in a pie.

We can buy wholesome, grassfed, pasture-raised chickens at the Auburn farmers market. Thanks to a couple of grants and generous donations, local farmers have the use of a mobile poultry processor. It lets the farmers butcher the birds in a USDA-approved portable facility.

This year is the first time farmers market shoppers have been able to buy chickens or turkeys directly from the grower. When I discover a farmer is selling birds, I pick up two or three, and freeze them. When it's time to cook the chicken, I simply move it to my refrigerator a couple days before chicken dinner. Slowly defrosted, the chicken meat is flavorful and tasty. Once you taste a walk-around chicken, a chicken that is raised in the out-of-doors with its feet on the ground, you will never be satisfied with anything else.

Baked Eggplant with Tomato Sauce and Mozzarella Appetizers

(Note: This recipe can be an appetizer for eight or a main course for four.)

Preheat oven to 350°F.

4 small eggplants, peeled and sliced into ½–inch thick slices

¼ cup plus 3 tablespoons olive oil

1 cup bell peppers, diced

3 cups tomatoes, blanched, peeled, seeds removed and diced

2 cups onions

1 pound fresh mozzarella sliced into 16 slices

½ cup Thai basil, diced

Salt and pepper to taste

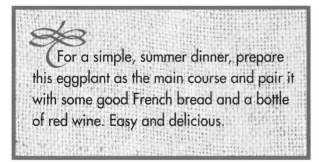

For a simple, summer dinner, prepare this eggplant as the main course and pair it with some good French bread and a bottle of red wine. Easy and delicious.

Brush olive oil on both sides of eggplant slices and place on parchment lined baking pan. Bake until eggplant is easily pierced with a fork. (Check after 15 minutes, then check every few minutes thereafter until done.)

Remove from oven, but leave on baking pan. Sauté peppers until soft in large sauté pan with 1 tablespoon olive oil. Add diced tomatoes to peppers and simmer for 10 minutes. Add diced basil and hold on very low heat. Salt and pepper to taste.

In another large sauté pan, place 2 tablespoons olive oil, and, over medium heat, caramelize onions until soft, 7 to 10 minutes.

Top each slice of eggplant with a small spoonful of onions, and then a slice of mozzarella. Sprinkle a small amount of salt on each slice of mozzarella, and return eggplant to oven until mozzarella melts.

On eight small plates spoon ⅓ cup of tomato sauce; top each pool of sauce with two slices of eggplant. Garnish with basil. Serve immediately.

Panzanella Salad

Preheat oven to 350°F.

¾ pound rustic bread
2 tablespoons olive oil
1 clove garlic, minced
Salt and pepper to taste
3 pounds heirloom tomatoes,
   cut into 1-inch pieces
1 tablespoon sherry vinegar
2 cucumbers, sliced
1 red onion, julienne
2 tablespoons olive oil
Salt and pepper

Remove crust from bread and cut into ¾-inch cubes.

In a medium bowl, toss the bread with oil, garlic, salt and pepper. Toast 10 to 15 minutes, until golden brown and crispy. Set aside.

Place tomatoes in a colander over a bowl and let juices drain. (Let the juices drain naturally, do not press.)

After about 20 minutes, measure out about ½ cup of the juice into a smaller bowl; add vinegar and season to taste with salt and pepper. (Any remaining juices will keep refrigerated 3 to 4 days for an addition to sauce or to another vinaigrette.) Gently toss tomatoes with cucumbers, onion, vinaigrette and croutons and serve.

Braised Chicken with Mushrooms and White Wine

Preheat oven to 350°F.

2 whole chickens, cut into 8 pieces each
Salt and pepper to taste
3 tablespoons grapeseed oil
2 tablespoons butter
2 pounds assorted mushrooms, quartered
1 yellow onion, julienne
1 cup white wine
3 to 4 cups chicken stock
Truffle salt
2 sprigs rosemary

Season the chicken pieces with salt and pepper. Heat half of the oil in a large sauté pan and sear chicken pieces until skin side is golden brown, about 2 minutes.

Remove from pan and place in a roasting pan. Repeat until all the chicken is seared, adding more oil as needed.

When the last batch is seared, add butter to the pan and sauté mushrooms over high heat until they begin to caramelize (don't overcrowd pan). Add the onions and continue to cook about 1 minute longer. Add wine, cook 1 minute more and then pour the mushrooms and onions over chicken in roasting pan.

Place the roasting pan on the stovetop, over medium-high heat and add enough chicken stock to barely cover. Season with truffle salt (sparingly) and salt and pepper. Add rosemary sprigs.

Bring to a gentle boil. Cover with foil and finish in oven, about 25 to 45 minutes longer.

When the chicken has reached an internal temperature of 160°F, remove from pan and hold on a large serving platter.

Return the pan to the stovetop over medium

high heat and reduce braising liquid by a third. If necessary, slurry with cornstarch to thicken. Check seasoning, adding more truffle salt if desired. Spoon mushrooms and some jus over chicken, serving the remaining jus on the side.

Sautéed Chard with Bacon

4 to 6 ounces bacon, diced
1 tablespoon butter
3 bunches chard, cut into pieces
Salt and pepper to taste

Slowly render bacon in a medium sauté pan until almost cooked through.
Remove from pan, drain, and then return bacon fat to the pan with butter. Sauté chard over high heat until wilted, add bacon back, and season to taste with salt and pepper.

Sautéed Green Beans with Garlic and Almonds

3 cloves garlic, minced
3 tablespoons butter
2 tablespoons olive oil
2 pounds green beans
¼ cup almonds, chopped

In a large sauté pan, cook garlic in 2 tablespoons butter and olive oil, until fragrant.
Add green beans and sauté until just tender; season to taste with salt and pepper.
Remove from pan and add remaining butter.
Cook until beginning to brown and add almonds, sautéing until golden brown and aromatic. Top green beans with nuts and serve.

august 10

Crème Brûlée with Almond Shortbread

Preheat oven to 325°F.

4½ cups heavy cream
1½ cups milk
1 vanilla bean, halved and scraped
Pinch salt
18 large egg yolks
1 cup plus ¼ cup sugar
Nine 6 to 8-ounce ramekins, placed in a
   large baking pan
Small kitchen torch (uses propane cylinder)

Heat the cream, milk, vanilla bean and salt in a saucepan over medium heat until bubbles begin to appear around the edges.

Remove from heat and let sit covered 20 minutes.

In a large bowl, whisk the egg yolks and sugar together until smooth. Slowly stir the cream mixture into the eggs, a little at a time, whisking constantly until combined.

Strain though a fine strainer and then pour into prepared ramekins about 5/6 full. If small bubbles appear, lightly torch the tops to eliminate.

Carefully place the pan into the oven and pour enough HOT water into the pan to come halfway up the sides of the ramekins.

Cover with foil and bake 30 to 35 minutes, or until firm, with a slightly jiggly center.

Remove from pan and let cool on a baking rack before refrigerating.

Refrigerate for at least 4 hours before serving. To serve, sprinkle sugar over tops of custards and using the torch, caramelize the tops to create a hard shell. Top with a few berries and garnish with almond shortbread.

Almond Shortbread

Preheat oven to 350°F.

14 ounces butter
5 ounces sugar
2 ounces brown sugar
1 teaspoon salt
2 teaspoons vanilla extract
1 pound bread flour
12 ounces ground almonds, or other nuts
Powdered sugar, for dusting

Cream the butter, sugars, salt and vanilla together until pale and fluffy. Set aside.

In a separate bowl, combine flour and nuts. Add slowly to butter mixture and combine.

Use ice cream scoop to scoop dough onto a sheet tray and bake for 20 to 23 minutes, until bottoms are golden brown. When cool, dust with powdered sugar.

pork & peas

Edamame with Sea Salt

Mixed Greens with Fresh Figs and Walnuts
and Thyme Honey Vinaigrette

Slow Roasted Pork Roast with Peppers

Fresh Pink-Eyed Peas with
Italian Sausage and Tomatoes

Sweet Corn Pie with Raspberries and Blackberries

Serves eight

Laura and I circle through the Auburn farmers market at least once to see what's new on the tables before we decide on a menu. We both got excited to see fresh, pink-eyed peas on the Muck Farm table, and black-eyed peas at the Cha Family Farm. The pink-eyed peas are a perfect match with Italian pork sausage from Coffee Pot Ranch.

In our excitement, we bought too many fresh peas. It took hours and hours to husk them, and many bags of peas went into the freezer. But it turned out to be a stroke of good luck. Peas freeze very well, and they were especially good a few weeks later when cooked and mixed with fresh corn for a picnic.

We were also excited to see mid-August berries well represented at the market, and we decided to try a corn pie recipe using our own local ingredients. The berries are a nice contrast to the sweet corn.

To me, August berries have a wider range of flavors than berries picked earlier in the season. It's the ideal time for preserving, and if we haven't already filled our freezer for winter berry pies, now is the time to do it.

august 17

Edamame with Sea Salt

1 pound fresh edamame
1 teaspoon sea salt

Blanch edamame in a large pot of boiling, salted water for about 20 seconds.
Immediately transfer to a bowl of ice water to cool. Drain well and season with sea salt.

Mixed Greens with Fresh Figs and Walnuts and Thyme Honey Vinaigrette

Preheat oven to 350°F.

1½ cups walnuts
1 teaspoon olive oil
Salt to taste
8 cups mixed greens
12 to 14 figs, quartered
¼ pound Roncal cheese (or other sheep's milk cheese)

Thyme Honey Vinaigrette

3 tablespoons fresh thyme, minced
2 tablespoons yellow onion, minced
3 tablespoons white balsamic vinegar
2 teaspoons honey
4 tablespoons extra virgin olive oil

Toss walnuts with olive oil and salt and toast in the oven until golden brown, about 12 to 14 minutes. Toss salad ingredients together. Whisk vinaigrette ingredients and toss with salad just before serving.

Slow Roasted Pork Roast with Peppers

Preheat oven to 250°F.

4 pounds pork shoulder roast

2 tablespoons olive oil

3 tablespoons garlic, minced

2 tablespoons rosemary, chopped

6 bell peppers, julienne

2 red or yellow onions, julienne

2 tablespoons grapeseed oil

Salt and pepper to taste

Season the pork with olive oil, garlic, rosemary, salt and pepper. Roast at 250°F 5 to 6 hours (internal temperature should be 160°F). Remove from oven and let rest at least 30 minutes.

In a large sauté pan, caramelize peppers and onions in grapeseed oil. Season to taste with salt and pepper.

Slice pork about ½-inch thick. Arrange on a platter over the peppers and onions.

august 17

Fresh Pink-Eyed Peas with Italian Sausage and Tomatoes

1 pound Italian sausage

1 large onion, diced

2 tablespoons garlic, minced

2 teaspoons rosemary

1 quart chicken stock

Salt and pepper to taste

3 pounds shucked fresh pink-eyed peas

3 cups tomatoes, diced

In a large pot, brown sausage, then add onions, garlic, rosemary and stock. Add peas. The stock should just cover the peas and sausage. Season to taste with salt and pepper.

Bring to a boil and then turn down to simmer, about 25 to 30 minutes. Check every 15 minutes to make sure there is enough liquid.

Drain any excess liquid (which can be reduced and added back in if desired), check seasoning and gently stir in tomatoes.

If you substitute dried beans, like black-eyed peas for the fresh pink-eyed peas, remember you'll have to use more water.

Sweet Corn Pie with Raspberries and Blackberries

Preheat oven to 275°F.

Meringue Crust

5 large egg whites

⅓ teaspoon cream of tartar

1 cup sugar

Beat egg whites until stiff. Add cream of tartar. Continue to beat, gradually adding sugar. Beat until stiff and glossy.

Spread in well-buttered 9-inch Pyrex pie pan. Bake 20 minutes. Raise oven temperature to 300°F and bake another 40 minutes. Cool on a wire rack for at least 1 hour.

Sweet Corn filling

3 ears fresh white corn

2½ cups half and half

½ cup plus 2 tablespoons sugar

1 teaspoon vanilla extract

Pinch of salt

5 egg yolks

3 tablespoons cornstarch

4 tablespoons unsalted butter, cut into small pieces

1 cup heavy whipping cream

1 teaspoon sugar

½ pint blackberries

¾ pint raspberries

Cut the kernels off the ears of corn and break cobs in half. Set aside 2 tablespoons fresh corn for the top of the pie.

Place remaining kernels and cobs in a medium saucepan and add half and half. Heat over medium-low until just boiling, then remove from heat and let steep for 30 minutes.

Remove and discard the cobs; puree corn and half and half in a blender or food processor. Strain through a fine meshed sieve. Discard corn in sieve.

Pour the strained corn and half and half cream back into the pot, add ½ cup sugar, vanilla and salt, and slowly heat until just beginning to boil. Meanwhile, in a mixing bowl whisk the 5 egg yolks with the remaining 2 tablespoons sugar and the cornstarch.

Remove the corn cream from the stovetop. Temper the yolks by slowing adding ¼ cup of the corn cream to the yolks while whisking constantly. Do this two more times, then pour the yolk mixture back into the pot, whisking constantly.

Over medium heat, whisk the mixture continuously until the custard reaches pudding consistency. Remove from heat and whisk in the butter piece by piece.

Pour into a bowl and cover the surface with plastic wrap to keep skin from forming. Cool slightly over cold water and then refrigerate for at least 2 hours or up to 12 hours.

Once the corn mixture has cooled, continue with the rest of the recipe: Whip cream to soft peaks. Blend sugar into cream. Gently fold half the whipped cream into the corn custard.

Starting in the center of the meringue crust, place blackberries in a circle. Top with custard mixture. Place raspberries on top of the custard in circles around the edge, then spread remaining whipped cream over the center of the pie.

Garnish with 2 tablespoons fresh corn kernels. Refrigerate 24 hours to allow custard top to firm up.

good stuffed peppers

Tomato and Corn Salad with Pea Shoots

Lamb Stuffed Peppers

Organic Brown Rice

Sautéed Summer Squash

Roasted Figs, Peaches and Raspberries
with Crème Fraîche

Serves eight

Frankly I've never been a fan of stuffed peppers. I'd eat them to be polite, but I didn't like them enough to prepare them. That changed when Laura suggested using ground lamb to stuff jumbo green bell peppers. Her stuffed peppers have forever changed my idea of how stuffed peppers should taste. In the future, stuffed peppers will definitely be served a couple times during the summer for a casual meal, and the peppers will be accompanied with a sweet corn and tomato salad. When available, the corn will come from a newcomer to the Auburn market, Four Frog Farm from Penn Valley.

Four Frog Farm, owned by Logan Egan and Andrew Meyers, is an organic farm, and sells some of the sweetest carrots, beets, and leeks in the market. Best of all, Four Frog grows sweet corn. It's exceptional sweet corn. Another newcomer to the Auburn farmers market is J. D. and Jenny Gardemeyer of Colfax Hill Family Farm. At 2,500 feet, Colfax Farm provides lettuce, radishes, spinach and peas much later in the season than lower elevation farms. The farm extends the season for spring greens another four to six weeks. It's encouraging to see younger people farming, and selling their delicious produce at the farmers markets.

august 24

Tomato and Corn Salad with Pea Shoots

6 to 8 heirloom tomatoes, sliced ¼-inch thick

4 ears corn

Salt and pepper to taste

2 tablespoons olive oil

2 teaspoons white balsamic vinegar

12 cups pea shoots

Shuck the corn and cut the kernels away from the cob. Set aside.

Arrange tomato slices on a large platter and then sprinkle corn overtop. Season lightly with salt and pepper.

In a small bowl, combine oil and vinegar and drizzle over. In the same bowl, gently toss pea shoots and place in the center of the salad.

Lamb Stuffed Peppers

Preheat oven to 350°F.

8 large bell peppers

2 tablespoons olive oil

Salt and pepper to taste

3 pounds ground lamb

1 tablespoon olive oil

2 tablespoons lamb seasoning (we used Penzeys
   Lamb Seasoning)

¾ cup yellow onion, minced

2 tablespoons garlic, minced

2 eggplants, peeled and small diced

½ cup basil, chopped

¼ pound Feta, crumbled

Toss peppers with oil, salt and pepper and roast
20 to 30 minutes. After removing from oven,
cover with plastic to steam 5 to 10 minutes
longer.

Cool slightly and peel the skin away, careful not
to puncture the pepper.

Remove the tops of the peppers. Remove seeds,
being careful not to tear peppers. Place peppers,
cut side up, on a sheet tray and set aside.

In a large sauté pan, brown the ground lamb in
olive oil. Add lamb seasoning, salt and pepper to
taste. When done, place in a medium bowl and
set aside.

In the same pan, sauté onions, garlic and
eggplant. Add more salt and pepper if desired.
Add ¼ cup basil. Mix 2/3 of the eggplant with the
lamb, and stuff peppers with this mixture. Top
with feta.

Reheat peppers in oven at 350°F.

Reheat remaining 1/3 eggplant and onion
mixture on stovetop.

Spread hot eggplant on platter. Arrange peppers
on top. Garnish with chopped basil.

Can't find Penzeys Lamb Seasoning?
Try making one of your own tailored to
your taste exactly. A good lamb seasoning
should include Greek oregano, rosemary,
cumin, garlic, celery seed, ginger, paprika,
pepper and onion.

august 24

Organic Brown Rice

3 cups brown rice
4½ cups water or stock
1 tablespoon salt

Rinse rice and drain well.
In a large pot, combine rice, water and salt. Bring to a boil, turn down to a low simmer, cover and cook 45 to 50 minutes, depending on the type of rice. You can also use a rice cooker.

Sautéed Summer Squash

3 tablespoons olive oil
3 tablespoons garlic
2 to 3 pounds assorted summer squash,
    large diced
2 teaspoons thyme
Salt and pepper to taste

In a large sauté pan, heat oil, and cook garlic until fragrant.
Add squash and thyme, and season to taste with salt and pepper. Be careful not to overfill pan; cook in batches if necessary.

There seems to be a continuous debate about the merits of brown rice versus white rice.

In a nutshell, brown rice is more nutritious, has fewer calories, has more fiber, is processed less, and is better for diabetics than white rice. Less processing means brown rice is more environmentally friendly than white rice, which must be further milled and polished. Buy organic brown rice, and you've really got a winner.

On the down side, brown rice takes longer to cook than white rice, and some people claim it is gummy.

Roasted Figs, Peaches and Raspberies with Crème Fraîche

Preheat broiler.

3 large peaches, sliced

20 small figs, sliced in half

1 pint raspberries

2/3 cup crème fraîche

1/3 cup brown sugar, firmly packed

1 tablespoon butter

Butter a 9-inch Pyrex pie pan. Layer peaches on bottom of pan. Layer sliced figs over peaches. Top with raspberries.
Stir crème fraîche and drizzle over fruit; sprinkle brown sugar on top of crème fraîche.
Turn oven to broil. Broil fruit 4 minutes or until bubbly and browned. Serve immediately.

This is the quickest, easiest dessert to make. It takes just a few minutes to prepare and it's beautiful to serve. You can use just about any combination of fruit you like. What's in season will guide you.

fresh fish and long beans

Figs with Goat Cheese and Honey

Sliced Tomatoes

Pan Seared Corvina with Romesco Sauce

Summer Succotash

Chinese Long Beans with Onions

Apple Crumble

Serves eight

Several years ago we noticed a strange-looking, very long green bean at the Auburn market. Mary Hada of Beauty Ranch explained it was a Chinese bean that tasted much like a western-style green bean, but didn't take as long to cook. The beans are 20 inches long, so of course I asked her how to prepare them. She suggested we cut them into shorter sections and sauté them in olive oil. I've discovered the beans are especially delicious when flavored with garlic or mixed with carrots.

Lucky for Auburn shoppers, several regional growers offer a variety of Asian vegetables throughout the year. Vie Family Farm owners, Kua and Lu Vue, drive from Elk Grove and offer white sweet potatoes, gai choy, yu choy, lemon grass, tatsoi, daikon and broccoli rabe.

Thar's Farm grows bok choy and broccolini. Donny Moua is from Sacramento and has heaping mounds of gai choy, okra, snow peas, joi choy, jicama, moqua, yo choy, and qos nqeeb.

The Cha Family brings thai basil, sugar peas, snap peas and India peas. Cha Xiong's stall is covered with a carpet of flowers, and Cha custom arranges them if a special blossom or color suits your taste. Cha has a good eye for the unusual, and many times several of his blossoms grace our fireplace mantel.

Figs with Goat Cheese and Honey

8 figs, halved
1 ounce goat cheese, crumbled
2 teaspoons honey

Lay figs, cut side up, on a sheet tray.
Place a small amount of cheese in the center of each one and broil about 5 minutes. Drizzle with honey and serve.

Sliced Tomatoes

8 to 10 assorted tomatoes
1 tablespoon olive oil
Salt and pepper to taste

Simply layer the tomatoes on a large platter and drizzle with olive oil, salt and pepper...a plate of summer.

Pan Seared Corvina with Romesco Sauce

2 tablespoons whole almonds

1 slice French–type bread
  (about 4 x 3 x ¼ inches)

1 clove garlic

3 to 4 roasted red bell peppers

2 tablespoons olive oil

1 tablespoon sherry vinegar

¼ teaspoon cayenne pepper

2 tablespoons grapeseed oil

3 to 4 pounds corvina

Romesco Sauce

Toast almonds in the oven until golden, about 5 minutes. Transfer to a food processor.
Toast the bread the same way and add to the processor with the garlic.
Process until finely chopped.
Add red pepper, oil, vinegar and cayenne.
Continue to process until the mixture is the consistency of mayonnaise. Set aside.

Pan Seared Corvina

In a large sauté pan, heat the grapeseed oil and sear the corvina on both sides, about 1 minute per side, depending on the thickness.
Immediately serve on a platter, topped with Romesco sauce.

Summer Succotash

2 tablespoons olive oil
1 cup yellow onion, diced
1 tablespoon garlic, minced
3 pounds shucked, fresh lima beans
2 cups chicken stock
Salt and pepper to taste
3 ears corn
2 cups tomatoes, diced
¼ cup basil, chopped
1 teaspoon chile flakes

Shuck corn and cut kernels away from the cob. Set aside.
In a large pot, heat olive oil and lightly sauté onion and garlic. Add limas and stock and season lightly with salt and pepper.
Bring to a boil and turn down to a low simmer. Continue cooking, about 20 to 30 minutes.
When the beans are tender, drain off excess liquid, check seasoning, and add the corn, tomatoes, basil and chile flakes. Stir to combine and serve.

Chinese Long Beans with Onions

2 bunches Chinese long beans, cut into
   bite-sized pieces
2 tablespoons olive oil
2 tablespoons butter
Salt and pepper to taste
2 shallots, thinly sliced

In a large pan, sauté the beans in 1 tablespoon olive oil and 1 tablespoon butter. Season to taste with salt and pepper. Set aside.
In the same pan, add remaining oil and butter and sauté shallots until golden. Pour over beans and serve.

Apple Crumble

Preheat oven to 375°F.

1 cup all purpose flour

1½ cups brown sugar

1 cup chilled butter, cut into ½-inch pieces

2½ cups old-fashioned oats

4 pounds apples, peeled, halved, cored and
  sliced ¼ inch thick

3 tablespoons lemon juice

1 tablespoon cinnamon

Vanilla ice cream

In a large bowl, combine flour and 1 cup brown sugar. With a pastry cutter or a fork, cut butter into flour and sugar mixture. Add oats and combine until mixture comes together in clumps. Set aside.

Butter the bottom and sides of a 9x13-inch baking dish.

Mix apples, lemon juice, cinnamon and remaining ½ cup sugar and arrange in baking dish.

Top with flour, sugar and oats mixture. Bake until apples are tender and top begins to brown, about 40 to 50 minutes.

Let cool slightly and serve with vanilla ice cream.

eating out(side)—
better than take-out

Sharlyn Melon Soup

Asian Pear Salad with Walnuts and Champagne Vinaigrette

Grilled Skirt Steak with Tomato Relish

Brown Rice with Tomatoes

Grilled Summer Vegetables

Fig Tart with Fruit Syrup Reduction

Serves eight

Several years ago, when I managed the Foothill Farmers' Market organization, J. R. Smith called to ask how his Blossom Hill Farm could participate in the market. J. R. worked with the telephone company, but he was spending a good deal of time raising crops.

I explained Blossom Hill Farm would need certification by the Placer County Agriculture Commissioner, and that many of our markets were already well represented with tomatoes, cucumbers and squash, and there was not room for more of the same. Quickly, and with pride in his voice, J. R. said, "I don't want to sell tomatoes, I want to sell melons."

Immediately, my attitude changed. We wanted melons at the market, especially organic melons. Turns out J. R.'s melons are some of the best I've ever eaten.

Today, J. R. and Claudia Smith's Blossom Hill Farm is the star grower of organic melons. Their varieties include red, orange, yellow and Mickey Lee watermelons; orange flesh Hales cantaloupe; Sharlyn, and Minnesota Midget melons, as well as specialty white flesh Sugar Nut, Canary, and St. Nick melons. Blossom Hill melons are extraordinary, and we serve them at our table with pleasure.

Sharlyn Melon Soup

1 Sharlyn melon, seeds and rind removed
Honey
Salt

Cut melon into 1-inch pieces. Purée in a blender until smooth. Season to taste with honey and salt.

Asian Pear Salad with Walnuts and Champagne Vinaigrette

1½ pounds mixed greens
5 to 6 Asian pears, finely sliced
¼ pound blue cheese, crumbled
½ cup walnuts, toasted

Champagne Vinaigrette

¼ cup Champagne vinegar
½ cup olive oil
1 lemon, juiced
1 teaspoon honey
Salt and pepper

Combine salad ingredients. Combine vinaigrette ingredients and season to taste with salt and pepper. Toss with salad.

Grilled Skirt Steak with Tomato Relish

Preheat grill.

1 tablespoon thyme, chopped

1 tablespoon rosemary, chopped

3 cloves garlic, minced

1 teaspoon chile flakes

1 teaspoon black pepper

2 teaspoons salt

⅓ cup olive oil

4 pounds skirt steak (you can
   substitute flank steak)

Combine herbs, garlic and oil and coat skirt steak. Let marinate at least 20 minutes before grilling.

On a hot grill, sear steak on both sides, about 2 minutes per side, depending on thickness.

Let the meat rest 10 minutes. Thinly slice meat and arrange on a platter with tomato relish.

Tomato Relish

3 cups tomatoes, diced

¼ cup basil, chopped

1 tablespoon red wine vinegar

2 teaspoons olive oil

Salt and pepper

Combine all ingredients and season to taste with salt and pepper.

Garnish steak and serve.

Brown Rice with Tomatoes

3 cups brown rice

6 cups water or stock

1 tablespoon salt

2 cups tomatoes, seeds removed, diced

Rinse rice and drain well.

In a large pot, combine rice, water and salt.

Bring to a boil, turn down to a low simmer, cover and cook 45 to 50 minutes, depending on the type of rice. You can use a rice cooker, if desired. After the rice is cooked, fluff with a fork and fold in tomatoes.

I feel a recipe is only a theme, which an intelligent cook can play each time with a variation.
Madam Benoit

205

september 7

Grilled Summer Vegetables

Preheat grill.

5 summer squash, sliced ¼ inch thick, lengthwise
2 eggplant, sliced ¼ inch thick
4 bell peppers, seeded and halved
4 red onions, halved
⅓ cup olive oil
Salt and pepper
¼ cup basil, chopped
3 tablespoons balsamic vinegar

Gently toss all the sliced vegetables with olive oil and season with salt and pepper. Grill until tender. To serve, cut the vegetables into smaller pieces if desired and sprinkle with basil and balsamic vinegar.

Fig Tart with Fruit Syrup Reduction

Fruit Syrup Reduction

3 cups fresh fruit (raspberries, blackberries, apricots, plums or peaches)

Macerate the fruit in a blender or food processor. Place in a 2-quart sauce pan and bring to a boil; reduce heat and simmer 5 minutes.
Pour sauce into a fine sieve placed over a bowl. Carefully stir sauce allowing the juices to separate from the pulp. Discard pulp.
Add a small amount of honey or agave syrup to juice if the juice is too sour or tart.
Return juices to sauce pan and simmer slowly until reduced to one third the original amount. The sauce will thicken slightly and be a syrup consistency. Save in a covered jar in refrigerator up to a month.

Fig Tart

Preheat oven to 400°F.

1 cup all purpose flour, plus 2 teaspoons
¼ cup sugar plus ⅓ cup
½ teaspoon salt, plus a pinch
4 tablespoons unsalted butter, softened
2 eggs
1½ tablespoons water
2 teaspoons powdered sugar
8 ounces mascarpone cheese
2 lemons, zested
Pinch of salt
⅓ cup heavy cream
16 fresh figs, stems removed and sliced lengthwise
1 pint fresh raspberries
⅓ cup fruit syrup reduction

Combine 1 cup flour, ¼ cup sugar and ½ teaspoon salt in a mixing bowl. Use a pie dough cutter or a fork to mix butter into flour mixture. Set aside.

In a small bowl, beat 1 egg with water. Using a fork, blend egg mixture into flour mixture until large pieces of dough form and the flour is totally incorporated. (You may have to add a couple teaspoons more water.)

On a lightly floured surface, shape dough into a 5-inch disk. Cover with plastic wrap and chill at least one hour.

Remove dough from refrigerator and roll out on a lightly floured surface to ⅛-inch thick, and 12 inches round.

Transfer dough to a 10-inch tart pan with a removable bottom. Press dough firmly in place and fold any overhang back toward the center. Press dough into sides of tart pan to shape the crust. Set aside.

In a bowl, stir together the powdered sugar and the remaining 2 teaspoons flour. Lightly dust the shell with the mixture. Chill 10 minutes.

In a bowl, combine the mascarpone, ⅓ cup sugar, lemon zest, and pinch of salt. Fold and stir the mixture with a rubber spatula until the sugar dissolves.

In a separate bowl, lightly beat the remaining egg with the cream. Fold the cream mixture into the mascarpone mixture and pour into the tart mold, spreading it to the edge.

Arrange the figs sliced side up in a circle along the edge of the tart with the stem ends facing the center. Make a slightly smaller circle of figs inside the larger one.

Place one large raspberry or two small raspberries on each fig.

Drizzle fruit syrup reduction over the figs.

Bake tart until the top is golden and puffed, about 30 to 35 minutes. Let sit 30 minutes before slicing.

sausage stuffed zucchini

Cucumber and Tomato Salad

Italian Pork Sausage Stuffed Zucchini

Late Summer Ratatouille

Sautéed Green Beans with Shallots

Asian Pear Galette with Pistachio Ice Cream

Serves eight

Everyone knows what a patch of zucchini looks like in September: there's zucchini everywhere. They seem to grow two inches overnight, and often get big as a club before you find them. When an enormous amount of zucchini fills growers' tables, it's time to use them in as many ways a possible.

A zucchini is the ideal stuffing container. The walls are firm enough to hold meat or other vegetables. Preparation is easy. Simply select the appropriate size, carefully spoon out some pulp, and you have a small oval-shaped bowl.

There's nothing better than ratatouille made the right way, with lots of zucchini, and I like it best after it's been in the refrigerator a day or two, and the various flavors blend together. A mound of ratatouille, a slice of fine Swiss or cheddar cheese, and a chunk of French bread is just right for lunch. Add a glass of Sauvignon Blanc and you have pure ambrosia.

September also signals the beginning of the nut harvest. Fortunately, in Placer County we have pistachio, almond, walnut, and pecan trees. Fiddyment Farm, a long-time West Placer pistachio grower, has a stall at the Auburn market. V & V Farms of Lodi sells almonds, and Salle Orchards of Wheatland, offers walnuts, flavored nuts and sun dried fruits. I'm especially fond of Salle's orange flavored walnuts, as well as their dried peaches and nectarines. I keep nuts and dried fruit in my freezer to have available for baking throughout the year.

Cucumber and Tomato Salad

8 to 10 medium cucumbers, sliced ⅛-inch thick

1 red onion, diced

¼ cup sea salt

¼ cup rice vinegar

4 tomatoes, diced

2 tablespoons olive oil

Salt and pepper to taste

1 bag pea shoots

In a medium-sized, flat-bottomed bowl, place a single layer of the cucumbers, then sprinkle with red onion and salt. Repeat until all the ingredients are layered. Cover and refrigerate for 2 to 8 hours.

Drain the water from the cucumbers and onions by pressing firmly; do not rinse.

Drizzle vinegar over and toss to combine. Set aside.

Toss the tomatoes in a small bowl with oil, and a little salt and pepper.

Place the cucumbers on a plate and garnish with tomatoes. Dress the pea shoots with any remaining oil in the bowl and use to top the salad.

september 14

Italian Pork Sausage Stuffed Zucchini

Preheat oven to 350°F.

4 large (fat) zucchini
1 tablespoon olive oil
Salt and pepper
3 pounds Italian sausage
1 onion, diced
3 cloves garlic, minced
2 teaspoons thyme, chopped
2 teaspoons chile flakes
¾ cup parmesan cheese, grated
Salt and pepper

Cut the zucchini in half, lengthwise, and hollow out the middle, being careful not to cut too close to the skin. (Reserve the insides for ratatouille.) Coat with olive oil, salt and pepper. Roast, cut side down, about 10 minutes. Let cool.

In a large sauté pan, brown sausage. When cooked through, remove from pan and place in a strainer over a bowl to drain any excess juices (reserve some for ratatouille).

Using the same pan, sauté onion, garlic and herbs in olive oil; season to taste with salt and pepper. Combine the onions with sausage and check seasoning.

When slightly cooled, stuff squash with sausage mixture and place on a sheet tray. Top with parmesan. Turn oven to broil, and broil until cheese begins to bubble. Serve on a bed of ratatouille.

Late Summer Ratatouille

2 eggplants, small diced

¼ cup grapeseed oil

Salt and pepper to taste

1 onion, small diced

5 bell peppers, small diced

3 summer squash (plus remaining from
   hollowing), small diced

6 large tomatoes, grated

½ cup basil, chopped

2 tablespoons balsamic vinegar

¼ cup olive oil

Salt and pepper to taste

In a large pan, sauté eggplant in 1 tablespoon grapeseed oil until slightly caramelized and tender. Season lightly with salt and pepper. Transfer eggplant from the pan to a sheet tray to let cool.

Repeat this process with the onion, peppers and squash, cooking each one separately. Set aside. In a large pot, bring the grated tomato and about ½ cup of sausage drippings from above to a simmer and slowly reduce by about one-third. Add the vegetables and stir just to combine and reheat. Stir in basil, balsamic vinegar and olive oil. Season to taste with salt and pepper.

Sautéed Green Beans with Shallots

2 pounds green beans

2 tablespoons butter

2 tablespoons olive oil

¼ cup shallots, sliced thinly

Salt and pepper

In a large pan, sauté green beans in 1 tablespoon butter and 1 tablespoon oil until tender. Season to taste with salt and pepper. Remove from pan into a serving bowl.

In the same pan, heat the remaining oil and butter and sauté shallots until soft. Season to taste with salt and pepper and toss with green beans.

Asian Pear Galette with Pistachio Ice Cream

Thanks to Jen Linn for this recipe.

Preheat oven to 350°F.

Crust

6 ounces all purpose flour
1½ teaspoons sugar
4 ounces cold unsalted butter
Large pinch of salt
2 ounces ice cold water

Mix flour, sugar and butter in a mixer until the butter forms pea to almond-size pieces. Set aside.
Dissolve the salt in the ice water and add to the flour mixture until it starts to come together.
With your hands, form dough into a disk. Wrap disk in plastic wrap and refrigerate at least an hour.

Filling

5 Asian pears, peeled, cored, sliced
   into ¼-inch slices
¼ teaspoon almond extract
¼ teaspoon vanilla extract
½ teaspoon cinnamon
Pinch of salt
¼ cup sugar
1 tablespoon all purpose flour
1 egg
1 tablespoon water
Demerara sugar for sprinkling

Toss pears with almond extract, vanilla extract, cinnamon, salt, sugar and flour. Let stand while you roll out the crust.

To assemble the galette:
Roll the crust a little thinner than ¼ inch. Arrange the pears leaving a 2-inch border along the edge. Pour excess juices from the pears over the top. Fold the edges of the crust over the pears.

Mix the egg and 1 tablespoon water in a small bowl. Brush the egg wash over all edges of the galette and then sprinkle entire galette with Demerara sugar.

Bake 55 minutes, until golden brown.

Pistachio Ice Cream

8 ounces unsalted pistachios
2 cups whole milk
2 cups heavy cream
⅓ cup sugar plus ½ cup
8 large egg yolks
1 teaspoon vanilla extract
Pinch of salt

In a food processor pulse the pistachios until coarsely ground. Set aside.

In a large saucepan combine milk, cream, ⅓ cup sugar and pistachios; bring to a boil over medium heat, stirring occasionally.

Remove the saucepan from the heat and let mixture steep 1 hour. Strain the mixture, discard the pistachios, and return the cream mixture to the saucepan.

Whisk together egg yolks and ½ cup sugar. Set aside.

Bring the cream mixture to a soft boil over medium heat, stirring occasionally. Reduce heat to low. Slowly whisk in 1 cup of the cream to the egg yolk mixture.

Add the egg mixture to the cream and return to medium heat stirring constantly until the mixture coats the back of a wooden spoon and you can draw a line through it.

Remove from heat, stir in salt and vanilla and put through a strainer to get rid of any egg pieces.

Chill the mixture at least 3 hours and process in a crank ice cream maker.

the best roasted chicken

Melon Salad with Mint and Honey

Roasted Chicken with Tomatillos and Cippolini Onions

Roasted Fingerling Potatoes

Sautéed Romano Beans with Tomatoes and Parmesan

Port Poached Pears with Crème Fraîche and Lace Cookies

Serves eight

Teri Ueki of Teri Ueki Garden Flowers is famous for her freshly picked, perky flower arrangements. She pours through seed catalogues to find unique and unusual flowers to grow. Get to the market early if you want to buy Teri's flower arrangements; she always sells out.

Teri also grows fine vegetables. A few years ago, she introduced me to Romano beans, sometimes called Italian flat beans. Similar to the common snap bean, Romanos come in green, purple and yellow. Sweet and buttery, they're broader and flatter than common green beans. Best of all, they're easy to cook. Simply steam or sauté them for one or two minutes; be careful not to overcook.

This week's chicken recipe blends Italian and Latin American favorites: cippolini onions and tomatillos. Yellow, flat and sweet, cippolini onions are favorites in Italian cooking. They're firm enough to hold their shape through roasting, and are visually pleasing on a platter. We find cippolinis at the Twin Brooks Farm stall. We combined the onions with tomatillos for a Latin twist.

Many Latin American sauce recipes include tomatillos for their green color and tart flavor. Tomatillos have a paper-like husk, and are easy to prepare. Four Frog Farm grows both purple and green tomatillos.

Before we cook with them, we use yellow, purple and green tomatillos as a centerpiece on the dinner table. After dinner, we remove the husk, and pop them whole in the freezer to use at a later time.

Melon Salad with Mint and Honey

2 summer melons, cut into 1-inch pieces
2 tablespoons mint leaves, thinly sliced
2 tablespoons honey

Toss all ingredients together and serve.

Roasted Chicken with Tomatillos and Cippolini Onions

Preheat oven to 375°F.

1 pound tomatillos, peeled
4 tablespoons olive oil
Salt and pepper
12 to 14 cippolini onions, peeled
2 whole chickens, about 4 pounds each
4 cloves garlic
8 sprigs of fresh parsley

Toss tomatillos and onions with 2 tablespoons olive oil and season lightly with salt and pepper. Set aside.

Season the chickens with 2 tablespoons oil, salt and pepper. Place 2 cloves of garlic and 2 sprigs of parsley inside each cavity. Roast 1 to 1½ hours. Halfway through roasting, arrange the tomatillos and onions around the chickens and continue to roast.

Remove chickens from oven and let rest 20 minutes.

Meanwhile, place tomatillos and juices from the chicken in a food processor and purée until smooth. Season to taste with salt and pepper.

To serve, carve the chicken and place slices on a large platter with onions. Garnish with tomatillo sauce and remaining sprigs of fresh parsley.

september 21

Roasted Fingerling Potatoes

Preheat oven to 375°F.

3 to 4 pounds fingerling potatoes
2 tablespoons olive oil
2 cloves garlic, minced
Salt and pepper to taste
2 tablespoons butter, melted

Toss the potatoes with oil, garlic, salt and
pepper.
Place on a sheet tray and roast 25 to 35 minutes,
until fork tender.
Toss with melted butter before serving.

Sautéed Romano Beans with Tomatoes and Parmesan

2 cloves garlic, minced
2 tablespoons butter
1 tablespoon olive oil
3 pounds Romano beans, cleaned
1 cup tomatoes, small diced
¼ cup parmesan cheese, grated
Salt and pepper

In a large sauté pan, heat garlic in butter and oil
and sauté Romano beans until tender, about 2
minutes.
Toss with tomatoes and cheese, season to taste
with salt and pepper.

Port Poached Pears with Crème Fraîche and Lace Cookies

Port Poached Pears with Crème Fraîche

3 cups Port

1 cinnamon stick

3 cloves

8 Bartlett pears, peeled

1 cup water

¼ cup sugar

¼ cup crème fraîche

In a medium pot, combine Port, cinnamon stick, cloves and pears.

Heat to a simmer and turn down to low to poach, about 20 minutes, depending on the size of the pears. When soft, remove from pot and refrigerate to cool. (Pears can be refrigerated in poaching liquid up to two days.)

After pears are cooled, remove them from liquid. Set pears aside.

Bring liquid to a boil, and reduce by ¾ to sauce consistency.

Cut each pear in half, and remove stem and core.

To serve, place a half pear in small bowl, put a spoonful of crème fraîche in the center, then lay the other half of the pear on top. Pour some of the reduced poaching liquid over the pear, and garnish with a lace cookie.

Lace Cookies

Preheat oven to 375°F.

3 tablespoons butter

1 cup brown sugar

4 tablespoons all purpose flour

1 egg, beaten

1 cup ground almonds

½ teaspoon almond extract

1 teaspoon vanilla extract

Beat butter and sugar together.

Add flour, egg, almonds and extracts and beat to combine.

Place 1 teaspoon of dough on a buttered sheet tray about 2 inches apart. Bake 8 minutes, until edges are golden brown and cookies are crisp. Let cool on a rack.

okra: the tasty way

Chilled Cucumber Soup

Arugula Salad with Pesto Dressing

Lamb and Okra Stew

German Butterball Mashed Potatoes

Sautéed Chard with Bacon

Chocolate Chip Cookie Ice Cream Sandwiches

Serves eight

Laura and I found okra on Jim Muck's table. As we started putting handfuls of okra in our basket, a very nice lady joined us at the stall. She, too, was excited to find okra. Quickly, she explained her favorite way to prepare it: Wash the okra, dry it, slice in 1-inch long pieces, dip in a whisked egg and milk mixture, roll in fine saltine cracker crumbs, and fry in olive oil until crispy.

I tried it and it's yummy. It makes a quick appetizer, and it's good. We like to use okra with lamb in a stew. The secret is to soak the whole okra in a vinegar and water mixture for 30 minutes. Remove the okra, dry and slice it, and add to the stew for the last 15 minutes. The okra should cook just long enough to be al dente.

What a nice surprise to discover September 28 is Laura's birthday. My husband, Jerry Burns, always makes ice cream for a family member's birthday, and after nine months of cooking every Monday night at our house, Laura Kenny is definitely a member of our family. For the occasion, Jerry made his famous vanilla ice cream. Laura baked chocolate chip cookies, and made cookie ice cream sandwiches. This is a nifty way to celebrate a birthday.

Jerry and I plan to make the same dessert for a grandchild's birthday. The children in the neighborhood will love it. Really, what better treat is there than chocolate chip cookie ice cream sandwiches?

Chilled Cucumber Soup

5 Mediterranean or Japanese cucumbers
3 scallions
1 large clove garlic, diced
1 cup chicken broth
1 cup buttermilk
Small pinch cayenne pepper

Peel cucumbers with about half the skin remaining. Dice white bottoms and ½ of the tops of the scallions. Sliver remaining green tops and set aside for garnish.
Place cucumbers, scallions, garlic, chicken broth, buttermilk and cayenne in blender. Add more broth if necessary. Chill at least 2 hours before serving.
Serve in small bowls or 6-ounce cups. Garnish with slivered scallions.

Arugula Salad with Pesto Dressing

½ pound arugula, torn into pieces
4 large tomatoes, sliced ¼-inch thick
4 cucumbers, medium diced

Pesto Dressing
1 cup basil
1 clove garlic
1 tablespoon pine nuts, toasted
2 tablespoons parmesan
½ cup olive oil

Toss all salad ingredients together.
Process dressing ingredients in food processor.
Thin with additional olive oil if desired.
(To store for later use, place pesto in airtight container and cover with thin layer of olive oil.)
Add 2 tablespoons of pesto dressing to salad just before serving.

september 28

Lamb and Okra Stew

2½ pounds lamb stew meat, after bones
   and fat removed
3 pounds okra, sliced
2 cups white wine vinegar
2 cups water
¼ cup grapeseed oil
2 onions, diced
3 pounds tomatoes, diced
Salt and pepper

Make stock with bones and fat. Set aside.
Place okra in a bowl and cover with white wine
vinegar and water. Set aside.

In a large pot, brown the lamb in the oil. Cook in
batches if necessary.
Add the onion and sauté until caramelized.
Add tomatoes and about 3 cups of lamb stock.
Simmer until the lamb is tender, about 20 to 30
minutes.
Drain, and add the okra to the stew and continue
cooking 8 to 10 more minutes.
Season to taste with salt and pepper.

German Butterball Mashed Potatoes

4 pounds German butterball potatoes
Salt to taste
1 cup milk
¼ pound (1 stick) butter

Cook the potatoes in salted water until fork tender. Drain and let dry. Set aside.
Heat milk in a small saucepan until scalded.
Pass the potatoes through a food mill with butter and add warm milk to desired texture.
Season to taste with salt.

Sautéed Chard with Bacon

3 bunches chard, stems removed and cut into
    1-inch diagonal pieces; leaves torn into pieces
½ pound bacon, small diced
1 tablespoon olive oil
1 shallot, minced
Salt and pepper to taste

Bring a small pot of salted water to a boil and blanch the chard stems about 20 seconds.
Transfer immediately to a bowl of ice water to shock. Drain and set aside.
In a medium sauté pan, render bacon until crispy, remove from pan and reserve fat. Set aside.
In a large sauté pan, heat the oil with some of the reserved bacon fat. Add shallot and cook until translucent.
Add chard leaves and sauté until wilted.
Add bacon and the blanched stems, and toss to combine. Season lightly with salt and pepper.

It's such a joy to visit your home – the flowers, the art, the tinkling chimes, the laughs, the conversations, the food.
        Laura Read, Tahoe City

Chocolate Chip Cookie Ice Cream Sandwiches
(Recipe from Cook's Illustrated)

Chocolate Chip Cookies

Preheat oven to 375°F.

1¾ cup all purpose flour

½ teaspoon baking soda

14 tablespoons (1¾ sticks) unsalted butter

½ cup granulated sugar

¾ cup packed dark brown sugar

1 teaspoon salt

2 teaspoons vanilla extract

1 egg and 1 yolk

1¼ cups Ghirardelli 60% bittersweet
   chocolate chips

¾ cup chopped pecans or walnuts, toasted

Sift flour and baking soda together in medium bowl. Set aside.

Heat 10 tablespoons butter in 10-inch skillet over medium heat until melted, about 2 minutes. Continue cooking, swirling pan constantly until butter is dark golden brown and has nutty aroma, about 1 to 3 minutes.

Remove skillet from heat and transfer browned butter to large heatproof bowl. Stir remaining 4 tablespoons butter into hot butter until completely melted.

Add sugars, salt, and vanilla to browned butter and combine thoroughly.

Add eggs and beat until mixture is smooth with no sugar lumps remaining, about 30 seconds. Let mixture stand 3 minutes, then beat an additional 30 seconds.

Repeat process of resting and beating 2 more times, until mixture is thick, smooth, and shiny. Add flour mixture and stir until just combined, about 2 minutes.

Stir in chocolate chips and nuts, giving dough final stir to ensure no flour pockets remain. Scoop dough into 16 to 18 portions, about 3 tablespoons each, and place on a sheet tray 2 inches apart.

Bake cookies one tray at a time until cookies are golden brown and puffy, and edges have begun to set but centers are still soft, 10 to 14 minutes, rotating baking sheet halfway through baking. Transfer baking sheet to wire rack; cool cookies completely before assembling sandwiches.

Homemade Ice Cream

3 eggs

1⅓ cups sugar

2 tablespoons vanilla

2 cups heavy cream

1 quart half and half

Mix together and add to ice cream maker cylinder. Follow freezer instructions for making ice cream.

To assemble the sandwiches, place eight cookies upside down on a flat surface. Put ¼ cup ice cream on center of each cookie. Top with another cookie. Store in freezer. Remove from freezer 5 to 10 minutes before serving.

yes, cioppino

Herbed Goat Cheese with Honey on Crostini

Roasted Almonds with Sea Salt

Tatsoi and Spinach Salad with Strawberries
and Balsamic Vinaigrette

Cioppino – San Francisco Style

Chocolate Pots de Crème with Raspberries

Serves eight

Tatsoi? Here's another new Asian vegetable for your salads. Tatsoi, a spoon shaped, dark green leafy vegetable, tastes slightly pungent, like mild mustard greens. It's super rich in calcium and vitamins and stands up well to spinach.

California's Pacific Coast is about 100 miles from Auburn. Fishermen catch fish every day of the year between Eureka and San Francisco. Many times, fish caught on Friday afternoon are processed and available for the Saturday Auburn farmers market. Brand Little of Little Fish Company supplies fish to several Placer County farmers markets. We needed a lot of seafood for our cioppino this week.

Laura shared the following cioppino story. In earlier days when fishing boats came into San Francisco Harbor after a day of fishing, someone walked among the boats and asked fishermen to "chip in" some of the day's catch for a stew. Something of everything on the dock ended up in the basket. If one of the boats brought in mussels or clams, they went in the pot. The same goes for crab and any white fish. Add some tomatoes and dry white wine, and a delicious cioppino dinner is on its way.

San Francisco is famous, of course, for its sourdough bread. For almost a year, Roke Whitson baked bread every Monday morning for the Monday night dinner. This meal featured a heaping basket of breads, including a loaf of sourdough, just right for dipping in cioppino broth.

october 5

Herbed Goat Cheese with Honey on Crostini

Preheat oven to 325°F.

1 baguette, thinly sliced

1 tablespoon olive oil

Salt and pepper to taste

4 ounces goat cheese

1 teaspoon thyme, chopped

½ teaspoon rosemary, chopped

1 tablespoon honey

To make crostini, brush the sliced baguette pieces with olive oil and season lightly with salt and pepper. Toast 10 to 12 minutes, until golden brown. Set aside.
In a small bowl, combine goat cheese with herbs. Spread each crostini with goat cheese and drizzle with honey.

Roasted Almonds with Sea Salt

2 cups fresh almonds

½ cup olive oil

Sea salt

Bring a quart of water to boil in a 2-quart sauce pan. Add almonds and boil 1 minute.
Quickly place in strainer and run cold water over almonds.
Lay a kitchen towel flat and distribute almonds on towel to dry. Once almonds are dry, remove skins by squeezing almonds between thumb and index fingers. (Almond skin is easier to remove when almonds are totally dry.)
In a large cast iron skillet heat olive oil until hot. Carefully distribute almonds across bottom of skillet. After 1 to 2 minutes, stir continuously and turn almonds until nicely browned. Almonds get soft quickly if not totally browned.
Using a slotted flat spoon, place almonds on a double layer of paper towels. Sprinkle generously with sea salt. Serve warm.

Tatsoi and Spinach Salad with Strawberries and Balsamic Vinaigrette

1 pound tatsoi (or other spinach–type
   salad green)
½ pound spinach, torn into pieces
2 pints strawberries, cut in quarters
¼ pound Petit Basque cheese, shaved
½ cup pistachios, toasted

Balsamic Vinaigrette

¼ cup balsamic vinegar
½ cup olive
½ lemon, juiced
Salt and pepper

Toss all salad ingredients together. Whisk
vinaigrette ingredients together and dress salad
just before serving.

october 5

Cioppino - San Francisco Style

2 tablespoons grapeseed oil

5 cloves garlic

2 onions, diced

1 head fennel, diced

2 red bell peppers, diced

Pinch saffron (optional)

1 tablespoon dried oregano

1 teaspoon chile flakes

3 cups tomato, diced

2 cups white wine

1 bottle clam juice

6 cups chicken stock

Salt and pepper to taste

2 pounds snapper, or other white fish, diced

1 pound mussels, cleaned and de-bearded

1 pound clams, cleaned

2 pounds cooked crab

¼ cup basil, chopped

2 tablespoons tarragon, chopped

2 tablespoons parsley, chopped

In a large pot, heat oil and sauté garlic, onions and fennel.

Add red peppers and continue sautéing until slightly tender.

Add saffron, oregano and chile flakes, and continue to sauté until fragrant. Add tomatoes and wine, then clam juice and chicken stock. Season lightly with salt and pepper.

Bring to a low a boil and simmer 25 to 35 minutes. Add white fish and cover to cook, about 5 minutes.

Add mussels and clams and cover again to let them steam open.

Add crab and check seasoning and consistency (thin out with chicken stock if desired).

Remove any shellfish that has failed to open.

Stir in basil, tarragon and parsley, and serve.

Chocolate Pots de Crème with Raspberries and Chocolate Heaven Cookies

Pots de Crème

Preheat oven to 300°F.

6 ounces semi-sweet chocolate, chopped
2½ cups plus ⅔ cup whipping cream
⅔ cup milk
½ cup plus 1 tablespoon sugar
1 vanilla bean, split
6 egg yolks
1 teaspoon sugar

Place eight 4-ounce ramekins in a baking pan. Combine 2½ cups cream, milk, 5 tablespoons sugar and vanilla bean and slowly bring to a boil. Turn off and let steep one hour. Return to low heat to warm again.

Whisk together egg yolks and remaining sugar. Slowly stir the cream mixture into the eggs, a little at a time, whisking constantly until combined. Return the mixture to a low heat once more.

Place chopped chocolate in a metal bowl and strain the warm cream mixture into it. Let sit 5 minutes to melt chocolate and then stir to combine.

Fill ramekins 5/6 full, pour about 2 cups of HOT water in the pan, cover with foil and bake 35 to 45 minutes, until almost set. Cool slightly in water bath and then transfer to refrigerator to cool completely.

In a small bowl, whip ⅔ cup cream until thick. Add sugar and continue whipping until peaks form. Top ramekins with whipped cream and serve with Chocolate Heaven Cookies.

Chocolate Heaven Cookies

Preheat oven to 325°F.

½ cup all purpose flour
½ teaspoon baking powder
1 teaspoon salt
6 ounces bittersweet chocolate, chopped
¼ cup butter
2 eggs
1 teaspoon ground coffee
1 cup sugar
½ cup semi-sweet chocolate drops
½ cup pecans, chopped

Sift together flour, baking powder and salt. Set aside.

Place bittersweet chocolate and butter in a double boiler and heat to melt, stirring until the mixture is smooth. Set aside.

In a mixer, beat the eggs and coffee about 30 seconds. Gradually add the sugar and beat for 2 minutes more, almost to ribbon stage.

Add bittersweet chocolate mixture and beat to combine. Add flour mixture and beat just to combine. Stir in semi-sweet chocolate pieces and pecans. Scoop dough onto a lined cookie sheet, about 2 inches apart.

Bake 9 to 13 minutes, depending on the size of cookies, until the tops are cracked and shiny (they may not appear totally set).

Cool on the tray 5 minutes before transferring to a wire rack to cool completely.

oktoberfest style

Melon, Asian Pear and Pomegranate Salad

Caraway Crusted Pork Roast

German Potato Salad

Sautéed Cabbage and Baby Carrots

German Apple Cake

Serves eight

When the heater came on this morning, it reminded me to slip on a jacket for our early morning market visit. It's fall, and mid-October mornings are chilly. It's the time of year for dressing in layers because once the sun is overhead, you'll want to shed your sweater or jacket.

As days become shorter, my taste buds yearn for food that's more filling and more substantial. Several varieties of cabbages show up on a number of market tables.

There's an abundance of sweet carrots, and some of the tried-and-true apple favorites are being picked by Colfax farmers whose orchards are at higher elevations. It's no wonder our thoughts turn to roasted pork, warm potato salad, and German apple cake.

This is the first week for Asian pears, and the bounty and variety of Asian pears at Beauty Ranch gives us an opportunity to showcase them in menus from now until early January. An Asian pear can be eaten much like an apple – fresh, baked or poached. In fact, in most recipes you can substitute Asian pears for apples. For a different taste, combine Asian pears and apples in a pie. The result is a unique blending of flavors, more complex and richer than using apples or Asian pears alone. Asian pears are sweet and crunchy, and add a nice contrast to an ordinary everyday fruit salad.

Be sure to ask the growers which pears are best for poaching, for baking, or for eating raw.

Melon, Asian Pear and Pomegranate Salad

4 cups melon, large diced
4 Asian pears, cored and sliced
½ pomegranate, seeded
2 tablespoons honey
Salt to taste

Toss all ingredients together. Season with salt if desired.

Caraway Crusted Pork Roast

Preheat oven to 350°F.

5 to 6 pound pork loin roast
2 tablespoons olive oil
1 tablespoon garlic, minced
2 tablespoons caraway seeds
Salt and pepper to taste
2 yellow onions, large diced
2 tablespoons rosemary, chopped

Rub pork roast with oil, garlic, caraway, salt and pepper. Let marinate at least an hour.
Spread onions on roasting sheet tray, and place roast on top of onions. Roast 1 to 1½ hours, depending on size of roast. Let rest at least 20 minutes.
To serve, arrange sliced pork on platter on top of roasted onions. Garnish with rosemary.

What was truly special about our Oktoberfest meal was it reminded us of what a dining experience could be. Not only did we have the finest, fresh ingredients cooked to perfection, but for a little while, we stepped away from the stress of our daily lives and simply enjoyed a gratifying evening of great food, fine wine and good conversation.

Kim Haswell, Auburn

German Potato Salad

2½ pounds Yellow Finn potatoes, quartered
1 pound bacon, diced
1 onion, diced
2 tablespoons all purpose flour
¼ cup sugar
1¼ cups apple cider vinegar
2 teaspoons celery seed
2 tablespoons parsley, chopped
Salt and pepper to taste

In a large pot of salted water, cook potatoes until tender. Drain and set aside.
In a large sauté pan, render the bacon, about 10 minutes. Add onion and continue to cook until onion is tender, but not brown.
Stir in flour and sugar; cook 1 minute. Add vinegar and cook until slightly thickened.
Pour bacon and onion mixture over potatoes. Season to taste with celery seed, parsley, salt and pepper. Serve warm.

Sautéed Cabbage and Baby Carrots

2 tablespoons olive oil
2 tablespoons butter
1 red onion, julienne
2 tablespoons garlic, minced
1 head each Napa, Savoy and red cabbage, sliced
3 bunches baby carrots, halved

In a sauté pan, heat 1 tablespoon olive oil and 1 tablespoon butter. Add red onion, garlic, and cabbage. Sauté until slightly wilted. Remove from pan.
Add remaining oil and butter, and sauté carrots until tender.
To serve, place cabbage in a bowl and surround with carrots.

october 12

German Apple Cake

Preheat oven to 350°F.

2 cups all purpose flour
1 teaspoon baking soda
½ teaspoon salt
2 teaspoons cinnamon
3 large eggs, beaten
1½ cups sugar
½ cup vegetable oil
1 teaspoon vanilla
¾ cup walnuts, chopped
5 cups baking apples, peeled and cored,
    finely sliced

Sift together flour, baking soda, salt and
cinnamon in a mixing pan. Set aside.
Combine eggs, sugar, oil and vanilla into a
large mixing bowl. Beat on low speed until well
blended.
Add dry ingredients, mixing until well blended.
Fold in walnuts and apples.
Spoon into a well-buttered 13x9x2-inch baking
pan.
Bake 45 to 50 minutes. Insert a toothpick to be
sure apples are totally cooked.

Whipped Cream
1 cup whipping cream
1 teaspoon vanilla
1 teaspoon sugar

Whip cream to very soft peaks. Add sugar and
vanilla gradually. Continue to whip to desired
consistency. Place a dollop on each slice of cake.

I buy apples in quantity, 10 or more pounds at a time, and put them on my counter. There they sit for weeks, even a couple of months because "aged" apples taste better in pies and other recipes. Their juices have had a chance to meld, their flavor time to develop. They're less watery and less crisp than just picked. We've become accustomed to hard, juicy apples, and yes, for eating fresh, they can't be beat. But for cooking, apples need some time to sit and mature.

salmon and brussels sprouts

Arugula and Grape Salad with Grape Vinaigrette

Pan Seared Salmon with Celery Root Rémoulade

Rice with Garlic and Parsley

Shaved Brussels Sprouts with Bacon

Asian Pear and Apple Pie

Persimmon Tea

Serves eight

I t's wonderful having friends who fish, especially friends who come bearing gifts of fish.

Our neighbor, Cindy Wachob, visits her family in Alaska every year, and always brings back a big box of frozen, vacuum-packed salmon. This year Cindy shared enough salmon for our Monday night dinner. The secret to perfectly prepared fish is never overcooking it. Sear the salmon a minute or two on one side, quickly turn the filets, and cook a brief minute on the other side. As a complement to the salmon, a creamy, gently seasoned celery root remoulade is delicate enough not to overwhelm the flavors of good salmon.

Brussels sprouts, which resemble miniature cabbages, were grown in the 13th century in what is now Belgium. The sprouts belong to the same family as kohlrabi, kale, broccoli and cabbage. The edible sprouts grow like buds in a spiral array on the side of long thick stalks that grow to three feet long. Be very careful not to overcook Brussels sprouts. Overcooking results in a sulfurous odor, and the odor is exactly the reason people dislike Brussels sprouts. Laura's method is quick and easy: finely slice the sprouts, then briefly blanch and sauté them. You'll like them.

october 19

Arugula and Grape Salad with Grape Vinaigrette

¾ pound arugula
1 cup grapes, whole
¼ pound soft cow's milk cheese
½ cup pistachios

Grape Vinaigrette

3 cups grapes
2 tablespoons Champagne vinegar
1 teaspoon honey (optional)
¼ cup olive oil
Salt and pepper to taste

Toss salad ingredients together. Set aside.
In a blender, purée grapes for vinaigrette. Strain
through a mesh strainer and add vinegar, honey
and olive oil. Season to taste with salt and
pepper. Dress salad just before serving.

Pan Seared Salmon with Celery Root Rémoulade

Celery Root Rémoulade

3 tablespoons crème fraîche

2 tablespoons Dijon mustard

2 tablespoons parsley, chopped

2 to 3 pounds celery root, peeled and julienne

Salt and pepper to taste

In a small bowl, combine crème fraîche, mustard and parsley. Add mixture to celery root and season to taste with salt and pepper.

Pan Seared Salmon

3 pounds salmon

Salt and pepper to taste

2 tablespoons grapeseed oil

1 tablespoon parsley, chopped

Season fish with salt and pepper. Set aside.
In a large pan, heat oil and sear fish on one side, about 1 to 1½ minutes. Flip and continue to cook about 30 seconds longer, depending on thickness.
To serve, layer celery root on a platter, arrange fish on top.
Garnish with parsley and a little more rémoulade.

october 19

Rice with Garlic and Parsley

2 cups Calrose rice

3 cups water or stock

2 tablespoons butter

2 tablespoons garlic, minced

2 tablespoons parsley, chopped

Rinse rice and drain well.

In a large pot, combine rice, water and salt. Bring to a boil, turn down to a low simmer, cover and cook 25 to 45 minutes, depending on the type of rice. You can also use a rice cooker.

In a small sauté pan, heat butter and lightly sauté garlic. Add parsley and pour over hot rice. Toss to combine; season to taste with salt and pepper.

Thank you for the wonderful dinner at your home. The food, conversation, your home and the wine made for a magical night.
    Steve and Leslie Galyardt, Auburn

Shaved Brussels Sprouts with Bacon

3 pounds Brussels sprouts, sliced ⅛-inch thick

½ pound bacon, diced

1 teaspoon garlic, minced

1 red onion, sliced

1 tablespoon olive oil

1 tablespoon butter

(The easiest way to slice the Brussels sprouts is with a mandolin or a food processor.)

Bring a small pot of salted water to a boil and blanch the sliced Brussels sprouts about 20 seconds. Transfer immediately to a bowl of ice water to shock. Drain and set aside.

In a large sauté pan, render diced bacon until just done. Remove from pan and drain fat.

In the same pan, combine bacon fat and butter. Sauté garlic and onion.

Add Brussels sprouts. Sauté until tender, add bacon and toss to combine.

(May need to be cooked in batches.)

Asian Pear and Apple Pie

Preheat oven to 400°F.

Two-Crust Pie Dough for 9-inch Pan

¼ cup vegetable shortening
¼ cup butter
1½ cups all purpose flour
½ teaspoon salt
¼ cup cold water
1 teaspoon half-cinnamon/half-sugar mixture
½ teaspoon Demerara sugar (optional)

Using a pie dough cutter, blend shortening, butter, flour and salt together to cornmeal stage. Place in a medium bowl and slowly add cold water, mixing with a fork, until dough comes together. Add more water if necessary. Form into a ball, cover and chill at least 2 hours before rolling out.

Cut the dough ball into two pieces, one slightly larger than the other. Roll out dough until ⅛-inch thick. Make dough 10 inches round for bottom, and 9 inches round for top.

Place the filling in the shell. Apply top crust. Trim, roll and crimp edges.

Sprinkle with cinnamon sugar; then sprinkle Demerara sugar on top.

Pie Filling

1 cup sugar
2 tablespoons flour
1 teaspoon cinnamon
Pinch salt
3 cups Asian pears, peeled, cored and sliced
3 cups apples, peeled, cored and sliced
1 tablespoon butter

Blend sugar, flour, cinnamon and salt. Set aside. Layer half of the apples and pears in pie shell and sprinkle ½ cup sugar mixture over apples. Repeat until done.

Top with remaining sugar mixture and distribute pieces of butter evenly over fruit.

Bake pie 50 minutes, or until a toothpick inserted comes out clean and juices are bubbling around the crust.

Serve with a scoop of vanilla ice cream. Garnish with chopped crystallized ginger.

Persimmon Tea

Persimmon tea is supposed to relieve acid reflux and heartburn, but I drink it because it's so delicious.

2 quarts water
½ cup thinly sliced fresh ginger
3 large cinnamon sticks
1 cup dried persimmons (hoshigaki), sliced

Simmer water, ginger and cinnamon sticks for 30 minutes. Strain, and stir in sliced dried persimmons. Add honey if you wish a sweeter tea. Add more water for a less flavorful tea. Do not strain out persimmons. Keep refrigerated. Serve chilled.

lamb and pickled figs

Mixed Greens with Roasted Beets and Goat Cheese
and Red Wine Vinaigrette

Roasted Leg of Lamb with Pickled Figs

White Corn Polenta with Peppers

Sautéed Mustard Greens

Persimmons and Asian Pears over Ice Cream
with Triple Ginger–Molasses Cookies

Serves eight

A persimmon, in ancient Greek, means "fruit of the gods." In the late 1800s, Japanese farmers introduced persimmons to the region, and along rural highways you'll see the remains of old persimmon orchards laden with tear-drop shaped fruit. It's a particularly lovely sight when the trees drop their leaves with just the dark red-orange fruit remaining. It's picture perfect.

There are two types of persimmon fruit: astringent and non-astringent. The heart-shaped Hachiya is the most common variety of astringent persimmon. When ripe and soft to the touch, the astringency disappears. The non-astringent Fuyu persimmon is flatter, like a tomato, and is eaten while firm, like an apple.

From mid-October through December, there's always a basket of both types of persimmons on the kitchen counter. We nibble on the Fuyus, and use them in salads and desserts. I also cut the top off a very ripe Hachiya, and spoon out the flesh for a quick snack. The Hachiya persimmon is the one we select for baking cookies, persimmon loaf and our favorite persimmon pudding (see February 9 recipe).

This is also the time of year, to find hoshigaki at the market. Hoshigaki is prepared using traditional hand-drying techniques, hanging the persimmons outdoors in the warm sun for two to three weeks. The fruit is further dried by exposure to heat for several days. Hoshigaki is great as a snack or a dessert. I like to use hoshigaki to replace raisins in cookies.

october 26

Mixed Greens with Roasted Beets and Goat Cheese and Red Wine Vinaigrette

Preheat oven to 350°F.

2 bunches beets, tops cut off
1 tablespoon olive oil
Salt and pepper to taste
2 heads red leaf lettuce
4 ounces goat cheese
¼ cup walnuts, toasted
½ cup watermelon radishes, sliced

Red Wine Vinaigrette

¼ cup olive oil
2 tablespoons red wine vinegar
Salt and pepper

Wash beets and season lightly with olive oil, salt and pepper. Roast 25 to 33 minutes, until fork tender. Cool slightly.

Peel away skin with your hands. Slice into bite-sized pieces.

Combine all salad ingredients together. Whisk vinaigrette ingredients together. Dress salad just before serving.

Watermelon radishes as appetizers are always a hit, and they're so simple to prepare. I slice the beautiful radishes very thinly, and put them in the refrigerator. Just as all the guests have been seated, I take the plate out of the refrigerator, sprinkle sea salt over them and take them to the table. Beautiful and delicious.

You can use many vegetables this way: kohlrabi, carrots, cucumbers, common radishes. Remember not to salt them too soon, or the salt will leach out all the moisture.

Sprinkle the salt just as you're going to pass the plate.

Roasted Leg of Lamb with Pickled Figs

Preheat oven to 325°F.

Roasted Leg of Lamb

6 to 8 pound bone-in leg of lamb
2 tablespoons olive oil
2 tablespoon rosemary, chopped
2 teaspoons salt
2 teaspoons pepper
Pickled figs (recipe follows)
4 ounces pea shoots

Season lamb with 1½ tablespoons olive oil, rosemary, salt and pepper. Place on a sheet tray and roast 2 to 3 hours, until internal temperature of 125°F is reached for medium rare.
Let rest at least 20 minutes.
Slice and arrange on a large platter with pickled figs.
Dress pea shoots with ½ tablespoon olive oil, salt and pepper and garnish lamb.

Pickled Figs

(Neta Burns' recipe)

½ cup baking soda
2 tablespoons salt
7½ pounds figs
5 pounds sugar
1 pint apple vinegar
1 tablespoon whole cloves
1 tablespoon ground cinnamon

Sprinkle baking soda and salt over figs. Cover with two quarts boiling water and let stand 5 minutes. Remove figs from water and drain well on a dry towel.
In a gallon pan, mix sugar, vinegar, cloves and cinnamon and bring to a boil. Add figs and simmer 10 to 15 minutes. Cover pan and let stand at room temperature.
The following day remove figs from pan. Bring sugar mixture (syrup) to a boil, return figs to syrup and simmer for 10 to 15 minutes. Cover pan, and keep at room temperature.
On day 3 remove figs from pan, bring syrup to a boil, add figs and boil for 5 minutes.
Put in sterile jars and seal while hot. Store in a cool, dry place.

october 26

White Corn Polenta with Peppers

8 cups chicken stock, milk or water
Salt and pepper to taste
2½ cups white corn polenta
2 tablespoons butter
½ cup parmesan cheese
4 tablespoons olive oil
1 pound assorted peppers, julienne
1 yellow onion, julienne

In a large pot, bring liquid to a boil. Season lightly with salt and pepper.
Stir in polenta. Reduce heat to simmer. Let simmer while stirring until tender, about 25 minutes.
Stir in butter and parmesan, and check seasoning.
Remove from heat. Spread polenta on a sheet tray lined with parchment paper to cool. Place in the refrigerator and cool completely.

Meanwhile, in a large sauté pan, heat 2 tablespoons oil and sauté peppers and onion. Sauté until just tender and remove from pan. When cool, cut polenta into 4-inch squares or triangles. Heat remaining oil in a large sauté pan and sear polenta squares until caramelized, about 1½ minutes per side. Place on a platter and top with peppers.

Sautéed Mustard Greens

1 tablespoon olive oil
2 tablespoons butter
1 tablespoon garlic, minced
1½ pounds mustard greens
1 lemon, juiced
Salt and pepper to taste

In a large sauté pan, heat oil and butter. Add garlic and cook until fragrant.
Add greens and quickly sauté to wilt.
Season to taste with lemon juice, salt and pepper.

Persimmons and Asian Pears over Ice Cream with Triple Ginger-Molasses Cookies

3 tablespoons butter
6 Fuyu persimmons, peeled and sliced
4 Asian pears, sliced
¼ cup brown sugar
½ pomegranate, seeded
Vanilla ice cream

In a large sauté pan, heat butter and quickly sauté persimmons and pears. Sprinkle with brown sugar and continue to sauté until sugar is melted and beginning to bubble. Toss in pomegranate seeds.

To serve, spoon fruit over scooped vanilla ice cream. Garnish with triple ginger molasses cookies.

Triple Ginger-Molasses Cookies

Preheat oven to 350°F.

1 cup sugar
¾ cup shortening
1 egg
4 tablespoons dark molasses
2¼ cups flour, sifted
1 teaspoon cinnamon
2 teaspoons powdered ginger
1 teaspoon fresh ginger, grated
2 tablespoons candied ginger, finely diced
2½ teaspoons baking soda
½ teaspoon salt
⅓ cup sugar

Cream sugar and shortening; beat in egg and molasses. Set aside.

Sift and measure flour. Add cinnamon, gingers, soda and salt. Blend into creamed mixture.

Take small amounts of cookie mixture, roll into balls, and roll balls in sugar. Do not flatten. Bake 15 to 17 minutes.

comfort food

Warm Fruit Salad

Meatloaf with Pancetta

Spaghetti Squash

Sautéed Green Beans with Walnuts and Garlic

Cinderella Squash Pie

Serves eight

The yard is bursting with color. The maples, oaks, and dogwoods are brilliant red or deep burgundy. The star magnolia doesn't want to be left out of the show, so it turns golden yellow. It's time to make sure the wood stack is high, the drains are unclogged for winter rains, the irrigation system is turned off, and the fall yard clean-up is finished.

Something about late fall means it's time to hunker down and enjoy the simple pleasures of the season. For me, that's cooking comfort food: meatloaf, roasted chicken, turkey. And, of course, mashed potatoes and pie are close to the top of the list.

Laura's meatloaf is among the best I've ever eaten, and our neighbor agrees. While making some big loaves for our Monday night guests, Laura prepared a small meatloaf and a pan of green beans for delivery to our long-time Auburn neighbor, Bob Mancini. Bob loves all things homemade, and meatloaf was a taste of home.

Warm Fruit Salad

2 tablespoons butter
6 Fuyu persimmons, peeled and sliced
6 Asian pears, sliced
½ pomegranate, seeded
¼ cup apple cider vinegar
1 tablespoon honey

In a large sauté pan, heat butter, and quickly sauté persimmons and pears.
Remove from heat, and add pomegranate seeds.
Whisk together vinegar and honey, and toss with fruit before serving.

Fall is the perfect season for using colorful produce as a centerpiece. After you enjoy it on the table, enjoy it as part of the next meal. Best choices include cauliflower, artichokes, apples, squash, pumpkins, peppers, tomatillos, eggplant, chestnuts, lemons, mandarins, persimmons, citrus, Asian pears. Let your imagination be your guide.

Meatloaf with Pancetta

Preheat oven to 375ºF.

5 pounds ground beef
4 red bell peppers, diced
1 red onion, diced
1 tablespoon garlic, minced
2 tablespoons dried basil
Salt and pepper to taste
5 eggs
3½ cups panko bread crumbs
¼ pound pancetta, thinly sliced
¼ cup barbecue sauce (your choice)

In a medium bowl, mix meat, peppers, onion, garlic and basil. Season lightly with salt and pepper. Add eggs and panko. Make sure all ingredients are mixed well.
Form mixture into a log and place on a sheet tray or loaf pan.
Top with pancetta slices, pressing down so they don't curl up while baking.
Bake 45 to 55 minutes.
When slightly cool, top with barbecue sauce, and slice to serve.

Spaghetti Squash

Preheat oven to 375ºF.

3 spaghetti squash, cut in half lengthwise
2 tablespoons olive oil
Salt and pepper to taste
½ cup water
2 tablespoons butter
2 tablespoons parsley, chopped

Brush squash with olive oil, salt and pepper.
Place on a sheet tray, cut side down. Add ½ cup water to tray, and cover with foil.
Bake 35 to 40 minutes, until fork tender.
When slightly cool, remove the seeds with a spoon.
With a fork, shred the pulp of the squash away from the skin and place in a large bowl.
Season with butter and parsley. Add more salt and pepper if desired.

Sautéed Green Beans with Walnuts and Garlic

1 tablespoon olive oil
1 tablespoon butter
1 tablespoon garlic, minced
2 pounds green beans
¾ cup walnuts
1 lemon, zest and juice
Salt and pepper to taste

In a large sauté pan, heat butter and oil, and cook garlic until fragrant.
Add green beans and continue cooking until slightly tender. Remove from pan.
Add walnuts and cook until butter gets foamy and nuts are toasted.
Add lemon zest and juice and toss with green beans. Season to taste with salt and pepper.

I sincerely thank you for the excellent food, hospitality, creativity, and social interaction that I so very much enjoyed last night. The variety of tastes and colors was more than I have experienced before.

Fred Vitas, Auburn

Cinderella Squash Pie

Preheat oven to 350°F.

Single pie crust
2 cups Cinderella squash purée
1 cup sugar
½ teaspoon salt
1½ teaspoons cinnamon
½ teaspoon allspice
½ teaspoon ginger
½ teaspoon nutmeg
½ teaspoon cloves
1½ cups evaporated milk
2 eggs well beaten
1 cup cream, whipped

To make the purée, cut squash, remove seeds, and roast until meat is soft. Cool slightly, remove skin, and purée.
Increase oven temperature to 425°F.
Mix squash with remaining ingredients (except whipped cream), and pour into unbaked pie crust.
Bake 15 minutes; reduce heat to 300°F, and bake an additional 45 to 60 minutes, or until knife inserted midway between edge and center of pie comes out clean. (It may take as long as 90 minutes to bake the pie, depending on the moisture in the squash.)
When cool, slice and serve with a dollop of whipped cream.

fall pears, pomegranates and persimmons

Butter and Romaine Lettuces with Asian Pears and Fleur de Maquis Cheese and Champagne Vinaigrette

Roasted Chicken with Pomegranate Glaze

Smashed Purple Potatoes

Sautéed Spinach

Persimmon Meringue Pie

Serves eight

November signals the beginning of the rainy season here in the Sierra foothills. It's definitely jacket weather. The nights are getting nippy, which is perfect for fall fruits.

Fall favorites, like pomegranates and persimmons, seem to be sweeter and more flavorful after a few nights of chill. It's as though the fruit is saying, "It's getting cold; we must develop flavor quickly so we'll be appreciated."

Pomegranates have always been grown in Placer County, and over the last several years more and more trees have been planted. Pomegranates add a cheerful spark of color to recipes, and they're easy to use. Open the pomegranate by scoring it with a knife, and then break it open. Separate the arils (seeds) from the peel and white pulp membranes. The simplest way to do this is by putting the broken-apart fruit in a bowl of cold water. The arils sink to the bottom of the bowl and the pulp floats. Or, freeze the entire fruit which makes it easier to separate the arils from the pulp. Left-over pomegranate seeds can be stored in the refrigerator for several days or frozen for future use.

This week's dessert features persimmons. They're less astringent this time of year after going through several hours of cold weather. Hachiya persimmons make a great persimmon pie. We topped this one with meringue, but Hachiya persimmons are also tasty prepared like a traditional pumpkin pie and topped with whipped cream.

Butter and Romaine Lettuces with Asian Pears and Fleur de Maquis Cheese and Champagne Vinaigrette

2 heads each romaine and butter lettuce, cleaned

4 ounces Fleur de Maquis cheese

2 pears, sliced

¼ cup almonds, toasted

Champagne Vinaigrette

3 tablespoons Champagne vinegar

½ cup olive oil

1 lemon, juiced

Salt and pepper to taste

Toss salad ingredients together. Whisk together vinaigrette ingredients and toss with salad just before serving.

Do you know how to make a proper vinaigrette, one that isn't too tart, yet not too oily? Most cooks find vinaigrettes a mystery they can't solve. Not to worry, help is here. Simply remember the proportion of oil to vinegar is three to one in most vinaigrettes, but two to one in sweet and sour vinaigrettes. Season to taste with salt and pepper, and you have a basic, neutral vinaigrette that will enhance, not mask, the flavors of your salad.

Further, vinaigrettes aren't just for greens; they pair well with pasta, fruits and vegetables.

Roasted Chicken with Pomegranate Glaze

Preheat oven to 375°F.

2 whole chickens, 3 to 4 pounds each
Salt and pepper to taste
4 cloves garlic
4 sprigs thyme

Season the chickens with salt and pepper. Place garlic and thyme in cavity.
Roast on a sheet tray 1 to 1½ hours. Thirty minutes into roasting, brush with half of the pomegranate glaze (below).

Glaze

1 cup pomegranate molasses
1 cup red wine vinegar
¾ cup honey
Salt and pepper to taste
¾ cup pomegranate seeds

In a small saucepan, combine molasses and vinegar. Simmer over medium-high heat. Add honey and simmer until reduced by half. Season to taste with salt and pepper.
Brush chicken with about half the glaze 30 minutes into roasting.
Add pomegranate seeds to remaining glaze and serve.

Smashed Purple Potatoes

1½ pounds purple potatoes
1 cup olive oil
8 cloves garlic
3 tablespoons butter
Salt and pepper to taste

In a large pot of salted water, cook potatoes until fork tender. Remove from pan and drain.
While potatoes are cooking, slowly heat olive oil and garlic over low heat. When the oil starts to bubble, turn off heat and let sit at least 20 minutes. Remove garlic from oil and smash. Reserve the oil.
Place the drained potatoes in a large bowl, and add garlic, butter, ½ cup garlic oil, salt and pepper.
Smash together, using a fork or potato masher. Season to taste with salt, pepper, or additional garlic oil.

Sautéed Spinach

1 tablespoon butter
1 tablespoon olive oil
1 tablespoon garlic, minced
1 tablespoon red onion, minced
3 pounds spinach
Salt and pepper to taste

In a large sauté pan, heat butter and oil. Add garlic and onion and cook until fragrant. Add spinach and cook just to wilt. Season to taste with salt and pepper. Serve immediately.

If we don't sing the songs, tell the stories, and make the foods that are dear to us, our children won't know what they missed, but I think they'll miss it just the same.

Laura Ward Branca

november 9

Persimmon Meringue Pie

Preheat oven to 325°F.

2½ cups Hachiya persimmon pulp (use very ripe, sweet persimmons)

½ cup sugar

1 teaspoon mace

1 teaspoon lemon zest

½ teaspoon salt

3 teaspoons butter

3 egg yolks, beaten (save egg whites for meringue)

1 baked 9-inch pie shell

Combine persimmon pulp, sugar, mace, zest and salt. Cook slowly for 5 minutes.

While pulp is cooking, combine butter and egg yolks.

Temper the egg yolks by adding a small amount of hot persimmon sauce to the butter and egg yolk mixture. Whisk to combine, and return to hot persimmon mixture.

Continue cooking over very low heat until slightly thickened.

Pour into pastry shell and cover with meringue.

Meringue

3 egg whites

¼ teaspoon cream of tartar

4 tablespoons sugar

1 teaspoon vanilla

Beat whites and cream of tartar until frothy.

Continue beating, and sprinkle sugar (1 tablespoon at a time) over whites until meringue forms definite peaks when beater is lifted.

Add vanilla, and beat briefly.

Spread on pie filling in swirls, covering completely to edge of crust.

Bake 15 to 18 minutes, or until meringue is a delicate brown.

I just made the time to relax and peruse the website, www.placercountyrealfood.com. It's beautiful, so informative, and the photographs captivated me for many minutes. I think I sat and watched them all, my mouth watering with each picture.

Betsy Newman, Utah

quintessential quince

Red Butter Lettuce Salad with Roasted Beets
and Red Wine Vinaigrette

Lamb Chops with Quince and Balsamic Vinegar

Baby Carrots and Onions

Roasted Acorn Squash with Walnut Brown Butter

Sautéed Purple Broccoli

Quince and Apple Pie

Serves eight

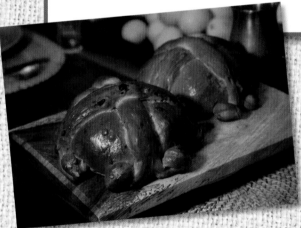

The Romans and Greeks grew quince, but it was only a few years ago I had my first taste of this often-ignored, misunderstood fruit.

I picked up a quince at the farmers market, and held it to my face to see if it had any fragrance. Quince has a subtle, unique scent, and the grower explained the fruit makes a good jam or jelly. I bought a bag, and put the fruit in the kitchen. I noticed every morning the quince perfumed the entire room, so now I buy quince for the experience of the fragrance as well as to eat. It's rare to find quince at the market, so when I find it on a grower's table, I pick up a bagful.

Most varieties of quince are too hard, astringent and sour to eat raw, and you won't want to eat them uncooked. Besides using them for jams and jellies, they can be used for quince pudding. Also, they can be peeled, then roasted, baked or stewed. The flesh turns a light red shade after a long cooking time. I like having a jar or two of quince preserves in my cupboard, but I also stew quince until it has little resistance when pierced with a fork. I keep a container of quince in the refrigerator, and use it to give purées a unique flavor, or as a complement to an apple pie.

253

Red Butter Lettuce Salad with Roasted Beets and Red Wine Vinaigrette

Preheat oven to 350°F.

2 bunches beets, greens removed
1 tablespoon olive oil
Salt and pepper to taste
3 heads red butter lettuce
¼ cup pistachios

Red Wine Vinaigrette
3 tablespoons red wine vinegar
½ cup olive oil
1 lemon, juiced
Salt and pepper to taste

To roast beets, toss with oil, salt and pepper and place on a sheet tray with ½ cup water. Roast 30 to 35 minutes, until fork tender. Let cool and peel skins off. Slice into bite-sized pieces. Toss with lettuce and pistachios.
Whisk vinaigrette ingredients together and toss with salad before serving.

Lamb Chops with Quince and Balsamic Vinegar

2 cups apple cider
½ cup sugar
3 quince, peeled, cored and cut into ¼-inch pieces
3 thyme sprigs
16 lamb loin or rib chops
Salt and pepper to taste
2 tablespoons grapeseed oil
2 tablespoons balsamic vinegar
1 teaspoon thyme, chopped
2 tablespoons butter
2 teaspoons rosemary, chopped

Combine apple cider and sugar in a small saucepan. Heat until sugar dissolves. Add quince and thyme.
Simmer until tender, about 25 minutes. Strain, and set quince and juices aside separately. Discard thyme.
Season lamb with salt and pepper. Heat oil in large pan and sear lamb on both sides, about 2 minutes per side, depending on thickness.
Remove from pan and cover to keep warm.
Discard oil in pan, and place pan over medium-high heat. Deglaze with reserved quince juices and reduce by one half.
Remove from heat; add vinegar, thyme, butter and 1 teaspoon rosemary.
Add quince back to sauce and season to taste with salt and pepper.
Arrange lamb chops on platter. Top with sauce and quince pieces. Garnish with remaining rosemary.

Baby Carrots and Onions

Preheat oven to 375°F.

16 small sweet whole onions, peeled
3 bunches small carrots, tops removed
Salt and pepper to taste
1 tablespoon butter
1 tablespoon sugar
2 tablespoons olive oil
1 teaspoon thyme, chopped
1 teaspoon parsley, chopped

Place onions in a small saucepan, and cover with water. Season lightly with salt.
Bring to a boil and turn down to simmer 20 to 30 minutes, until tender. Remove from heat and drain. In a medium sauté pan, heat butter and add onions. When slightly caramelized, add sugar and cook to dissolve and glaze the onions. Cover and set aside.
Toss the carrots with oil, salt and pepper. Roast on a sheet tray 10 to 15 minutes. Toss with onions, and garnish with thyme and parsley before serving.

Roasted Acorn Squash with Walnut Brown Butter

Preheat oven to 350°F.

3 acorn squash, cut into wedges, seeds removed
2 tablespoons olive oil
Salt and pepper to taste
¼ cup butter
½ cup walnuts, chopped
2 tablespoons parsley, chopped

Season squash with oil, salt and pepper. Place on sheet tray. Cover with foil, and roast 30 to 40 minutes, until tender.
Meanwhile, in a large sauté pan, heat butter. When foamy, add walnuts and continue to cook until brown flecks appear in the butter. Season lightly with salt and pepper.
To serve, place squash on a platter, skin side down, and top with brown butter. Garnish with chopped parsley.

Sautéed Purple Broccoli

1 tablespoon olive oil
1 tablespoon butter
1 tablespoon garlic, minced
2 heads purple broccoli, cut into small pieces
Salt and pepper to taste

Heat oil and butter in a large sauté pan and add garlic. Cook until fragrant, and add broccoli. Sauté until just tender. Season with salt and pepper.

Quince and Apple Pie

Preheat oven to 400°F.

Two-Crust Pie Dough for 9-inch Pan

¼ cup vegetable shortening

¼ cup butter

1½ cups all purpose flour

½ teaspoon salt

¼ cup cold water

1 teaspoon half-cinnamon/half-sugar mixture

½ teaspoon Demerara sugar (optional)

Using a pie dough cutter, blend shortening, butter, flour and salt together to cornmeal stage. Place in a medium bowl and slowly add cold water, mixing with a fork, until dough comes together. Add more water if necessary. Form into a ball, cover and chill at least 2 hours before rolling out.

Cut the dough ball into two pieces, one slightly larger than the other. Roll out dough until ⅛-inch thick. Make dough 10 inches round for bottom, and 9 inches round for top.

Place the filling in the shell. Apply top crust. Trim, roll and crimp edges.

Sprinkle with cinnamon sugar; then sprinkle Demerara sugar on top.

You can – and should – reduce the amount of sugar in recipes. For example, most pie recipes call for a cup of sugar. However, that much sugar isn't necessary because we use such generous amounts of fresh fruit in recipes. Use ¾ or even ½ cup of sugar instead. I encourage you to focus on the fruit, to feel confident about taking a portion of the sugar out of every recipe. It's an easy, painless way to cut calories, and you'll still enjoy the full flavor of the fruit or custard or whatever it is you're making.

Quince and Apple Pie

1 cup sugar

½ teaspoon salt

2 tablespoons all purpose flour

2 cups poached quince slices (recipe follows)

4 cups baking apples, peeled and sliced

1 tablespoon butter

In a small pan blend sugar, salt and flour. Set aside.

Place alternate layers of sliced apples and quince in a pie shell until half full. Sprinkle half of the sugar and flour mixture over fruit. Continue layering apples and quince, top with remaining sugar mixture and distribute pieces of butter evenly over fruit.

Bake 50 to 60 minutes, or until toothpick inserted in pie meets no resistance.

Poached Quince

2 cups water

½ cup sugar

2 large ripe quince, peeled, cored and sliced into ½-inch sections

Place water in saucepan, add sugar and quince (quince should be covered with water; add more if necessary).

Bring to a boil. Reduce heat, and simmer until quince can be easily pierced with a fork.

turkey and trimmings

Fruit Salad

Roasted Turkey with Mushroom Gravy

Apple–Raisin Herb Stuffing

Cranberry, Mandarin and Ginger Relish

German Butterball Mashed Potatoes

Roasted Marina de Chioggia Squash with Onions and Sage

Sautéed Green Beans

Chocolate Pomegranate Torte

Serves eight

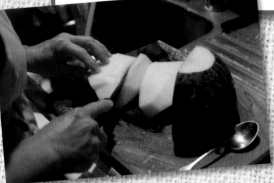

Thanksgiving at our house isn't Thanksgiving without a turkey. Fortunately, Bryan Kaminsky's Natural Trading Company is seven miles from our front door; this short distance allows us the privilege of serving a truly local, organic bird. The moist, full-of-flavor turkey was the best tasting turkey served in all the decades of Thanksgiving dinner at the Neft table; the gravy the most memorable.

To honor the season, we added mandarin juice to the soup, hoshigaki to the dressing, St. Nick melon to the fruit salad, and pomegranate lacing to the chocolate tart. The mandarin juice gave the squash soup a nice citrus flavor. Served with a dollop of crème fraîche and a touch of mandarin zest, the soup is just right served in small, hand-held soup cups as an appetizer.

Each year J. R. and Claudia Smith of Blossom Hill Farm bless us by growing St. Nick melons. The melon is sweet and nicely textured. We buy several melons when told "these are the last of the season." The melons store well; in fact, many times we serve them for breakfast on Christmas day to celebrate the name.

november 23

Fruit Salad

½ St. Nick melon, cubed

6 Fuyu persimmons, peeled and sliced

2 Asian pears, sliced

½ pomegranate, seeded

Combine all fruit and toss together before serving.

Roasted Turkey with Mushroom Gravy

12 to 14 pound turkey, brined (instructions below)

2 cups Kosher salt

8 quarts water

6 sprigs fresh rosemary

6 sprigs fresh thyme

6 sprigs fresh sage

5 Meyer lemons, halved

½ cup butter, room temperature

Salt and pepper to taste

Brine turkey the afternoon before roasting. For brine, combine salt and water in a 5-gallon bucket. Place turkey in bucket. Use a 1 gallon freezer bag filled with water to keep turkey submerged in the brine. After 6 hours, wash off salt brine with fresh running water. Totally dry bird with an old towel. Place turkey, breast side up, on a wire rack in a large pan. Put in refrigerator, uncovered, to air dry overnight. Don't be alarmed if the skin looks wrinkled.

Preheat oven to 450°F.

Place the bird breast side down on a V-shaped rack so there is air around it.

Place 3 lemons in cavity, with open slices toward the breast. Insert sprigs of rosemary, thyme and sage over lemons.

Rub the bird thoroughly with butter. Season with pepper and a little salt.

Distribute the juice of remaining 2 lemons on the bottom of the pan. (The lemon juice results in very dark drippings which gives rich flavor and colored gravy.)

Place turkey in oven and immediately reduce temperature to 275°F. (If you're cooking an organically grown turkey, remember it takes less time to cook.)

Keep your eye on the clock. After 2½ to 3 hours, check temperatures. Roast bird until breast is 160°F.

Remove bird from oven, and let it rest at least 1 hour before carving.

Mushroom Gravy

Turkey pan drippings

6 tablespoons all purpose flour

6 cups neck and giblet stock and chicken stock (add enough chicken stock to neck and giblet stock to make 6 cups; recipe follows)

1 pound crimini mushrooms, sliced

Salt and pepper to taste

Remove pan drippings from the bottom of the roasting pan with a flat spatula. Pour drippings into a 2 quart bowl and purée with a hand blender until all lumps are gone. Return drippings to roasting pan.

Add flour to pan. Whisk and blend flour with drippings. Cook at least 5 minutes (otherwise gravy will taste like flour).

Slowly add chicken broth or stock. Whisk until blended, add mushrooms and simmer at least 30 minutes before serving. Turkey gravy is better if simmered for at least 1 hour.

If gravy is not thick enough, simmer until it reaches desired consistency. If gravy is too thick, add more chicken broth or white wine. Season to taste with salt and pepper.

Neck and Giblet Stock

Neck and giblets from inside turkey

3 carrots, sliced

1 cup celery, sliced

1 onion, sliced

½ teaspoon salt

Place all ingredients in a 2-quart sauce pan. Cover with water and bring to a boil. Immediately reduce to simmer at lowest temperature for 2 to 3 hours. Strain. Discard vegetables and save neck. Pick meat off neck bones and add meat to gravy or save for snacking. Use this stock and enough chicken stock to yield 6 cups of gravy.

Apple-Raisin Herb Stuffing

(This recipe makes enough stuffing for a 12 to 14 pound turkey)

Preheat oven to 350°F.

8 cups dried bread cubes (12 slices bread dried overnight)

3 cups Granny Smith apples, skin on, cored and chopped

¾ cup golden raisins (soaked overnight in ¼ cup Gran Marnier or Cointreau) and slightly diced

½ cup onion, chopped

1½ teaspoons ground sage

1 teaspoon dried thyme leaves

1 teaspoon dried rosemary leaves, crushed

1 cup chicken broth

6 tablespoons butter, melted

Combine bread, apples, raisins, onions, sage, thyme and rosemary. Add broth and butter. Toss to mix. Transfer to a buttered 3-quart baking dish. Bake 50 minutes, or until apples are easily pierced.

You can use hoshigaki instead of raisins in any stuffing recipe, and in November, that's an easy thing to do. In Japanese, "hoshi" means "dried" and "gaki" means "persimmon."

November is hoshigaki season at Placer County's Otow Orchard. Each fall they pick fresh persimmons and dry them slowly. The persimmons are hung by a string on a rack, watched carefully and massaged every three to five days for several weeks. The entire process is done by hand. The result is a sugary delicacy that is tender and moist with concentrated persimmon flavor. They are simply stunning to see.

november 23

Cranberry, Mandarin and Ginger Relish

One 12-ounce bag cranberries
½ cup crystallized ginger chips
⅓ cup brown sugar
2 tablespoons mandarin juice
2 whole mandarins
2 peeled mandarins

Wash cranberries, and lay out in a jelly-roll pan in order to easily pick out and discard soft or damaged cranberries. Set aside.
In a food processor pulse ginger chips until broken up. Set aside.
Over low heat, dissolve brown sugar in mandarin juice. Add to food processor. Pulse 3 or 4 times to blend.
Add whole cranberries to mixture and pulse briefly until cranberries are broken up. Remove mixture with a spatula to a bowl.
Place whole mandarins in processor, pulse briefly, and add to bowl. Place 2 peeled mandarins in processor, pulse briefly, and add to bowl. Stir relish until blended.
Put relish in a covered container and refrigerate until ready to use.
(Can be made a day or two in advance.)

German Butterball Mashed Potatoes

4 pounds German Butterball potatoes
Salt to taste
1 cup milk
¼ pound (1 stick) butter

Cook the potatoes in salted water until fork tender. Drain and let dry. Set aside.
Heat milk in a small saucepan until scalded.
Pass the potatoes through a mill with butter and add warm milk to desired texture.
Season to taste with salt.

In addition to German butterball potatoes, we've used Yukon Gold for mashing, and, surprisingly, Peruvian Purple. We don't mash the Peruvian Purple potatoes as thoroughly as we would other varieties of potatoes. We intentionally leave them a bit rough, and we like describing that as "rustically mashed."

A trip to a farmers market will show you potatoes come in an amazing array of tastes, textures and colors. There are white-fleshed potatoes, as well as ones that are golden, red or bluish-purple inside. They come round as a ball, long and thin like fingers, even lumpy and oddly shaped. We're drawn to the oddly shaped ones because we think they have an offbeat personality.

Potatoes can be waxy textured, creamy, mealy, and even dry. The names are as exotic as the potatoes themselves: Yellow Finn, Cranberry Red, Russian Banana, and Swedish Peanut.

Roasted Marina de Chioggia Squash with Onions and Sage

Preheat oven to 350°F.

1 Marina de Chioggia squash, peeled and
  cut into cubes
2 tablespoons olive oil
1 tablespoon butter
1 tablespoon sage, chopped, plus leaves
  for garnish
Salt and pepper to taste
1 red onion, julienne

Toss together squash, 1 tablespoon oil, butter,
sage, salt and pepper. Roast on sheet tray 15 to
20 minutes, until tender.
Meanwhile, heat remaining oil in large sauté
pan and add onion. Cook over medium heat to
caramelize. Season lightly with salt and pepper.
Toss squash and onions together and serve in a
large bowl. Garnish with sage leaves.

Sautéed Green Beans

1 tablespoon butter
1 tablespoon olive oil
1 tablespoon garlic, minced
1½ pounds green beans
Salt and pepper to taste

Heat butter and oil in a large sauté pan. Add
garlic and cook until fragrant. Add green beans
and sauté until tender. Season to taste with salt
and pepper.

november 23

Chocolate Pomegranate Torte

Preheat oven to 350°F.

6 ounces bittersweet chocolate

4 tablespoons butter

3 tablespoons water

3 eggs, separated

¾ cup sugar

⅛ teaspoon cream of tartar

½ teaspoon salt

½ cup all purpose flour

1 cup Twin Peaks Pomegranate Jelly

For the cake, lightly grease the sides of a 9x2-inch round cake pan, and line the bottom with parchment paper. Set aside.

Finely grate or chop 2 ounces of chocolate. Set aside.

In a double boiler, combine the remaining chocolate with butter and water, and melt over low heat until smooth.

In a large bowl, whisk egg yolks and ½ cup sugar until thick and pale in color. Set aside.

Separately, in a mixer, beat egg whites and cream of tartar to soft peaks. Gradually add remaining sugar and beat to stiff peaks, 1 to 2 minutes more. Sift salt with flour, and gradually add to yolk mixture. Stir to combine. Whisk in the warm chocolate.

With a rubber spatula, carefully fold the egg whites into the chocolate mixture, ¼ at a time. Before adding the last ¼, sprinkle with chopped chocolate and continue to fold.

Pour the batter into the prepared cake pan and spread evenly.

Bake 20 to 25 minutes, until a toothpick comes out smudged with a few crumbs.

Cool in the pan 10 minutes before running a knife around the edge and turning out onto a wire rack. Let cool completely.

Remove any loose crumbs that may be attached to the sides of the cake. Top with an even layer of pomegranate jelly and place in the refrigerator.

Glaze

6 ounces bittersweet chocolate

6 tablespoons butter

1 tablespoon honey

½ teaspoon salt

2 tablespoons cold water

¼ cup pomegranate seeds

Place the chocolate, butter, honey and salt in a double boiler. Stir to melt, and combine until smooth.

Remove from heat, and stir in cold water.

Let cool to room temperature. When cool, it should have the consistency of thick, pourable cream.

Remove the cake from the refrigerator and place the wire rack over a sheet tray.

Using a ladle, slowly pour the glaze over the top and sides of the cake, spreading gently with a rubber spatula if necessary. Repeat by scraping the excess from the sheet tray below and reglazing.

Top with pomegranate seeds. Let set 10 minutes on the rack before moving to a cake plate. Store at room temp before serving.

november 30

mandarins and rock cod

Red Leaf Lettuce with Mandarins and Mandarin Vinaigrette

Pan Seared Rock Cod with Almond Crust

Creamy Polenta with Goat Cheese and Peppers

Sautéed Kale

Roasted Baby Carrots

Warm Apple Compote

Serves eight

Days are getting shorter, which means most farmers market shoppers prefer to sleep in or get a later start on the day, so they don't show up at the market until after 9 a.m. The pace is a little slower, and it seems at this time of year the growers have more time to visit for a few minutes, to recall a son's recent football game, or to talk about a favorite fishing experience. And although everyone is wearing a heavier jacket, it's a warmer, friendlier time of the year. Time seems to slow down, even if for just a few minutes.

Stalls at the market are filling up with a variety of root vegetables and leafy greens. Spinach, kale, rutabaga, parsnips, and turnips started during the warmer fall months are now mature enough to harvest. And some of the leafy lighter greens are available, too. Even carrots, which are available most of the year, taste sweeter and are crunchier now, thanks to a few cool nights.

Placer County mountain mandarins are developing the full, sweet, complex flavors everyone appreciates. The big orange bags are everywhere, announcing mandarins are ready for eating one after the other, for juicing for a breakfast treat, or for shipping to friends and relatives across the country. Traditionally, I wait until the first week of December to ship mandarins so I'm sure they're at their peak of flavor.

Red Leaf Lettuce with Mandarins and Mandarin Vinaigrette

3 small heads red leaf lettuce, torn into pieces
6 mandarins, segmented
¼ cup walnuts, toasted

Mandarin Vinaigrette

3 mandarins, juiced
2 tablespoons rice wine vinegar
2 tablespoons olive oil
Salt and pepper to taste

Toss all salad ingredients together. Whisk together vinaigrette ingredients and toss with salad just before serving.

Pan Seared Rock Cod with Almond Crust

Preheat broiler.

Almond Crust

1 cup almonds
2 cloves garlic
1 lemon, zest and juice
½ cup olive oil
Salt and pepper to taste

Place almonds and garlic in a food processor and pulse until chopped. Add lemon zest, juice and olive oil and continue to pulse until it becomes a paste. Season to taste with salt and pepper. Set aside.

Pan Seared Rock Cod

4 pounds rock cod (snapper)
Salt and pepper to taste
2 tablespoons grapeseed oil
Salt and pepper to taste
2 Meyer lemons, sliced

Season fish with salt and pepper.
Heat oil in a large sauté pan, and sear fish on both sides, about 1 minute each, depending on thickness. Place on a sheet tray, top with almond mixture and broil 2 to 3 minutes to toast. Serve on a large platter with sliced Meyer lemons.

Creamy Polenta with Goat Cheese and Peppers

4 cups chicken stock

4 cups milk

2 cups white cornmeal

4 ounces goat cheese

2 tablespoons butter

Salt and pepper to taste

1 tablespoon olive oil

1 tablespoon garlic, minced

6 peppers, julienne

2 tablespoons parsley, chopped

In a large pot, heat chicken stock and milk. When simmering, whisk in cornmeal.

Turn down heat to low and continue to cook, 20 to 30 minutes longer, stirring frequently.

Remove from heat, whisk in goat cheese and 1 tablespoon butter. Season to taste with salt and pepper.

Meanwhile, heat oil in a large sauté pan. Add garlic; cook until fragrant. Add peppers and quickly sauté. Season to taste with salt and pepper.

To serve, pour polenta into a serving bowl, and top with peppers and chopped parsley.

You'll be pleased to know, I now shop at the farmers market every week, and I love it!
Pat Rubin, Meadow Vista

Sautéed Kale

1 tablespoon butter
1 tablespoon olive oil
1 tablespoon garlic
1½ pounds kale, stems removed
2 tablespoons Mirin
1 lemon, juiced
Salt and pepper to taste

In a large sauté pan, heat butter and oil. Add garlic; cook until fragrant. Add kale and sauté to wilt.
Add Mirin and lemon juice; season to taste with salt and pepper.
Serve with roasted carrots.

Roasted Baby Carrots

Preheat oven to 350°F.

4 bunches baby carrots
1 onion, julienne
1 tablespoon olive oil
Salt and pepper to taste

Toss carrots with onion, oil and salt and pepper. Roast on a sheet tray 15 to 20 minutes, until tender. Serve with sautéed kale.

Warm Apple Compote

Thanks to Jen Linn for this recipe.

2 cups apple cider

2 tablespoons brown sugar

1 teaspoon cinnamon

¾ cup butter

6 Pink Lady apples, peeled, cored,
   and cut into 1–inch cubes

6 Granny Smith apples, peeled, cored
   and cut into 1–inch cubes

1 cup sugar

Mix cider, brown sugar and cinnamon in a
saucepan. Bring to a boil, and then reduce heat.
Let the mixture simmer until it has reduced by
half.

Meanwhile, melt butter in a large saucepan,
and mix in apples. Stir together, and cook over
medium heat for 10 minutes.

Stir in sugar, and cook 10 to 15 minutes longer.
When done, the apples should still be a little firm.
Pour the cider mixture onto the apples.

Serve warm with a dollop of whipped cream.

mandarin magic

Spinach Salad with Mandarins and Kiwi and Mandarin Vinaigrette

Roasted Leg of Lamb with Mandarin Marmalade

Sautéed Romanesco with Bacon

Smashed Sweet Potatoes

Spiced Mandarins with Pomegranate and Kiwi

Serves eight

This morning I woke to find eight inches of snow on the ground.

At 1,234 feet elevation, Auburn enjoys the reputation of being below the snow and above the fog. We may get a dusting of snow once every four years or so, but it doesn't stick. According to Jerry Burns, the last time he remembers this much snow was in the early 1940s.

The roads are icy, snow is piled up everywhere. In Aeolia Heights, where we live, early this morning two cars slipped on the ice and ended up in the olive orchard. How do we handle Monday night dinner tonight, our 49th meal? Dinner guests are coming from Roseville and Newcastle, which had less than two inches of snow. Do guests know how to drive on the ice? Do they have four-wheel drive vehicles? Can they get down our long, narrow driveway?

Somehow we knew it would all work out. We set the table.

It's mandarin season, so the meal featured mandarins in practically every dish, including flutes of mandarin and Champagne for a starter, and boneless leg of lamb glazed with Ann's Orchard Satsuma Mandarin Marmalade.

Magically, the snow didn't chill our spirits. Dinner was delicious, and the big snow turned out to be star of the show.

Spinach Salad with Mandarins and Kiwi and Mandarin Vinaigrette

1 pound spinach
4 mandarins, sectioned
2 kiwi, peeled and sliced
4 ounces cow's milk cheese
½ cup walnuts, toasted

Mandarin Vinaigrette

½ cup mandarin juice
2 tablespoons red wine vinegar
1 tablespoon agave nectar
¼ cup olive oil
Salt and pepper to taste

Combine salad ingredients. Whisk vinaigrette ingredients together and toss with salad just before serving.

december 7

Roasted Leg of Lamb with Mandarin Marmalade

Preheat oven to 400°F.

2 boneless legs of lamb, about 3 pounds each
2 tablespoons olive oil
Salt and pepper to taste
1 (9.5 ounce) jar Amy's Orchard Satsuma
   Mandarin Marmalade
3 mandarins, sectioned

Season lamb with oil, salt and pepper. Roast on a sheet tray 10 minutes.
Turn oven down to 325°F, and continue to cook 30 to 35 minutes longer. Remove from oven, and increase heat to broil.
Glaze lamb with marmalade, and return to oven 5 to 10 minutes longer to caramelize.
Let meat rest before carving.
Serve on a large platter with mandarin sections.

Sautéed Romanesco with Bacon

¾ pound bacon
1 tablespoon olive oil
1 red onion, julienne
1 head romanesco, cut into small pieces
Salt and pepper to taste

Cook bacon in a large sauté pan until just crispy. Remove from pan, and drain fat. Set fat and bacon aside.
Return pan to stove, and heat 1 tablespoon bacon fat with olive oil. Add onion and cook until tender.
Add romanesco, and sauté 45 seconds to 1 minute, until tender.
Add bacon to pan, and toss to combine. Season to taste with salt and pepper.

Smashed Sweet Potatoes

3 pounds purple sweet potatoes, cut into 2-inch
   pieces, skins left on
3 tablespoons butter
Salt and pepper to taste

Place sweet potatoes in a large pot, cover with salted water, and bring to a boil.
Turn down to simmer, and cook until fork tender.
Drain water, and return potatoes to pot.
Stir in butter, smashing the potatoes slightly.
Season to taste with salt and pepper.

Spiced Mandarins with Pomegranate and Kiwi

2 cups sugar

3 cups water

2 cinnamon sticks, each about 4 inches long

14 whole cloves

½ cup fresh ginger, peeled and thinly sliced

8 green cardamom seeds

6 whole star anise

12 Satsuma mandarins

1 to 2 kiwi, peeled and thinly sliced

½ cup pomegranate seeds

Dissolve sugar in water and bring to a boil. Add cinnamon, cloves, ginger, cardamom and anise. Simmer 10 minutes. Remove from heat.

Cover pan, and let steep 15 minutes.

Using a sieve, strain spices and discard.

Chill syrup in covered pan several hours.

Cut peel from mandarins, being sure to remove pith. Slice mandarins in 3/8-inch rounds and put in large serving bowl. Cover with syrup and refrigerate two hours.

Serve in small dessert bowls; top with kiwi and pomegranate seeds.

ham and potatoes

Red Leaf Salad with Mandarins and Pistachios
and Mandarin Vinaigrette

Mandarin Glazed Ham

Zucchini Pickles, Watermelon Style

Twice Baked Potatoes

Baby Cabbages with White Wine

Plum and Raspberry Buckle

Serves eight

Wheh Bob Sorenson of Coffee Pot Ranch announced he'd have plenty of ham and bacon at the next market, Laura and I immediately ordered ham for tonight's dinner. And we ordered several packages of his famous bacon for the freezer. Bob's signature meat at the ranch is pork, and there's nothing better tasting than locally grown pork chops, bacon or roast.

People often ask about the ranch name, Coffee Pot. The land on Karchner Road near Sheridan, as pictured on a map, is in the shape of an old-fashioned coffee pot, and the name held through several generations of ranchers.

Neft family tradition says whenever we serve ham, mom makes double-roasted baked potatoes; this recipe is one I've made for at least 40 years. Cottage cheese with a touch of Parmesan cheese is the unique ingredient. While you're at it, make extra halves for the freezer; that takes care of potatoes for another meal.

Fortunately we have space for two big freezers. Freezing food allows us to purchase meat and produce at the peak of the season. That's when produce is abundant, and the lowest cost. For example, when raspberries are in season at Amber Oaks Raspberry Farm, we pick at least 30 pounds for the freezer. Black Amber plums are another favorite for freezing. We quarter the plums, remove the seeds, and freeze them in freezer bags. The combination of raspberries and plums not only tastes good, but offers rich color and gives a nice presentation.

Red Leaf Salad with Mandarins and Pistachios and Mandarin Vinaigrette

2 heads red leaf lettuce, torn into pieces
4 mandarins, segmented
½ cup pistachios

Mandarin Vinaigrette

¼ cup mandarin juice
2 tablespoons rice wine vinegar
¼ cup olive oil
Salt and pepper to taste

Combine salad ingredients. Whisk together vinaigrette ingredients and toss with salad just before serving.

Mandarin Glazed Ham

Preheat oven to 325°F.

2 cups mandarin juice
1 teaspoon thyme
Salt and pepper to taste
5 to 6 pound ham
3 mandarins, sectioned
1 cup pea shoots

To make the glaze, place mandarin juice in a small saucepan, and reduce by three-fourths. Add thyme and season to taste with salt and pepper. Set aside.
Place ham on a sheet tray, and cover with foil. Bake 25 to 35 minutes.
Increase oven temperature to 400°F.
Remove ham from oven, uncover, and glaze with mandarin reduction. Return ham to oven 10 minutes longer.
Slice and serve on a large platter with mandarin sections and pea shoots.
Pairs well with zucchini pickles.

There are almost 70 mandarin orange groves in South Placer County. Warm days and cool nights are perfect for producing sweet, intensely-flavored mandarins. Mandarin season runs from November through January.

Fresh mandarins are a staple on holiday tables, and are used in recipes from salads to desserts, sauces and syrups. The most commonly grown variety is the Owari Satsuma Mandarin, a Japanese hybrid that is easy to peel and seedless. Despite the year trees are planted, the yield is usually heavy in alternate years, as though the trees have their own communication system.

december 14

Zucchini Pickles, Watermelon Style

Thanks to Kay McCreary for the recipe.

10 cups zucchini, cut in chunks
1 cup slacked lime
6 cups cider vinegar
10 cups sugar
1 teaspoon salt
2 tablespoons whole allspice
2 sticks cinnamon
2 tablespoons celery seed
Green food coloring

Peel and scoop out seeds of a super large zucchini. Cut in pickle-size chunks (enough to make 10 cups). Set aside.

Dissolve slacked lime in 1 gallon of water. Add zucchini. Stir every 3 hours for 24 hours.

After 24 hours, wash zucchini in water 3 times, then soak in clear COLD water another 24 hours (add ice cubes and keep refrigerated). Mixture must be kept cold.

Drain zucchini.

In a large pan mix vinegar, sugar, salt, allspice cinnamon and celery seed. Bring to a boil, add zucchini, and turn off heat. Let stand 6 hours or overnight.

Bring to boil again, and cook 30 minutes.

Add a few drops of food coloring and remove from heat.

Seal in hot jars. Makes 7 pints.

Twice Baked Potatoes

Preheat oven to 400°F.

4 large russet potatoes, without blemishes
1 tablespoon olive oil
1 pound small curd cottage cheese
⅓ cup mayonnaise
1 cup Parmesan cheese, grated
1 tablespoon Worcestershire
2 tablespoons fresh chives, finely cut
½ teaspoon salt
Paprika

Wash potatoes, dry, and brush with olive oil. Pierce potatoes several times with a long tined fork. Place potatoes on a baking sheet. Bake potatoes until easily pierced with a fork, about 1 hour. Remove from oven, and let cool 10 minutes. With a serrated knife, cut potatoes in half from stem to bottom. Use a small spoon to carefully remove potato from the skin, and place in a bowl, leaving a boat-shaped potato skin. Set skins aside. Mash potatoes with a hand masher or electric mixer. Add cottage cheese, mayonnaise, ½ cup Parmesan cheese, Worcestershire sauce and chives. Blend until mixed.

Fill potato skins, top with remaining Parmesan cheese and paprika, and place on a large baking sheet. Refrigerate at least 2 hours.

Reduce oven to 350°F, and bake until brown and bubbly on top, about 30 minutes. Be careful not to over bake; the potatoes will flatten out.

Potatoes can be frozen and used at a later date. Slightly defrost before baking.

Baby Cabbages
with White Wine

1 tablespoon olive oil
1 tablespoon butter
6 small heads Savoy cabbage, about 5 inches in
   diameter, quartered (not cored)
Salt and pepper to taste
½ cup white wine

Heat oil and butter in a large sauté pan, and sear
cabbage on two sides. Season lightly with salt
and pepper. Add wine and cover to steam, 1½ to
2 minutes.
Serve on a large platter with zucchini pickles on
the side.

Plum and Raspberry Buckle

Preheat oven to 350°F.

1⅓ cups plus ¼ cup all purpose flour
1¼ cups sugar
1 teaspoon cinnamon
1 teaspoon salt
4 tablespoons cold butter, cut into cubes
1½ teaspoons baking powder
¾ cup butter, softened
1½ teaspoons vanilla extract
¼ teaspoon almond extract
3 eggs
2 cups Black Amber plums
2 cups frozen raspberries
Powdered sugar for dusting
Whipped cream

Butter a 9-inch square baking dish.
For streusel topping, combine ¼ cup flour, ¼
cup sugar, cinnamon and ½ teaspoon salt in a
medium bowl. Cut in cold butter until mixture is
the size of peas. Set aside.
To make the buckle, sift together 1⅓ cups flour,
baking powder and remaining salt. Set aside.
In a mixer, beat softened butter on medium
speed about 1 minute. Add 1 cup sugar, vanilla
and almond extract; beat until pale and thick.
Reduce speed to low, and add eggs, one at a
time, mixing to incorporate. Add sifted flour
mixture in two stages, and stir to combine.
Remove from mixer, and fold in half of the plums
and half the raspberries.
Spread the batter in buttered dish, top with
remaining fruit, and sprinkle with reserved
streusel topping.
Bake 45 to 50 minutes, until a toothpick inserted
in the center comes out clean. Let cool to room
temperature before serving.
To serve, slice cake into eight pieces. Sprinkle
with powdered sugar and top with whipped
cream.

christmas dinner

French Onion Soup

St. Nick Melon Salad

Standing Rib Roast with Garlic and Rosemary

Horseradish Crème Fraîche

Garlic Mashed Potatoes

Roasted Brussels Sprouts with Balsamic Vinegar

Roasted Cauliflower and Broccoli

Chocolate Jelly Roll

Serves eight

It's Christmas.

A pine tree decorated solely with things from the garden, three oversized poinsettias, icicle lights lining the roof, and the dining room filled with candlelight announce Christmas is here. Sounds of Christmas music play softly in the background, and Champagne glasses filled with mandarin juice and Champagne hint at the festive meal to follow.

Memories come from traditions, and one of the Christmas traditions at our house is French onion soup. During October and November, I save every beef bone and end piece, and stow them in the freezer. Mid-December is the time to make good hearty beef stock. Beef stock is the basis for flavorful French onion soup. I stop at Newcastle Produce for Gruyere cheese and the largest yellow onions I've ever seen. On Christmas Eve, we serve big bowls of piping hot Swiss Gruyere cheese-topped French onion soup. Nothing warms holiday spirits more than hot soup on a chilly Christmas night.

For Christmas dinner, we cooked a beef rib roast we'd ordered from Bob Sorenson of Coffee Pot Ranch. The horseradish to go with the beef came from Gary Romano of Sierraville. The gorgeous display of beautifully colored cauliflower in orange, purple and white came from Francis Thompson. The colorful cauliflower combined with one dark purple head of broccoli gave Laura's Christmas dinner a truly festive look. The Christmas cake with a raspberry sauce was the grand finale to a fine seasonal dinner.

december 21

French Onion Soup

Preheat oven to 350°F.

6 large yellow onions, peeled and thinly sliced

¼ cup olive oil

½ teaspoon sugar

4 cloves garlic, minced

8 cups beef stock

½ cup dry vermouth

2 bay leaves

½ teaspoon thyme

Salt and pepper to taste

8 slices French bread, toasted

1½ cups Swiss Gruyere cheese, finely grated

In a large saucepan, sauté the onions in olive oil until caramelized, 30 to 40 minutes. Add sugar the last 10 minutes.

Add garlic and sauté another 2 minutes.

Add stock, vermouth, bay leaves and thyme. Simmer another hour. Discard bay leaves. Season to taste with salt and pepper.

Ladle soup into small soup bowls. Cover with toast, and sprinkle on cheese.

Bake until cheese is browned and bubbly, about 10 minutes.

Serve immediately.

St. Nick Melon Salad

1 St. Nick melon, peeled and cut into
   bite-size pieces
½ cup pomegranate seeds
5 mandarins, sectioned
1 tablespoon honey

Toss all ingredients together and serve.

Standing Rib Roast with Garlic and Rosemary

Preheat oven to 425°F.

1 standing rib roast, 4 to 5 ribs
3 tablespoons olive oil
Salt and pepper to taste
6 cloves garlic, minced
2 tablespoons rosemary, chopped

Season roast generously with oil, salt, pepper,
garlic and rosemary.
Place in a roasting pan, and roast 20 minutes.
Turn oven down to 325°F and continue to roast
40 to 60 minutes longer, depending on the size.
Let meat rest at least 30 minutes before slicing.
Serve with horseradish crème fraîche.

Horseradish Crème Fraîche

½ cup crème fraîche
¼ cup fresh horseradish, peeled and grated
½ lemon, juiced
Salt and pepper to taste

Combine all ingredients. Let sit at least 1 hour
before serving to develop flavor.

Garlic Mashed Potatoes

3 pounds German butterball potatoes,
   peeled and quartered
Salt to taste
1 cup olive oil
10 cloves garlic
3 tablespoons butter
½ cup half and half

In a large pot of water, bring potatoes and salt
to a boil. Turn down to simmer and continue to
cook until fork tender. Drain well.
Meanwhile, heat oil and garlic in a small pot.
When garlic starts to bubble, turn off heat, and
let stand 20 to 30 minutes. When slightly cool,
mince garlic and set aside.
Mash potatoes with a food mill or masher. Add
garlic and oil to taste, butter, half and half, and
salt. Combine well before serving.

Roasted Brussels Sprouts with Balsamic Vinegar

Preheat oven to 375°F.

3 pounds Brussels sprouts, halved
2 tablespoons olive oil
Salt and pepper to taste
2 cloves garlic, minced
1 cup balsamic vinegar

In a large bowl, toss Brussels sprouts with oil, salt, pepper and garlic. Roast on a sheet tray until slightly tender, about 20 to 30 minutes. Meanwhile, in a small saucepan, reduce balsamic vinegar by three-fourths.
When Brussels sprouts are roasted, toss with reduced balsamic vinegar, and serve.

Roasted Cauliflower and Broccoli

Preheat oven to 375°F.

1 head orange cauliflower, cut into pieces
1 head purple broccoli, cut into pieces
2 tablespoons olive oil
Salt and pepper to taste

Toss vegetables, separately, with oil, salt and pepper.
Roast on a sheet tray until tender, about 15 to 20 minutes. Remove from oven and serve.

Chocolate Jelly Roll

Preheat oven to 375°F.

1 cup cake flour, sifted
1½ teaspoons baking powder
¼ teaspoon salt
2 eggs
¾ cup sugar
3 tablespoons milk
½ teaspoon vanilla extract
¼ cup powdered sugar
1 jar Beauty Ranch Strawberry Raspberry Jam

To make the cake, sift together the flour, baking powder, and salt. Set aside.
In a separate bowl, beat eggs until thick and lightly lemon colored. Add sugar gradually, beating well. Fold in flour mixture a little at a time.
Spread batter into a jelly roll pan lined with buttered parchment paper. Bake until cake bounces back when lightly touched with finger, about 15 minutes.

Turn cake out onto a flour sack kitchen towel generously sprinkled with powdered sugar. Remove paper quickly and cut off crispy edges. Roll cake WITH the towel inside immediately, and let stand 10 minutes.
Unroll; spread cake with jam. Roll up again without the towel, cover and refrigerate.

Vanilla Frosting

1 pound powdered sugar
¼ cup butter
1 teaspoon vanilla extract
¼ cup milk
Shaved chocolate (to garnish)

In a mixing bowl, combine powdered sugar, butter, vanilla extract and milk. Beat on medium-high 7 to 10 minutes, stopping to scrape down the sides a few times.
When well combined and fluffy, spread evenly over cake. Shave chocolate over top to garnish. Refrigerate at least 30 minutes before serving.

new year's supper

Green Leaf Lettuce with Roasted Beets,
Cabbage and Radishes and Red Wine Vinaigrette

Chicken Mole

Brown Rice with Scallions

Roasted Baby Carrots and Chard with Cilantro

Meyer Lemon Pudding

Serves eight

It's celebration time!

It's the 52nd Monday night dinner, and the last dinner of the year. We poured Champagne, and toasted the Placer County and regional farmers market growers who provide us with the finest of sweet fruits, savory vegetables, grassfed meats, fresh eggs, and healthy nuts throughout the year. We toasted each other, and how, as a team, we fulfilled our goal to prepare, in a simple and easy fashion, in-season meals that would nourish and please our guests.

Every Saturday, at the Auburn farmers market, we purchased everything for the Monday night dinner. Laura took the raw ingredients, and with careful preparation, showcased each bold flavor with subtle restraint. Each platter of food was delicately prepared, each dish exquisitely blended with another, and the plates were alive with just the right combination of color and taste. Laura presented platters of edible art. Every meal was a symphony of flavors.

More than 300 dinner guests shared our home. Most were people we first met as they walked through the front door. People came from throughout the region, and many had never shopped at local farmers markets. Guests wrote thank you notes describing the positive experience.

Let's continue to celebrate healthy, fresh, in-season local food that's good for us and good for the earth.

Green Leaf Lettuce with Roasted Beets, Cabbage and Radishes and Red Wine Vinaigrette

Preheat oven to 350°F.

2 bunches beets, tops removed
1 tablespoon olive oil
2 heads green leaf lettuce
½ head red cabbage, thinly sliced
1 watermelon radish, peeled and thinly sliced

Red Wine Vinaigrette

2 tablespoons red wine vinegar
¼ cup olive oil
1 lemon, juiced
Salt and pepper to taste

To roast beets, toss with olive oil. Place on a sheet tray with ½ cup water, and roast until tender, about 20 to 30 minutes. Peel when cool and slice.
Combine with remaining salad ingredients. Whisk together vinaigrette ingredients, and toss with salad before serving.

Chicken Mole

Thanks to Peg Tomlinson-Poswall for sharing this recipe.

Mole Sauce

⅔ cup vegetable oil

1 large yellow onion, plus ½ cup, peeled and large diced

8 garlic cloves, peeled

2 cups almonds, blanched

1 cup roasted peanuts, unsalted

6 whole cloves

12 whole peppercorns

1 stick cinnamon, 4 inches long

1 cup bread, pulled in pieces

4 cups tomatoes, small diced

7 large dried ancho chiles, stems and seeds removed, rehydrated in 1 cup boiling water

3 tablespoons vegetable oil

In a large pan, heat oil. Add large onion, garlic, almonds, peanuts, cloves, peppercorns, cinnamon and bread.

Cook slowly for 1 hour.

Turn off heat. Add tomatoes and chiles and stir well. Pour mixture in a food processor and blend until liquefied. Set aside.

Add vegetable oil and ½ cup onions to the pan. Cook until onions are slightly browned.

Add nut and tomato mixture to pan. Cook 25 to 30 minutes, at medium heat, until sauce thickens. At this point, mole sauce can be held overnight in refrigerator or frozen.

Tom and I will move mountains on our schedules to have dinner at Joanne's. The evenings are always about enjoying great local food, beautifully prepared and presented, lively and interesting conversation where we always learn something new, and lots of laughter. We leave, completely filled - body, mind and spirit.

Susan Dupre and Tom Neary, Auburn

Chicken

2 chickens, 2 to 3 pounds apiece, or one 5-pound whole chicken

2 large carrots, peeled and cut in 3-inch lengths

4 celery stalks, cut in 3-inch lengths

1 large yellow onion, thickly sliced

8 whole cloves

2 bay leaves

1 teaspoon salt

Cut up chickens, and place entire back, neck and wing tips into large pot. Add carrots, celery, onion, cloves, bay leaves and salt. Cover with water. Bring to a boil, lower heat and slow simmer for 2 hours.

After two hours, put legs and thighs into simmering pot, and cook 10 minutes.

Then add breasts and wings and simmer another 25 minutes.

Remove chicken, and set aside in a large bowl. Empty contents of pot into a strainer, and drain the broth into pan. Discard vegetables and bones. Set aside broth.

(Both chicken meat and mole sauce can be made the day before serving and refrigerated.)

Blending Chicken and Mole Sauce

¼ cup almonds, diced

2 tablespoons cilantro, chopped

An hour before serving, add 2 cups or more of reserved chicken stock to the mole sauce. The mixture should be the consistency of gravy. For a hotter sauce, add a slight pinch of chile powder. Add more salt if necessary.

Bring thinned sauce to a boil, and add chicken pieces. Simmer until heated through, about 20 minutes.

Serve in a large bowl; garnish with almonds and cilantro.

december 28

Brown Rice with Scallions

4 cups brown rice
8 cups liquid (water or stock)
Salt and pepper to taste
1 cup scallions, sliced

Rinse rice and drain well.
In a large pot, combine rice, liquid, salt and pepper. Bring to a boil, turn down to a low simmer, cover and cook 50 minutes. You can also use a rice cooker.
Turn off heat and let sit 10 minutes.
Fluff rice with a fork and stir in scallions. Season to taste with salt and pepper.

Roasted Baby Carrots and Chard with Cilantro

Preheat oven to 375°F.

Carrots

2½ pounds baby carrots, peeled
2 teaspoons garlic, minced
1 tablespoon olive oil
Salt and pepper to taste
½ cup cilantro, chopped

Toss carrots with garlic, oil, salt and pepper. Roast until tender, about 15 to 20 minutes. Toss with cilantro.

Chard

1 tablespoon olive oil
1 tablespoon butter
1 teaspoon garlic
2 bunches chard, stems removed
Salt and pepper to taste

In a large sauté pan, heat oil and butter. Add garlic and cook until fragrant. Add chard and quickly sauté to wilt.
To serve, place chard on a large platter. Arrange carrots in the center.

Meyer Lemon Pudding

Preheat oven to 350°F.

1 cup plus 2 tablespoons sugar

5 large eggs, separated

⅓ cup flour

½ cup fresh Meyer lemon juice

3 tablespoons Meyer lemon zest

2 cups whole milk

½ teaspoon salt

1 cup whipping cream, whipped

Butter eight 1-cup custard bowls. Set aside. Whisk 1 cup sugar and egg yolks in large bowl. Add flour, lemon juice and lemon zest to bowl and whisk. Add milk and blend. Set aside.
In electric mixer set at low speed, beat egg whites and salt until frothy. Increase speed, and slowly add 2 tablespoons sugar until soft peaks form.
Gently fold egg whites into lemon mixture.
Place mixture in custard cups and put cups in a roasting pan. Add hot water to roasting pan until water comes halfway up custard cup sides.

Bake custard 30 minutes, until tops are slightly browned.
Remove cups from roasting pan.
Serve with a dollop of whipping cream topped with candied lemon rind.

Candied Lemon Rind

Preheat oven to 300°F.

3 Meyer lemons

2 cups sugar

1 cup water

Peel lemons from top to bottom, carefully removing skin without the pith. Slice into ⅛-inch lengths. Set aside.
In a medium saucepan, bring sugar and water to a rolling boil. Add lemon pieces. Cook until 230°F.
Drain sugar water.
On parchment lined baking sheets, place individual lemon pieces. Be sure rinds are not touching. Place pan in oven. Immediately turn off heat. Remove pan after 8 to 10 hours, or overnight.

harvest calendar

RD. NEWCASTLE CA. 956
COUNTY GROWER

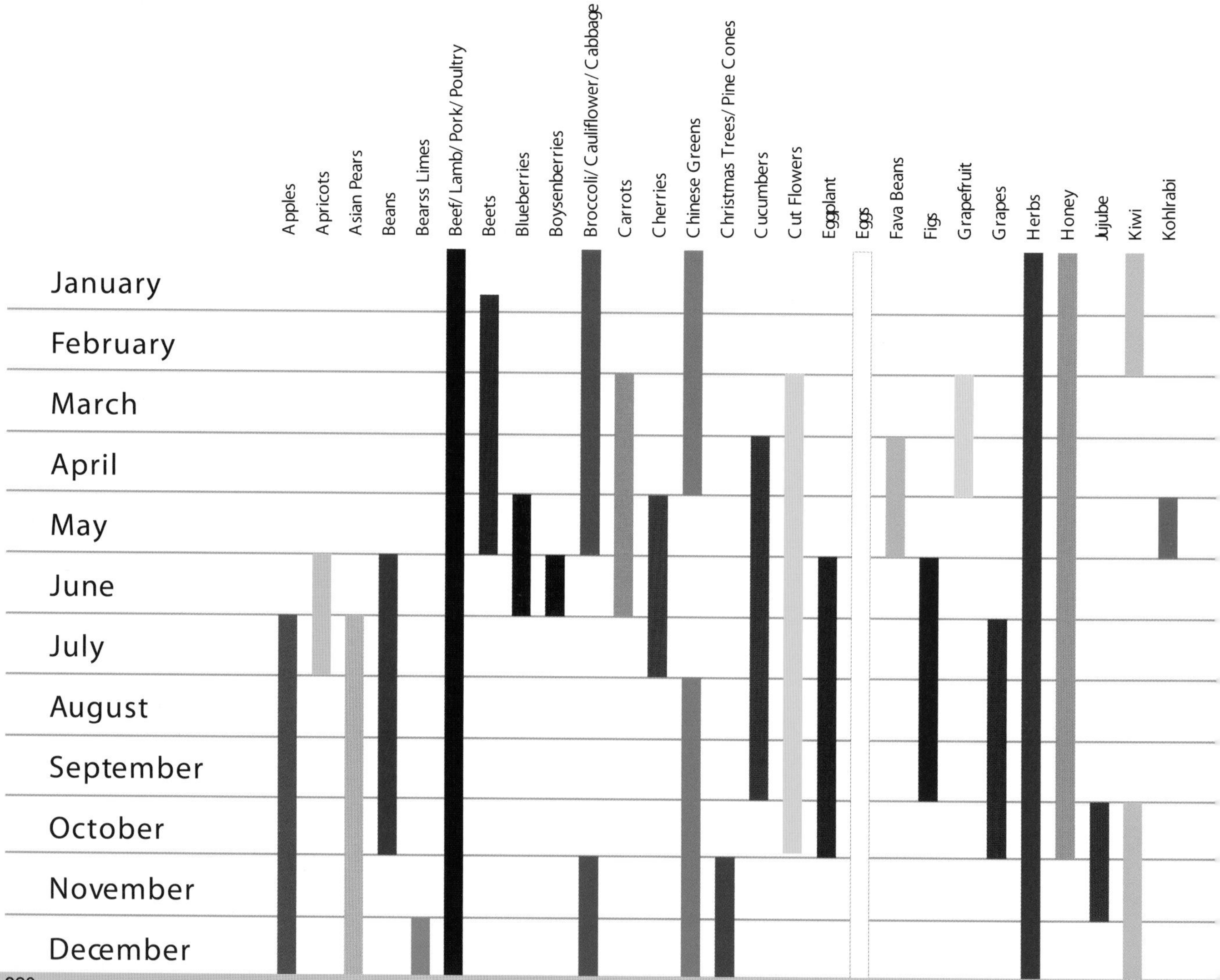
Apples
Apricots
Asian Pears
Beans
Bearss Limes
Beef/ Lamb/ Pork/ Poultry
Beets
Blueberries
Boysenberries
Broccoli/ Cauliflower/ Cabbage
Carrots
Cherries
Chinese Greens
Christmas Trees/ Pine Cones
Cucumbers
Cut Flowers
Eggplant
Eggs
Fava Beans
Figs
Grapefruit
Grapes
Herbs
Honey
Jujube
Kiwi
Kohlrabi
January
February
March
April
May
June
July
August
September
October
November
December

harvest calendar

Kumquats
Mandarins
Melons
Meyer Lemons
Nectarines
Nursery Stock
Nuts/Rice
Onions
Oranges/Blood & Navel
Pears
Peas
Peaches
Peppers
Persimmons
Pomegranates
Potatoes
Pluots
Plums
Pummelo
Pumpkins
Quince
Radishes
Raspberries
Rhubarb
Salad Greens/Spinach/Arugula
Squash (Summer)
Squash (Winter)
Strawberries
Sunflower Sprouts/Wheatgrass
Sweet Corn
Swiss Chard/Mustard Greens/Kale
Tomatoes
Wine

the end